C000262559

REVIVAL
AND
REVIVALISM
IN
BRITAIN

1735 – 1957

Norman A. Lloyd

Acorn Independent Press

CONTENTS

SECTION TWO
REVIVAL IN THE NINETEENTH CENTURY

SECTION THREE
REVIVAL IN THE TWENTIETH CENTURY

SECTION FOUR
REVIVAL AND REVIVALISM IN THE
NINETEENTH AND TWENTIETH CENTURY

PREFACE

Much of the material of this book was originally written in the late 1990s. It was in response to the author, as a Minister and Trustee of the Countess of Huntingdon's Connection, who had already written articles on the Connection and a history of each of three C. of H. Churches he pastored, and which each could trace their beginnings, ultimately, to the great spiritual Awakening in the eighteenth century under John Wesley and George Whitefield. The project was to produce a Church History module, as part of a training course for trainee ministers belonging to three small denominations: the Wesleyan Reformed Union, the Independent Methodists and the Countess of Huntingdon's Connexion.

It was thought too that the subject of Revival might be generally acceptable and appropriate, since each of the three denominations trace their origins to the eighteenth-century Revival. Also, that something, at least, should be known of that so-called "Methodist" Revival, as the adherents of the Countess of Huntingdon's Churches were also called "Methodist" at that time, though the Connection was the Calvinistic wing of the Revival. The course, with questions and a list of further reading on each chapter was then used for several years by some ministers of these denominations on a distant learning basis. Since that time it has been suggested that the main body of these accounts might prove of interest to a wider Christian public.

INTRODUCTION

Perhaps another book on revival may be justified on the grounds that there is still no greater need in the Christian Church at this time than that of revival. It is good to remind ourselves of how God has greatly blessed our land in the past, even in the darkest and most desperate times, in answer to the earnest prayers of his people. There was a time when God's people expected revival as the normal means God used to build up his Church and this occurred in frequent local Awakenings, as well as in the more well-known national ones. In more modern times, however, the Church has tended to rely rather on evangelistic campaigns of various kinds. It is hoped, therefore, that the following accounts will not be considered as simply theoretical but that they will have the practical effect of reminding us of what God has done in the past and of encouraging us to pray, "Will you not revive us again, that your people may rejoice in you"? Psalm 85:6.

Revivals have taken place in so many countries, particularly since the Reformation, that any comprehensive account of them would be impossible. Therefore these accounts are only concerned with the major revivals that have occurred in Britain, from the eighteenth century to the present. The book is divided into four sections. The first three sections deal with the 18th, 19th and 20th centuries, respectively, and the three most significant revivals in each of those centuries. The final section of three chapters then deals with what may be regarded as the difference between classical Revival, as evidenced in the first nine chapters, and what many would regard simply as Evangelistic Campaigns or as Revivalism.

This final section may be considered controversial. There has been, at least from the beginning of the nineteenth century, a division of opinion among Christians as to what constitutes revival and as to whether it is possible to promote one. It is questionable whether a satisfactory answer can be given. As Professor Joad used to say on the Radio Programme, "Brains Trust" many years ago, "It all depends what you mean by..." Readers will come to their own conclusions, if they haven't reached them already! One thing is clear, however, and that is that when God is about to revive a church or district or nation, he prompts some of his people, at least, to prepare their hearts and to seek him in prayer for such a visitation.

With regard to the phenomena that often occurred following the preaching of the Gospel during these times of revival, it is naturally regarded by many now as it was by many then, as extremely bizarre and dismissed as mere hysteria. However, the preachers did not encourage it and some sought to suppress it, but the radical and lasting change in the moral and spiritual lives of those affected and, as a result, the consequent change for the better in society, shows that these responses were more than a passing human emotion. Rather, they were the result of sinful human souls having an overwhelming sense of the holiness and judgement of God and then the total relief of experiencing his forgiving love in Christ.

Over a century has passed since the last nationwide revival in Wales and almost a century since there was a visitation in England, and that only in a localized area, and almost seventy years since the spiritual Awakening in the Hebrides. Our land has been so favoured by God by these revivals in the past but there has never been, perhaps, a greater need of another great Awakening in our land, than at the present. Knowing the increasing secularization of our society we can pray humbly with the psalmist, "It is time for you to act, O Lord; your law is being broken". Psalm 119:126.

SECTION ONE

REVIVAL IN THE EIGHTEENTH CENTURY

Left to Right: George Whitefield; Henry Venn; Howell Harris;
Daniel Rowland; John Fletcher; William Romaine
John Berridge; Rowland Hill and Augustus Toplady

CHAPTER ONE
THE EIGHTEENTH CENTURY REVIVAL IN WALES 1735-1790

The spiritual condition of Wales before the Revival.

The first signs of religious revival in Britain in the eighteenth century were seen in Wales which, in the early years of the century, was in an even worse state morally and spiritually than England. Drunkenness and dissipation of all kinds were prevalent among clergy and laity while the lives of the poor were characterized by ignorance, superstition and immorality. Those who thought at all denied the need for divine revelation and supernatural grace, and outward morality was regarded as enough for this life and the next. Few people acknowledged the need of personal salvation through faith in Christ. Howell Harris wrote:

> A universal deluge of swearing, lying, reviling, drunkenness, fighting and gaming had over-spread the country, like a mighty torrent ...ministers were ...not in earnest, and did not appear to have any sense of their own danger, nor any sense of the love of Christ. [1]

---

[1]   Evans, Eifion, Fire in the Thatch, p. 88

Griffith Jones

Unlike several revivals in Britain in the nineteenth and twentieth centuries that were largely, it seems, independent of the endeavours of great preachers, the eighteenth century "Methodist" Revival centred on certain evangelists whom God raised up and empowered in a unique way. The story of this revival, therefore, is the story of these great men of God and how they were used by the Holy Spirit to spiritually awaken the people in Wales, England and Scotland at this time. A quarter of a century before the conversion of the Wesleys in 1738, God was raising up men who would prepare the way for the Great Awakening that would begin in the late 1730s.

Griffith Jones of Llanddowror, (1683-1761), "The Morning Star of the Methodist Revival".

The most significant of the men whom God used to prepare people for the great Awakening in Wales was Griffith Jones. He was ordained in 1708, became the curate of Laugharne in Carmarthenshire in1710 and rector of Llanddowror in 1716, where he remained until his death. In 1739, when he made his first visit to Wales, Whitefield said of him:

> I think Wales is excellently well prepared for the Gospel of Christ. They have many burning and shining lights among both Dissenting and Church ministers, amongst whom Mr. Griffith Jones shines in particular. No less than fifty Charity Schools have been erected by his means, without any settled visible fund, and fresh ones are setting up every day. People make nothing of coming twenty miles to hear a sermon and great numbers there are who have not only been hearers, but doers of the Word; so that there is a most comfortable prospect of the spreading of the Gospel in Wales. [2]

---

[2]   Whitefield, George, *Journals*, p. 231

Griffith Jones, the Preacher

As early as 1713 it is said that, although Griffith Jones' parish had only ten or twelve small families, his congregations consisted of five hundred or six hundred and sometimes a thousand people. They came to hear the Gospel powerfully preached in Welsh, and the following year there was a spiritual awakening there, which had a considerable impact on the locality. Because he attracted people from other parishes over a wide area, and sometimes preached in other places, Jones had to appear before the Bishop of St. David's on the false charge that he neglected his parish, while he intruded into the churches of other clergy without their permission. The charge was dismissed as it was proved that he was always invited to preach elsewhere. It was also explained that he had to preach outside his church as the building was unable to hold the large number of his hearers. When further attempts were made to silence him, he wrote to the Bishop concerning the people's need of the Gospel and he gently suggested that the Bishop would do better, "in stirring up those (clergy) that preach not than silencing those that do"![3] This must have had some effect for he was appointed rector of Llanddowror soon afterwards.

It was then, as a preacher, that he first became famous and, as a pioneer of field preaching in Wales he prepared for the revival that followed. At a time when spiritual death and ignorance of the Gospel prevailed, he exercised a unique ministry preaching the need of repentance, faith, the new birth and holiness. He was an excellent elocutionist and orator and made passionate appeals to the conscience of his hearers, often breaking into tears and causing the congregation to weep, as he described the sufferings and love of Christ. When clergy refused him their pulpits, he preached in the graveyards and thousands

[3]   Wood, A. Skevington, *The Inextinguishable Blaze*, p. 43

were converted through his itinerant ministry, some travelling twenty miles to hear him. He also had a puritan zeal against the demoralizing effect of fairs and wakes and transformed the social and moral condition of numerous districts. From 1748 he was also closely associated with the Countess of Huntingdon. She invited him to England, where he supplied some of her chapels, and he also accompanied her on a tour of Wales, preaching to great crowds.

Griffith Jones, the Educationalist

Jones was not, however, simply concerned with combating sin. When he started a catechetical class in his parish, he found a number of parishioners were grossly ignorant and unable to read. He decided, therefore, that he had also to combat ignorance if he was to influence people with the Gospel, and not only in his parish but throughout the nation, by establishing a system of basic education. The system, begun in 1731, consisted of setting up "Circulating Welsh Charity Schools", and he trained men of various denominations to teach people to read the Welsh Bible, the catechism and to sing the psalms. He then sent them on a circuit from parish to parish, to remain a few months at a time in each. All ages from the very young to the very old were taught to read and supplied with books free. The system grew rapidly and, by his death in 1761, about three thousand five hundred schools and a hundred and fifty eight thousand scholars had been taught, a quarter of the population. [4] He also wrote catechisms and expositions of the Ten Commandments, the Lord's Prayer, the sacraments and other books.

In those days, Bibles in Wales were virtually unknown, so Jones persuaded the Society for the Propagation of the Gospel to

---

[4]   Evans, Eifion, *Fire in the Thatch*, p. 65

publish thirty thousand Welsh copies, which were sold cheaply to the poor. He also anticipated the circuit system, which was a principle feature of the Methodist section of the revival movement. Few men did more for the spiritual good of Wales. His schools and his provision of Bibles prepared the minds of the people for the preaching of the revivalists, Whitefield, Wesley, Harris and Rowland, the latter being converted under his ministry. On the eve of the revival he spoke of atheism, infidelity and other various fatal errors coming into Wales like a flood but his prayers during the previous twenty-five years for an awakening were about to be answered.

The Ministry of George Whitefield, John Wesley and Howell Harris

Both Whitefield and John Wesley preached with great success in Wales from 1739, sometimes in association with Griffith Jones, Howell Harris or Daniel Rowland and many were converted through their ministry. Wesley made about twenty visits, visiting most towns in the principality and Whitefield travelled four hundred miles on one visit, preaching forty times in thirteen towns in seven counties. Whitefield was also moderator of the Welsh Calvinistic Methodists from the formation of the first Association in 1743 until 1748. Even so, their influence was not so great in Wales as that of the famous Welsh preachers of the time. By 1767, almost thirty years after the commencement of Wesley's ministry in Wales, there were only two hundred and thirty-two Wesleyan Methodists there, a tenth of those in Cornwall, the great majority of the converts following Harris and Rowland, the principal leaders in the Calvinistic Methodist movement. Another revivalist of the period was Howell Davies, a pupil of Griffith Jones, who became rector of Prengast, but his parishioners had him dismissed from his parish for his plain preaching. He then exercised an itinerant ministry in Pembrokeshire, preaching to crowds and many lives were changed through his ministry. It was, however, Harris and Rowland particularly, who made the greatest impact on Wales and it is on them, as God's chief instruments in this revival that this study now focuses.

Howell Harris of Trevecca (1714-1773)

Harris was converted in nearby Talgarth church on Whitsunday, 1735, when he received the assurance that his sins were forgiven. Shortly afterwards, feeling a further spiritual need, he sought God in Llangasty church. He said:

> Being in secret prayer I felt suddenly my heart melting within me like wax before the fire with love to God my Saviour. I felt not only love and peace, but also a longing to be dissolved and to be with Christ; and there was a cry in my inmost soul, which I was totally unacquainted with before, it was this, "Abba Father'; 'Abba, Father"! I could not help calling God my Father; I knew I was His child, and that He loved me; my soul being filled and satiated crying, "It is enough, I am satisfied; give me strength, and I will follow Thee through fire and water". There was in me "a well of water, springing up into everlasting life", yea the love of God was shed abroad in my heart by the Holy Ghost.[5]

After his conversion, Harris sold his few possessions and gave away his money and the clothing he regarded as too gaudy for a Christian. He was appalled at the moral and spiritual condition of his district and, that summer, he began to testify to his friends and neighbours, first by reading Scriptures and prayers to those

---

[5]   Evans, Eifion, *Fire in the Thatch*, p. 78

who gathered in his mother's cottage to hear him and then by witnessing in house to house visitation, not only in his own parish but also in adjacent villages. A remarkable change took place in the religious and moral condition of the place. People made peace with one another and appeared concerned about their eternal state and religion became a common subject of conversation. Family worship began in many homes, the local churches were crowded and the number of communicants greatly increased.

Howell Harris the Exhorter

In November, persuaded by his family, he went to Oxford to prepare for the ministry but apparently because of the irreligion and immorality there, he wrote,

> I soon tired of the place and I longed for my freedom, which I soon obtained. I came home, and my brother offered to have me live with him; but God had such a hold on me that I could not go. Soon afterwards I left my school (in Llangasty where he had taught for about a year) and devoted myself to exhorting everyone I met to flee from the wrath to come. [6]

When the numbers attending his exhortations became too large to accommodate in a house, he started to hold open-air services, such as at the Talgarth fairs where, he says, he denounced:

> The swearers and cursers without fear or favour. At first I knew nothing at all, but God opened my mouth (full of ignorance), filling it with terrors and threatenings. I was

---

[6] Bennett, Richard, *Howell Harris and the Dawn of Revival*, p. 36

given a commission to break and rend sinners in the most dreadful manner. I thundered greatly, denouncing the gentry, the carnal clergy and everybody. My subjects, mostly were death and judgement without any mention of Christ. I had no order and hardly any time to read except a few pages now and then, because of constant busyness and haste. But when I came to the people matter enough was given to me and I received a fluency of speech and great earnestness, although I was inclined by nature to levity and frivolity. [7]

The messages Harris spoke were with such spiritual power that men cried out on the spot for the forgiveness of their sins. He hoped the clergy would help him in his efforts but he was disappointed and was soon forbidden to speak publicly. Harris, however, was unable to keep quiet. Sometimes he preached six sermons a day to crowded congregations. The whole country was in a corrupt, careless and godless state, gentry, clergy and common people alike being in spiritual darkness. Harris declared, no doubt in exaggeration, that he didn't know anyone who had the true knowledge of the God they pretended to worship. He saw that the ministers were not in earnest nor did they appear to have any sense of their own danger or experience of the love of Christ. Their deadness and indifference, he said, made him speak of death and judgement and the fire of God burned in his soul, so that he could not rest day or night without doing something for his God and Saviour.

Increasing Opposition

Yet the more Harris preached, the more the opposition against him grew. Despite the beneficial effect he had on the community, the gentry, magistrates and clergy were angry at his

7 Ibid., p. 42

unauthorized preaching and threatened him with prosecution. They also imposed crippling fines on poor people who went to hear him, with the result that he was unable for a time to continue to witness openly. That year, 1736, he was also refused ordination. At the same time he opened a school in Trevecca, but he was turned out of the school the next year and then devoted himself to itinerant preaching, often being assaulted by violent mobs. He was a large, fearless and aggressive man who could face down mobs by sheer force of will. Sometimes, however, these were stirred up by clergy who preached against him and who distributed alcohol to mobs to incite them against him. Also, at times, the shouting, threatening and swearing of the mob drowned his voice.

Some of his escapes from violent mobs were little short of miraculous. He was beaten, stoned and trampled on. More than once he was left for dead and one of his companions was killed. Pistols were fired at him, he was covered with dirt and ditch-water and all kinds of intimidation were used against him. His male hearers were seized by press gangs, while women had their clothes torn off and were physically and sexually assaulted. On one tour he didn't undress for a week, being obliged to preach at midnight or very early in the morning to avoid persecution. Within seven years, however, he and his revivalist friends had changed the religious and moral condition of Wales, ending many vicious and licentious practices.

Howell Harris and George Whitefield

In 1739 Harris met Whitefield in Cardiff and went on a preaching tour with him, Whitefield preaching in English and Harris in Welsh. If any church was closed to them, they preached in the open-air or, if it was wet, in a public house. In Cardiff they preached in the Town Hall and, during their stay there, a considerable number of the population responded to the Gospel. Whitefield said of Harris at this time:

> A burning and shining light he has been in these parts, a barrier against profaneness and immorality and an indefatigable promoter of the true Gospel of Jesus Christ... For the past three years he has discoursed twice a day for three or four hours at a time. He has been in seven counties going to Wakes etc. to turn people from such lying vanities. Many alehouse people, fiddlers, harpers sadly cry out against him for spoiling their business and had constables sent to apprehend him. He loves all who love our Lord Jesus Christ and is, therefore, styled by bigots a Dissenter. All who are lovers of pleasure more than lovers of God condemn him, but God has greatly blessed his endeavours. Many call him their spiritual father and, I believe, would lay down their lives for his sake. He discourses generally in a field but at other times in a house, from a wall, a table or anything else. He is full of faith and of the Holy Ghost...Blessed be God, there seems to be a noble spirit gone out into Wales; and I believe ere long there will be more visible fruits of it.[8]

On the same tour, Harris, preaching in the streets of St. David's, Pembrokeshire, was described as preaching with such convicting power that his hearers were terrified and fearful that the Day of Judgement had overtaken them and strong men, being seized with fainting fits through fear and terror, fell as corpses in the streets. On the other hand, believers were filled with joy at his descriptions of the union of the child of God with Christ in language reminiscent of the Song of Solomon. In 1740, visiting North Wales, Harris was grieved

---

[8] Wood, A. Skevington, *The Inextinguishable Blaze,* p. 51

over the spiritual darkness, superstition and immorality that characterized the area. He cried out

> O Lord I can't help mourning over the darkness of the country of North Wales! North Wales! Thy guides are blind, the magistrates are persecutors, and the instruments for thee (clergy) are all weak...dreadful things do I hear of all the ministers in these parts" [9]

By the middle of the century, however, the Gospel was spreading throughout Wales and other ministers were being raised up to preach to thousands in the open-air. Harris could testify that God was pouring down His Spirit upon them more abundantly than ever before, and that in various places the Word of God was going forth in great power everywhere. God was making all fall before the Gospel of His dear Son. In order, however, to ensure that the converts would make spiritual progress by regular fellowship and exchange of spiritual experiences Harris also, from 1736, formed societies in nearly all the places where his preaching had been successful.

Howell Harris and "The Family" at Trevecca.

After fifteen years of continual evangelism, however, Harris' health broke down and, though he was as zealous as ever, he was forced to rest for seven years. At the same time a rift took place between himself and Daniel Rowland over Harris' adoption of the Moravian view that God Himself died on the Cross, and the Calvinistic Methodists went into a temporary decline, being split into two camps. During that time Harris established a self-supporting Christian community at Trevecca called "The Family", for over a hundred men, women and

---

[9] Evans, Eifion, *Revivals – their Rise, Progress and Achievements,* p. 6

children from all over Wales and some from England. Many of them were his converts, who brought their possessions and put their money into a common pool. In the meantime, from 1759-1763, at the time of the Seven Year War in Europe Harris, having formed a company of men from his community, served as an officer in the Breconshire Militia, on the understanding he would be free to preach the Gospel, wherever he was posted.

After this period in the militia and twelve years' separation from the Welsh Calvinistic Methodists, Rowland and Williams of Pantycelyn, the hymn-writer and a convert of Harris, sought reconciliation with Harris. The dispute was settled and he re-joined his old friends. After this he did occasional itinerant preaching but, although his old converts welcomed him, his former spiritual power and authority was gone. His wife, formerly Anne Williams, whom he married in 1744, predeceased him in 1770, and he died three years later at Trevecca, on July 21st 1773. His funeral was one of the most spectacular ever seen in Wales and twenty thousand people are said to have attended it. Three ministers, in turn, attempted to read the funeral service without success, each breaking down in tears and Harris was buried without a service, amidst a weeping congregation, in Talgarth church where he came to faith in Christ. The inscription on his memorial states:

Near the Communion Table lie the remains of Howell Harris, Esquire; born at Trevecca, January 23rd, 1714. Here, where his body lies, he was convinced of sin, had his pardon sealed, felt the power of Christ's precious blood at the Holy Communion. Having tasted grace himself, he resolved to declare to others what God had done for his soul. He was the first itinerant Preacher of Redemption in this period of Revival in England and Wales. He preached the Gospel for the space of thirty-nine years, till he was taken to his

29

final Rest. He received those who sought Salvation into his house. Then sprang up the Family at Trevecca, to whom he faithfully ministered unto his end, as an indefatigable servant of God and a faithful member of the Church of England. His end was more blessed than his beginning. Looking to Jesus Crucified, he rejoiced to the last that death had lost its sting. He fell asleep in Jesus at Trevecca, July 21st 1773, and now rests blessedly from his labours. [10]

Daniel Rowland of Llangeitho (1713-1790).

Rowland was born near Llangeitho, Cardiganshire, where his father was the rector. His father died when he was eighteen and his elder brother John became rector and, two years later, Daniel was ordained at an unusually young age, becoming his brother's curate. At this time he was ignorant of the Gospel and renowned in the district for his levity and addiction to all kinds of pleasures and foolish amusements, even after service on the Sabbath. He was, however, conscious that his congregations were being drawn to a Nonconformist preacher named Pugh, so Rowland decided to discover what was Pugh's secret of success. He found that Pugh preached powerful, convicting sermons on fearful texts about the certainty of a future judgement for the impenitent, so he began to do the same, preaching with eloquence and force on the most terrible texts on the wrath of God against the wicked. As a result, his church was soon crowded with attentive and awe-struck listeners and a hundred or so people came under deep conviction and began to cry out for spiritual help, while Rowland himself was still without a spiritual concern.

He was not, however, to remain in that condition for long. One day he heard Griffith Jones preaching at nearby Llanddewi

---

[10] Bennett, Richard, *Howell Harris and the Dawn of Revival*, p. 182

Brefi. The preacher was so concerned at the cynical attitude of the young clergyman that he stopped in his sermon and prayed that God would touch his heart and make him a means of turning thousands to Christ. The message and the prayer resulted in Rowland's conversion and his life and ministry were completely changed. He continued to "thunder" in his sermons on the wrath of God against sin until Pugh advised him that his convicted people now needed the Gospel of God's love and forgiveness. If he went on thundering out the curses of the law in such a terrible way, Pugh said, he would drive half the country mad, for no-one could stand before him. As a result, his preaching changed, many came to rejoice in God's forgiving mercy and the parish experienced a remarkable revival.

Rowland, the Field Preacher.

Rowland is commonly regarded as the greatest preacher Wales has produced and, in a day of great preachers, it was thought that only Whitefield was his equal. People came on foot from all parts of the country, travelling fifty or sixty miles to hear him, often in companies. Crowds filled churchyards as well as churches and, on Holy Communion days, even in his small remote parish, it was not uncommon to have two thousand communicants. He was soon led to preach outside his parish at the earnest request of a woman from Ystradffin, Carmarthenshire, who was one of his regular hearers. For six months she walked a round trip of over forty miles each weekend to attend his services. It is reported that one day she said to him:

> Sir, if what you say is true, there are many in my neighbourhood in a most dangerous condition, going fast to

eternal misery. For the sake of their souls come over, sir, to preach to them. [11]

Rowland could not refuse, although it was against Church policy for a clergyman to preach outside his parish and, from that time, he never hesitated to do so whenever there was an opportunity for him although it led, as it did in the case of Griffith Jones and Howell Harris, to his being bitterly opposed by the clergy. Several attempts were made on his life too, including one to blow him up with gunpowder, but nothing deterred him from his ministry. His success, humanly speaking, was largely due to his single-minded devotion to God and preaching the Gospel and to constant, fervent prayer. Rowland then, like Harris, established religious societies over most of Wales for building up the converts of the revival and these, with those of Harris, ultimately developed into the Welsh Calvinistic Methodist Church. The societies met four times a year and, after 1748, Rowland generally acted as Moderator.

Rowland's voice was said to be remarkably powerful and, in some respects, even excelling that of Whitefield and other leaders of the Revival. It was said to be:

Like a clear and melodious trumpet, and its control so perfect that hundreds of persons were often melted to tears, after only a few sentences of his sermon had been delivered [12]

He didn't normally preach long sermons but it is reported that, one Sunday morning, he continued preaching for about six hours, until sunset, while the people are said to have listened with intense eagerness! One of the seven revivals which broke out in Llangeitho during his fifty years' ministry there took

[11]   Ryle, J.C., *Five Christian Leaders*, p. 93

[12]   Johnson, Henry, *Stories of Great Revivals*, p. 173

place when he was reading in such an impressive way the Anglican Litany, "By Thine agony and bloody sweat; by Thy Cross and passion; by thy precious Death and Burial, by thy glorious Resurrection and Ascension; and by the coming of thy Holy Ghost, Good Lord deliver us".[13] It so affected the whole congregation that all broke down and wept and another spiritual Awakening began, which extended throughout the neighbourhood, with many being brought to faith in Christ.

The Physical Manifestations under Rowland's ministry.

In 1743, Harris said of his preaching:

> I was last Sunday at the Ordinance with brother Rowland, where I saw, felt, and heard such things as I can't send on paper any idea of. The power that continues with him is uncommon. Such crying out and heart-breaking groans, silent weeping and holy joy and shouts of rejoicing I never saw. Their 'Amens' and crying, 'Glory in the highest' would enflame your soul It is very common when he preaches for scores to fall down by the power of the Word, pierced and wounded or overcome by the love of God...and lie on the ground... Some lie there for hours, some praising and admiring Jesus...others wanting words to utter...Others meeting when the word is over to sing and you might feel God among them there like a flame; others falling down one after another for a long time together, praying and interceding... others mourning and wailing for the Comforter...This is but a very faint idea of it, but what words can express spiritual things.[14]

---

[13] Ryle, J.C. *Five Christian Leaders*, p. 104

[14] Evans, Eifion, *Fire in the Thatch*, p. 82

Rowland himself writing to Whitefield said that the Lord came down among his congregation in such a way he could not describe and that, although he had tried to prevent people falling down and crying out etc., yet such was the vision and power of God which was given to many through the preaching that they could not help crying out, praising and being quite swallowed up in God. One hearer wrote of Rowland that he dwelt on the love of God and the greatness of His gift to man, with such overwhelming thoughts, that he was swallowed up in amazement. He did not know whether he was on earth or in heaven. On one occasion Rowland, too, was so overcome as he described the love and sufferings of Christ that he fainted in the pulpit.

Rowland evicted from the Church.

When his elder brother died in 1760, the Bishop of St. David's refused to give the living to Daniel, although he had served as curate for twenty-seven years and he gave it instead to Daniel's son. It seems that the Bishop's reasoning was that if Daniel became rector it would be difficult to remove him, whereas if he remained curate he could get rid of him more easily. Three years later, it seems, his licence was revoked, simply for preaching outside his parish to multitudes of people who otherwise would not have heard the Gospel As a result, a great number of people left the Established Church with him and a chapel was built for him in Llangeitho, while his son allowed him to continue living in the rectory. The Church of England gained nothing by evicting him and it lost a great deal, for another secession then took place with yet another denomination, the Welsh Calvinistic Methodist Church, being formed by his followers.

John Wesley Preaching in the Fields

Charles Wesley

Lady Huntingdon

CHAPTER TWO
THE EIGHTEENTH CENTURY 'METHODIST' REVIVAL IN ENGLAND C. 1738-1790

Conditions in England before the Revival.

The religious, moral and social conditions in England in the early eighteenth century were probably worse than at any time in English history. After the religious fervour of the sixteenth and early seventeenth century a reaction set in, from the time of the restoration of the Stuarts in 1660. It was an age of doctrinal drift when vital changes in belief were regarded with little concern and any experimental knowledge of the Holy Spirit's work in the heart was derided as fanatical, the popular idea being that the worst sin was religious "enthusiasm"! The doctrinal drift affected Nonconformists as well as Anglicans and a large proportion of Presbyterian churches settled down into Unitarianism, as did many Congregational and some Baptist churches. The prevalent religious view among educated people was Deism, the idea that God was too remote and indifferent to the affairs of men to take any interest in them and so there was no faith in prayer or desire to know God or to please Him. In fact, as Bishop Butler said in his *Analogy of Religion*, published in 1736:

> It is come, I know not how, to be taken for granted by many that Christianity is not so much a subject of inquiry but that it is now, at length, discovered to be fictitious. And, accordingly, they...set it up as a principal subject of mirth and ridicule, as it were by way of reprisals for having so long interrupted the pleasures of the world. [15]

Many prominent politicians were unbelievers and noted for their immoral lives, drunkenness and foul language. Marriage and fidelity in marriage was sneered at and literature and drama were so corrupt that visitors from abroad were shocked. Bishop Atterbury said men and women had left off even to study the outward appearance of piety and virtue, and were not content merely to be but affected to be thought loose and lawless. Crime was rampant and few towns had any kind of police force but, to protect the privileged classes criminal justice was ruthless, with almost two hundred offences, many petty, being punishable by death and the weekly public executions were attended by vast, ghoulish crowds. Robbers and murderers abounded and gangs of drunken ruffians paraded the streets assaulting women and violently attacking men. The whole nation seemed given over to gambling and drunkenness and innumerable gin shops invited people to get, "drunk for a penny, dead drunk for two pence with free straw to lie on". There was virtually no schooling for the masses, little harmless entertainment and the sports were brutal, such as cock fighting, bear baiting, bull fights and savage dog fights.

There were many absentee clergymen who received their parish revenues without going near their parishes. One Bishop boasted he had only seen his diocese once and, in ten parishes around Cheddar, there was not one resident clergyman. Church services were neglected and church buildings fell into

---

[15] *Works of Bishop Butler,* Vol. II, pp. lxxv-lxxvi

disrepair. There were some faithful godly ministers but more were known for their "hunting, shooting and fishing" or worse and, during the revival, numbers of them, ignorant of the Scriptures and prejudiced against Gospel preaching, led riots against the revivalists.

So great was the religious ignorance that a Methodist preacher was charged before the magistrates with swearing because he quoted the text, "he that believeth not shall be damned" (Mark 16:16). Even Bishop Butler, who had sought to defend orthodoxy with his *Analogy of Religion,* had no sympathy for the revivalists and refused to allow Wesley to preach in his diocese saying,

> Sir, the pretending to extraordinary revelations and gifts of the Holy Ghost is a horrid thing; yes, sir, it is a very horrid thing".[16]

Twenty or thirty years after the revival broke out, the clergy in general seem to have been unaffected. Sir William Blackstone, going from church to church in London to hear every clergyman of note, said that in each sermon he heard it was impossible for him to discover whether the preacher was a follower of Confucius, Mohammed or Christ! It was said of them that they determined to know everything *but* Jesus Christ and Him crucified!

John Wesley, 1703-1791 and Charles Wesley, 1707-1788.

The Great Spiritual Awakening in the eighteenth century is often called the Wesleyan Revival because John Wesley, assisted by his brother Charles, was clearly the leader of it. The revival is

---

[16] Pollock, John, *Wesley the Preacher*, p. 133

more often called the "Methodist" Revival, however, from the nickname given to the Wesley brothers and their friends in the early days of the movement, because of their methodical way of living. John Wesley preached in more places, to more people and for more years than any other of the revival preachers and, with his genius for organization, he did more to preserve the results of the revival. At the Foundation of the City Road Chapel, he said:

> Multitudes have been thoroughly convinced of sin and, shortly after, so filled with joy and love, that whether they were in the body, or out of the body, they could not tell: and, in the power of this love, they have trampled underfoot whatever the world counts either terrible or desirable, having evidenced in the severest trials, an invariable and tender goodwill to mankind, and all the fruits of holiness. Now, so deep a repentance, so strong a faith, so fervent love and so unblemished holiness, wrought in so many persons in so short a time, the world has not seen for many ages. [17]

John Wesley was born in 1703 and was the fifteenth of nineteen children of Samuel Wesley, the Anglican rector of Epworth and his wife Susannah, both of whom were brought up as Nonconformists. Susannah was a most godly and disciplined woman who ran her household according to a detailed timetable, including regular times each day for prayer, reading, meditation and self-examination. She also set aside time each week to talk individually with each child about the Scriptures, Christ and their spiritual condition and she expected the very highest standards of behaviour from them. She has rightly been called "The mother of the Revival".

---

[17] Wesley, John, *Works*, Vol. VII, p. 426

When John was six, disgruntled parishioners set fire to the rectory and, after the rest of the family had escaped outside, they realized that John was still inside. He was rescued just as the roof fell in and ever afterwards he saw a spiritual significance in his being, "a brand plucked from the burning", (Zechariah 3:2). From the age of eleven, until he was seventeen, he went to Charterhouse boarding school, where he again endured strict discipline and hardship, being deprived of food by older boys. In later years he attributed his continued good health to exercise and a simple diet! From Charterhouse he went, in 1720, to Christ College, Oxford, graduating in 1724 and being ordained in 1725. The next year he was appointed Fellow of Lincoln College, Oxford and became lecturer in New Testament Greek and, the following year, received his M.A.

During his time in Oxford John Wesley continued to live the strict, disciplined life he had learned at home. From 1730, he and his brother Charles met with a dozen or so students to study the New Testament and to pray and celebrate Holy Communion together. They lived by strict rules, fasting, practising self-denial and self-examination and always seeking each day to practice some virtue. They aimed never to waste a moment and, to the disgust of the university authorities, visited the poor and prisoners, giving them all the material help they could and teaching them to read and pray. Their enemies derisively called them, "The Holy Club".

In 1735, John and Charles went to America as missionaries to the colonists and Indians. It seems they did much good but John was disillusioned with himself and his work and complained, "I who went to America to convert others was myself never converted to God". In May 1738, however, in a Methodist society meeting in Fetter Lane, London, he received the assurance of salvation, four days after Charles had received a similar experience. In later days it seems he was uncertain himself as to whether the Fetter Lane experience was one of conversion or simply of assurance. Six months later, on New Year's Day, 1739, he had a further experience which prepared him for the great work to which God was calling him. The Wesleys, Whitefield and sixty or so others, in an all-night prayer meeting in Fetter Lane, received a mighty baptism of the Holy Spirit, which has been called the Methodist Pentecost. Then, that week, the leaders spent several nights in prayer and became convinced that God was about to do great things in the land.

In April 1739, John Wesley, who was reluctant at first, thinking it was not "proper" to preach outside a church, was persuaded by Whitefield to join him as a field preacher in Bristol and he was surprised at the success of his preaching. Thousands gathered and well-dressed mature people, as well as the poor, were suddenly crying out in an agony of conviction and were falling to the ground as though they had been struck. When Wesley prayed for them they soon found peace and rejoiced in the assurance of salvation. Some objected to these prostrations but then they too were smitten to the ground in an agony over their own sins. Wesley didn't encourage these phenomena, nor did he discourage them, believing it was evidence of the work of God.

At first John Wesley's centres were London, Bristol and later, Newcastle. Wherever he went, however, he would attract a crowd within minutes of beginning to speak. His sermons were closely reasoned and it is surprising that many who were illiterate, hung on his every word, at five o'clock in the morning! Only the power of God in his ministry can account for his success and the fact that his audiences were often swept by emotion, despite his calm, unemotional delivery. Excluded from parish churches he and his companions now preached everywhere they could gather a crowd, in houses, barns, market squares, churchyards, open fields or on hillsides and race courses. Without a pulpit they used horse blocks, churchyard walls, doorsteps and windowsills. On one occasion he stood with a helper at the end of a street in a poor district of Newcastle and began to sing psalm one hundred. Three or four people came out to see what was happening and, before he had finished speaking, about one thousand five hundred had gathered and were staring at him with astonishment, never having seen a clergyman in canonicals outside a church. He announced that he would be preaching that evening and was astonished himself when a vast multitude assembled, greater even than the crowds that gathered at Moorfields or Kennington Common.

When he went to Epworth, his father's successor refused him any part in the church service so, in the evening, Wesley stood and preached on his father's tombstone in the churchyard. If he recognized an individual in the crowd he would seek him out and ask him if he was a believer in Christ and did he know the regenerating influence of the Holy Spirit. The spiritual need was so great that he stayed in the village for a week, visiting in the surrounding villages and preaching in Epworth churchyard at night, with the result that revival broke out. Here, too, the revival phenomena were seen, with people falling to the ground under conviction and the cries and praises of those repenting and receiving assurance of salvation drowning his voice.

Wesley was not such an orator as Whitefield, but no preacher in the eighteen century revival exercised a greater and more lasting influence. People felt he was speaking to them alone and the effect on them was overwhelming as they were gripped with the solemnity of eternity and judgement, heightened by Wesley's calmness, certainty and authority, which brought a sense of God's nearness, holiness and power. At times he was so anointed by the power of God that he found it difficult to stop, speaking for two or three hours. He had the welfare of others on his heart until the last and he corresponded with more people on spiritual matters than anyone else in his day.

His last letter, written a few days before he died was to William Wilberforce, urging him to continue to take his stand against slavery:

> Your glorious enterprise in opposing that execrable villainy which is the scandal of religion, of England, and of human nature ... O be not weary in well doing! Go on, in the name of God and in the power of his might, till even American slavery (the vilest that ever saw the sun) shall vanish before it.[18]

Wherever there were responses to the Gospel, Wesley organized the converts in "religious societies" of twelve members each, with weekly class meetings for mutual encouragement, edification and discipline and with the penalty of expulsion for moral failure. The class leaders themselves were brought together for instruction and guidance in the Annual "Methodist" Conferences. Wesley encouraged all members to remain loyal members of the Church of England since he had no intention of starting another denomination. At first, he believed only an Episcopal ordained minister could administer baptism and Holy Communion but, in time, he realized that apostolic succession could not be proved and that he was as scriptural a Bishop as anyone. When, therefore, Bishops refused to ordain his helpers, he ordained them himself. He never wanted to separate from the Church of England but he couldn't stop his itinerant preaching nor dissolve his societies or forbid lay preaching.

Wesley's Christianity was always essentially practical, doing all he could to help the poor and needy, living frugally himself and giving most of his income away. He also attacked abuses in public life such as corruption in politics, the press gang

---

[18] Pollock, John, *Wesley the Preacher*, p. 258

and slavery, as well as evils such as smuggling and plundering wrecked ships. When he was eighty-one, he walked through the streets of London for five days begging two hundred pounds to buy clothes for the poor in his societies. He said it was hard work, because most of the streets were filled with melting snow which was ankle deep, so that his feet were steeped in snow water from morning to night. He kept at it pretty well until the fifth evening but he became seriously ill as a result.

From 1739 Charles, like John, undertook itinerant and open air preaching, although he was by no means such an eminent preacher as John. As time went on however, John and Charles who had been so close to each other grew apart. In February 1751 John married a rich widow, Mrs. Molly Vazeille, but it was a very unhappy match and she left him in 1771. Charles had happily married in April 1749, and gave up itinerant preaching in 1756, settling in Bristol until 1771 and then in London. He continued to preach when his health allowed and assisted in Methodist administration, as well as making his greatest contribution to the movement in writing his many hymns, but it could be said that he retired from active service in 1756. The majority of his six thousand or more hymns did not become popular, nevertheless he was the greatest as well as the most prolific hymn-writer of all time. John complained that Charles was not wholehearted in his loyalty to the movement and to him. He also criticized Charles for his close links with the Countess of Huntingdon and Whitefield, and for his likely agreement with predestination. Charles on the other hand, as a high Anglican, was critical of John's doctrine of Perfectionism, but more so of his lay preachers and of the influence he thought they were exercising on John to break with the Church of England. Charles' support was very important to John and, from the 1760s, he tried hard to persuade Charles to support him on their points of difference. When, in 1788, he heard of

Charles' death, he broke down in public for the first time in his life.

Wesley, as other revival preachers, travelled about the country without regard to any weather conditions and the apostle Paul's "in perils" etc., (2 Cor.11: 26-29) could be written of him. Roads were infested with highwaymen and robbers. Also, road conditions were incredibly bad and sometimes he had to push through deep mud or floods or snow drifts. When roads were impassable he would take long detours, walking with his horse as much as twenty miles. He planned his visits so that he could stop and preach at as many places as possible, but occasionally he was overtaken by darkness, and had no shelter but a hovel. Notices of his coming would be sent ahead of him and he would rarely break his schedule. He took the opportunity when he was walking or travelling on horseback to read and prepare his sermons so that no time was lost. When he was sixty-nine he was injured and the following year his friends bought him a carriage. Even then, when the carriage broke down, he would borrow a horse and if that became lame he would walk. In his eighties nothing would stop him in his efforts to preach the Gospel in every place. It is estimated that, over fifty years or so, he travelled two hundred and fifty thousand miles and preached forty-six thousand times. Although failing in health, John continued preaching until a week before his death, on March 2nd 1791, his last words being, "The best of all is, God is with us".

Wesley's lay preachers were poor, godly, self-sacrificing men like him and shared the same hardships and persecutions as he did. Some died as a result of injuries inflicted on them and others were taken by press gangs. A clergyman, who was also a magistrate, imprisoned one young lay preacher but he continued to preach through the gaol window! People were so impressed that they brought him bedding and food until he was released. Wesley said he didn't know anyone who won so many souls for Christ within such a short time as this young man did. He spent all his time and energies in soul winning and died of tuberculosis aged twenty-eight.

George Whitefield, 1714-1770.

Whitefield, "The Awakener", was born in the Bell Inn in Gloucester, owned by his parents, and was educated at the Crypt Grammar School, Gloucester, where he excelled at elocution and acting and dramas were composed especially for him. After serving for a short time in the Bell Inn, he went up to Oxford in 1732 and, a year or so afterwards, became acquainted with the Wesleys and joined the so-called Holy Club. At this time Whitefield was under conviction and trying to save his soul by good works and mortifying his body to an extent that was extreme, even by Puritan standards. He practised fasting and self-denial in fact to such an extreme that he became ill for almost two months. The college authorities thought he was mad and he was advised to return home for a time! He stayed in Gloucester for about nine months and, while he was reading and praying with the poor and those in prison there and in Bristol, he began to see that the grace of God was free and he was soon converted. He returned to Oxford but was soon in Gloucester again to prepare himself by prayer and fasting for his ordination, on Trinity Sunday, 1736. He said that as the Bishop laid his hands upon him, "my heart was melted down and I offered my whole spirit, soul and body to the service of God's sanctuary".

From that time Whitefield preached with great power. He was only twenty-two but, wherever he preached, people gathered in huge crowds to hear him. He said he slept very little and had he a thousand hands he would employ them all in Christ's service and he wanted a thousand tongues to praise Christ. The next Sunday after his ordination he preached in his parish church, St. Mary de Crypt, and this resulted in such conviction that some complained to the Bishop that he had made fifteen people mad by it! In fact, there were later, frequent cases of hysteria, when people cried out and were prostrated under his ministry, as under Wesley's, which disturbed him. Lady Huntingdon wrote to him advising him not to remove them from the meetings as had been done, for it seemed to bring a damper on the meetings. "Let them cry out" she said, "It will do a great deal more good than your preaching"! After preaching this first sermon in Gloucester, he returned to Oxford to receive his B.A. degree and, during that summer, he continued to visit the prisoners and poor in Oxford.

In August 1736, he supplied the pulpit of a London church. He said that, when he went up into the pulpit, almost all the congregation began to sneer at him on account of his youth but he preached with such power that when he came down they showed him great respect. He immediately created an immense sensation with constant news of him in the press and, wherever he travelled, news of him spread and crowds appeared as from nowhere to hear him. The numbers wishing to hear him were so large that buildings were unable to accommodate them and additional services had to be held. Wesley said of him, "have we ever read or heard of any other person who called so many thousands, so many myriads of sinners to repentance?".

In February 1738 Whitefield sailed for Georgia to minister to the colonists and Indians, returning in December that year. Before he left England he was extremely popular but he found attitudes among the clergy had changed when he returned. Within a year, fifty pamphlets were written condemning him and his ministry and church doors were closed against him. He was regarded as an enthusiast and fanatic and the clergy were especially offended by his teaching that baptized Anglicans needed to be born again. Whitefield then began to lead the way in preaching in the open air. Seeing thousands everywhere not attending any church and spending Sundays in idleness and sin, he resolved to go after them and "compel them to come in". In February 1739, he began by preaching in the open air to vast crowds of colliers, regarded as depraved savages, in the notorious district of Kingswood, Bristol. The effects of his preaching were seen, he said, in "the white gutters made by their tears which fell plentifully down their black cheeks".

Whitefield has never been equalled as a preacher. Benjamin Franklin calculated that, over thirty thousand people could hear him clearly in the open air while David Garrick, the great British actor of the time, said that Whitefield could reduce an audience to tears by merely saying the word "Mesopotamia"! It was, however, the extraordinary power of God upon him that produced the amazing results from his ministry. The power of his preaching was seen on one occasion when he described the unconverted person being like a blind beggar going along a road near the edge of a steep cliff. At last the man was about to take the step which would have hurled him down the precipice and Lord Chesterfield, the well-known sceptic, was so carried away that he jumped up as if to save the man saying, "Good God, he is gone"! An example of how revival broke out under Whitefield's preaching is given in a letter of Henry Venn to Lady Huntingdon, in 1768. Venn attempts to describe what happened when Whitefield preached from a tombstone in Cheltenham parish churchyard, after he had been refused permission to preach in the church.

> To give your Ladyship any just description of what our eyes have witnessed and our hearts felt within the last few days exceeds my feeble powers... Under Mr. Whitefield's first

sermon there was a visible appearance of much soul concern among the immense crowd that filled every part of the burial ground, so that many were overcome with fainting: some sobbed deeply, some wept silently and a solemn concern appeared on the countenance of almost the whole assembly... his words seemed to cut like a sword upon several ... so that whilst he was speaking they could no longer contain but burst out in the most piercing, bitter cries. At this juncture, Mr. Whitefield made an awful pause of a few seconds-then burst into a flood of tears...O with what eloquence, what energy, what melting tenderness did Mr. Whitefield beseech sinners to be reconciled to God-to come to Him for life everlasting and rest their weary souls in Christ, the Saviour. When the sermon was ended the people seemed chained to the ground. Mr. Madan, Mr. Talbot, Mr. Downing and myself found ample employment in endeavouring to comfort those who had broken down under a sense of guilt. We separated in different directions among the crowd and each was quickly surrounded by an attentive audience, still eager to hear all the words of this life... Intelligence of the extraordinary power attending the word soon spread and, the next day, we had Mr. Charles Wesley and many friends from Bristol, Gloucester, Tewkesbury, Rodborough and the villages in the neighbourhood, but all loud weeping and piercing cries had subsided and the work of conversion went on, though in a more silent manner. [19]

When the London pulpits were closed to Whitefield, the first Moorfields Tabernacle was built, in June1741, which was supported by the Countess of Huntingdon. His routine was to preach in the Tabernacle in the winter and to tour other

---

[19] Seymore, A.C.H., *The Life and Times of Selina, Countess of Huntingdon*, Vol. I, p. 430

parts of the United Kingdom in the summer. He also went to all the large open spaces around London where many pleasure seeking people gathered on Sundays, and there preached to an estimated thirty to forty thousand people, although sceptical early Methodist historians said we should divide the numbers by ten! One week, after preaching in the open air at Moorfields, he received a thousand letters from people seeking spiritual help. Much of his ministry was spent in America, where he did immense good, winning tens of thousands to Christ. In 1769, he crossed the Atlantic for the thirteenth time. He never returned. On September 30th 1770 he preached his last sermon to a vast multitude and died early the next day at Newburyport, Massachusetts, where bells tolled and ships fired their guns in salute. He was buried in the crypt of the Old South Presbyterian Church and Memorial services were held all over New England and Britain and large congregations attended.

Selina, Countess of Huntingdon, 1707-1791.

Lady Huntingdon became a Christian in 1738, through the witness of her sister-in-law, Lady Margaret Hastings, who had been converted through the ministry of the Rev. Benjamin Ingham, whom Lady Margaret later married. Ingham was one of the members of the Holy Club and a close associate of the Wesley brothers, accompanying them on their mission to America in 1735. From the time of her conversion Selina was a regular attender of the first Methodist society, which was formed in Fetter Lane, London, in September 1738. She was, therefore, involved in the revival throughout her long life and she gave her full support and protection to the preaching of the Wesleys, Whitefield and other notable evangelical clergymen, some of whom became her chaplains. The influence she exercised on behalf of the Gospel was incalculable, equalling if not surpassing, that of any other woman and she was called, by her contemporaries, "The Queen of the Methodists". She favoured, however, Calvinistic preachers, such as William Romaine, Henry Venn, John Berridge and William Grimshaw, after adopting Calvinistic views herself. It seems this was a result of a closer association with Whitefield, from the time of his return from America in 1748, when she appointed him her chaplain.

In particular, in her endeavour to reach as many of her aristocratic friends as she could she made the drawing rooms of her Leicestershire and other homes available for the preaching of the Gospel, which was a remarkable break with tradition in those times, when religion was only thought to be proper and respectable in churches. Her efforts were not always appreciated by many of her social class, who thought she was a fanatic and pleaded, unsuccessfully, with her husband to forbid her to act as she did. Selina was also concerned for the conversion of all classes, and she sought to do well to her servants and the poor on her various estates, numbers of whom were converted through her personal witness. When her husband, the Earl of Huntingdon died, she was able to devote her whole wealth and energy to the cause of evangelism, selling her jewels and possessions worth several million pounds in current value. As a Countess, she felt justified in appointing her own chaplains to preach in her private chapels, and so she began to acquire or erect residences for herself with chapels attached, in various places. In addition to George Whitefield, her chaplains included the most famous and successful evangelical preachers of the day such as Martin Madan, Walter Shirley, Thomas Haweis and Romaine and other famous revival leaders such as Venn, Grimshaw and Berridge, who worked closely with her. The latter, the most eccentric and independent was very plain in addressing her saying his instructions must come from the

Lamb, not the Lamb's wife! As the spiritual work sponsored by the Countess grew she saw the need to train others to assist her select band of evangelical clergy. In 1768, therefore, the Countess opened a theological college in Trevecca, Breconshire, although students were free to serve under her patronage or enter any other Christian ministry.

Ten years later, a more serious division took place when the Countess lost the court case brought against her by William Sellon, Incumbent of Clerkenwell, who objected to the unauthorized preaching sponsored by the Countess in his parish. The judgement applied to such preaching in any parish, so she was then faced with the problem of either closing her chapels, which had been societies within the Established Church, or of protecting them under the Toleration Act by registering them as Nonconformist places of worship. Reluctantly, she chose the latter course and left the Church of England. Romaine, Thomas Haweis and other of her Anglican chaplains then resigned, although Haweis was appointed a trustee and executor at her death.

Opposition to the "Methodist" Preachers.

From the beginning of the revival, individuals and mobs used every means to disrupt the meetings and to drown the preacher's voice such as by drums and church bells. Horses and hounds and mad bulls were driven at them. Dead cats, every kind of missile and all kinds of filth were thrown at them and they were punched and attacked by a variety of weapons. Sometimes their clothes were torn to shreds and they were rolled in mud until they were unrecognizable. Even houses were attacked and some pulled down by mobs determined to reach the preachers who were staying or preaching in them. Wesley, however, was not shaken by persecution, whether by attacks on his body or reputation. Because he was so short, stones thrown at him often went over his head and hit one of his opponents! In the midst of the most violent persecution he was always amazingly courageous and calm. Once, when he was about to be thrown in a river, his only concern was that papers in his pocket would be spoiled! One account describes his visit to Wednesbury in the West Midlands, on October 20th 1743. The former support of the vicar of Wednesbury had turned to hatred and Wesley said of the sermon he preached in his hearing that he had never heard so wicked a sermon and delivered with such bitterness of voice and manner. Other local clergy were also antagonistic and stirred up mobs in their parishes telling them that cockfighting, bullbaiting and prize fights were in danger from the Wesleyan preachers. After preaching in Wednesfield Wesley went to the house of the leader of the society, which was surrounded by a mob shouting, "Bring out the minister, we'll have the minister". Wesley was then dragged by the mob to a local magistrate, who dismissed him, but a mob from Walsall arrived to attack him. He was ultimately rescued by a prize fighter, called "Honest Munchin", who later became a pillar of the Methodists in Wednesbury and Walsall and was himself persecuted for years until his death forty-six years later. In an account based on Wesley's recollections in later years it was reported:

> The screaming mob pulled Wesley toward Walsall down the steep and wet cobbled streets. One slip and he would have gone down, and they would have pummelled him to death, but he kept his feet, with his heart at peace. Several blows with bludgeons were deflected – he didn't know how except his small size made him a difficult target in a melee. And one man who "came rushing through the press, and raising his arm to strike, on a sudden let it drop and only stroked my head", saying, "What soft hair he has"... Wesley shouted,

"Will you hear me?" "No, No! Knock his brains out! Kill him!" The mob roared again, "Bring him away! Strip him". "You needn't do that: I will give you my clothes". Suddenly, a prize fighter called Honest Munchin, said, "Sir I will spend my life for you: follow me and not one soul shall touch a hair of your head". Others said the same and one cried, "Shame! Shame! Let him go". But he was again attacked and hit in the face and blood gushed out. However a new escort got Wesley safely away. Charles wrote; "My brother came delivered out of the mouth of the lion. He looked like a soldier of Christ. His clothes were torn to tatters. Munchin has been constantly under the Word since he rescued my brother. I asked him what he thought of him. "Think of him" he said, "That he is a man of God and God was on his side, when so many of us could not kill one man".[20]

Clergy and magistrates everywhere continued to be united against the Methodists and stirred up mobs against them, but King George insisted that they be respected and protected and, in time, attitudes changed. Not all magistrates, however, were biased against them. At Epworth, after Wesley's visit in 1742, a wagonload of them were arrested and taken before the magistrate. He asked what their crime was and one person said that they made people get up at four o clock and they were always praying and had converted his wife. "What have they done to her", the magistrate asked. "Well", the man replied, "before she was the biggest scold in the parish but since she has been quite a quiet soul". The magistrate then told the Methodists to go home and convert all the scolds in the parish!

In later years, Wesley was warmly welcomed and cheered by thousands as he entered a town and his visit treated as a public holiday. Those who had opposed him most bitterly regretted

[20] Pollock, John, *Wesley the Preacher*, pp. 179-181

they had done so and he lived to be almost idolized by his followers. Sadly the revival preachers opposed one another. The doctrinal differences between Whitefield and Selina and their followers on the one hand, and those of Wesley on the other, came to a head in 1770 when Wesley's London Conference issued Minutes, contrary to Calvinistic views, which Selina found offensive. She stated that, "all ought to be deemed papist who did not disown the Minutes". Wesley had formerly supported Trevecca, calling it "our college", but things now changed there when the Arminian tutor was dismissed and the president, the saintly John Fletcher, also Arminian, resigned. Some attempts were made on both sides to achieve reconciliation but the bitterest acrimony was shown by some Calvinists such as Toplady, who made disgraceful accusations against Wesley, suggesting he should be hanged or transported for his supposed crimes.

The Results of the Revival.

When Wesley died there were, in Methodism, about three hundred itinerant preachers, a thousand local preachers, and one hundred and twenty thousand or more members in the societies, with many more adherents. Moreover, Methodism had spread overseas. Most important of all, English society had been transformed and many believed that the revival saved England from the revolution which overtook France. In his address at the Foundation of the City Road Chapel John Wesley said:

> How extensive it (the revival) has been. There is scarcely a considerable town in the kingdom where some have not been witnesses of it... Consider the swiftness as well as the extent of it. In what age have such a number of sinners been recovered

from the error of their ways? When has true religion, made so large a progress in any nation within so short a time? I will not say since the Reformation but since the time of Constantine the Great. We may likewise observe the depth of the work.[21]

Almost all the revival leaders were converted when they were already in holy orders. Their experience led them to a new conception of their pastoral duties and their tireless efforts set an unprecedented standard of ministerial faithfulness and effectiveness. Thomas Grenville wrote "I have seen no change in my long life equal to the change in the habits and manners of the clergy". Church life as a whole was affected. Congregations greatly increased, as did weeknight services, the celebration of Holy Communion and Scriptural instruction. Worship was also greatly improved as dreary hymns were replaced by the vast output of new hymns by Charles Wesley, as well those by Watts, Cowper, Toplady and Newton, many of which we sing today. Nonconformist denominations were also revived. The drift towards Unitarianism was reversed and the churches were filled with the spiritual life of newly born-again members. Moreover, many agencies for the promotion of Christian work were established. These included the Sunday School Movement in 1780, the Baptist Missionary Society in 1792 and, shortly afterwards, The London Missionary Society, The Church Missionary Society and The Religious Tract Society, among others, all in the same decade. The departure of the Methodist clergy and their followers left a gap in the ministry of the Established Church. The gap was filled, however, by a second generation of evangelicals who, unlike the itinerant Methodist clergy, confined their ministry within their own parishes and infused new life into the Established Church itself.

---

[21] Wesley, John, *What hath God wrought,* Sermons, No. 132 on Numbers 23:23

George Whitefield

CHAPTER THREE
Scotland's 1742 Revival In Cambuslang

The Religious Situation in Scotland in the early Eighteenth Century

In the early part of the eighteenth century, religion was generally at low ebb in the United Kingdom. The Act of Union of England and Scotland was passed in 1707, followed by the Oath of Abjuration in 1712, by which all ministers had to swear to defend the succession of the Crown, as settled by the English Parliament. Presbyterianism, however, remained the faith of the national Church of Scotland, retaining the strong Calvinistic doctrine of the Reformation period, from which the Church of England had, in practice, largely departed. Like the English Church, however, the Scottish Church was in a low spiritual state in the early decades of the century. The spirituality of the Reformers of the sixteenth century, who protested against the errors of the Church of Rome at that time, and of the Covenanters of the late seventeenth century, who were martyred for objecting to what they regarded as the unscriptural nature of episcopacy, was no longer prevalent in Scotland.

There was rather, at this time, a new generation of ministers who regarded the Covenanters with contempt and who had a greater concern for culture and popularity with the gentry than for the spiritual welfare of their parishioners. After the "Glorious Revolution" of 1688 and the accession of William and Mary, the Scottish General Assembly met again after a suspension of thirty-seven years. By royal command, however, it had to be made up of men with very different characters and beliefs-those who had been cruelly tortured for their faith under the Stuarts and those of little conviction and spirituality who had compromised in order to keep their livings. It was a mixture, which was not promising for the future unity of the church, and the division between the two groups was to widen as time went by. Nevertheless, there were numbers of ministers and church members who were longing and praying for better times.

A book had been published in London, in 1645 entitled, *The Marrow of Modern Divinity*, containing choice extracts from the writings of Calvin, Luther and other well-known evangelical leaders. It emphasized that the Gospel was to be offered to all men, which was in contrast to the prevailing hyper-Calvinism in Scotland at the time, which stressed a divine sovereignty in predestination, which bordered on fatalism. The book was discovered by Thomas Boston, at the turn of the eighteenth century, and proved to be so popular among his friends that it was re-published in 1718 and was widely read by all classes. In 1720, however, the book was condemned by the General Assembly of the Church of Scotland and the "Marrow Men", as they were called, were persecuted and ministerial students sympathetic to them were prevented from entering the ministry. Eight of the "Marrow" ministers, who were dissatisfied with the spiritual condition of the Scottish national Church and were opposed to the system of patronage, were finally deposed from the Church. These men and their followers were known as Seceders and they founded a group which they named The Associate Presbytery, in 1733, and their first church was formed in Glasgow in 1740, the year of their expulsion from the national church. In the next twenty-five years the number of Seceding churches grew to one hundred and twenty, with one hundred thousand members. Had the Cambuslang Revival not taken place, meeting the spiritual needs of those who had been dissatisfied within the national church, the drift to the Seceders would have been much greater.

The dissatisfaction of the Seceders was well founded. The divinity students in Glasgow had hardly any teaching in theology throughout the 1730s, due to the suspension of the professor on charges of heresy. Expositions of Scripture or appeals to the conscience by preachers were not encouraged and Christianity was taught more as a moral code with some hope of immortality, than as Good News for repentant sinners. Moreover, about this time, there were far fewer meetings for prayer than there had been for very many years. It was reported that in Glasgow the number fell from more than seventy, at the turn of the century, to four or five in the 1720s and that there was nothing like meetings for prayer among the ministerial students, many of whom met in various clubs for drinking. But there were also from the beginning of the century signs of a spiritual renewal. In Donald Macfarlane's classic account of the revival he states:

> From almost the very commencement of the century there were in Scotland indications of returning power. The habitations of cruelty abroad, and the abominations of immorality at home, being both glaring, began to engage the public mind. The country was not so far gone as not to feel, at least in many places, a want of gospel light and gospel warmth in the pulpit, and the tyranny of ecclesiastical moderation in the Church courts; and for a time the few strove against the many, in seeking to arrest the downward

61

progress in both; the secession broke the strength of the reclaiming party within the Church, and their attention was perhaps all the more directed to other and brighter scenes. [22]

Sadly, however, the Seceders, who had prayed for revival for years, rejected it when it came because it was not according to their own prejudices. And, in the purpose of God, it was through the evangelical ministers who remained in the Church of Scotland that the revival came. Skevington Wood comments:

> When the spreading flame reached the Scottish border it by-passed the splinter groups as well as the Moderate strongholds and found its fullest scope in the Evangelical parishes. Many of these faithful ministers must have been sorely tempted to follow in the train of the Seceders. But they could not bring themselves to believe that the Church they loved so well could best be served by their departure. They longed for the opportunity to reform from within. And as they waited on the will of God that opportunity came. Their decision to remain within the fold proved crucial in paving the way for the revival. [23]

The Parish and Minister of Cambuslang.

In 1731, the parish of Cambuslang had been without a minister for ten years or more. For most of that time the parishioners had resisted the attempts of the patron, the Duke of Hamilton, to impose on them a candidate whom they regarded as totally unfit for the charge. This stalemate continued until, finally, the Duke reluctantly gave his consent that the people's choice, a William M'Culloch, should be appointed and he was received

---

[22] Macfarlane, D., *The Revivals of the Eighteen Century*, p. 31

[23] Wood, A. Skevington, *The Inextinguishable Blaze*, p. 116

by the parish in April that year. M'Culloch was forty years old when he began his ministry, having been a probationer for nine years, during which time he served as a private chaplain and tutor, and he then remained as pastor in Cambuslang until his death, forty years later. The apostle Paul reminds us that, "God chose the weak things of the world to shame the strong... so that no-one may boast before Him". And in this revival, as in others, the instrument God chose was not one others would have expected.

M'Culloch, though scholarly, having been educated at the universities of Edinburgh and Glasgow, and godly, was not regarded as a good preacher, his manner being slow and cautious and very different from the popular orators. It was said, in fact, that when he stood up to speak, many of the congregation left to quench their thirst in the public house! The parish itself was five miles south-east of Glasgow, with a population of less than a thousand people, consisting of about two hundred families. It was in a beautiful situation with the Clyde running along the boundary of the parish but the main road was narrow and rough, hardly passable for carts in the summer and too deep in mud to be passable for horses in the winter. Most of the people were employed in agriculture, but there were many others in coal-mining and weaving.

When M'Culloch began his pastorate in 1731, he found the parish in a state of spiritual neglect, including the fairly small church building. His predecessor had died in 1724 and had been unable to perform his duties for several years before that because of ill health, although he had a temporary assistant between 1721 and 1723. As a result, it was said two years before M'Culloch's appointment, that no-one under sixteen years of age had been catechized. For the first three years M'Culloch felt unable to administer the sacrament of Holy Communion partly, he said, because of illness and partly because he did not have enough elders, and he needed to first instruct the people and get to know them better. He was obviously a sensitive and conscientious man, so much so that soon after his ordination a colleague, whom he consulted as to whether he thought he was fit for the ministry, said he was of rather a melancholy disposition and assured him that it was thoughtful, studious persons who were mainly troubled with doubts. He also predicted that the Lord would do well by M'Culloch and that He was training him to be useful.

At the beginning of his ministry, there were still many in the parish who had had personal experience of the bitter persecution by the royal forces under Charles II and James II, in the attempt to impose episcopacy on Scotland. Thousands of those who signed the Covenant with their own blood to uphold the truth that Christ alone was Head of the Church were hunted down, tortured and killed or imprisoned for years in appalling conditions. In the 1730s, however, there was no longer the Christian love in the congregation that there had been fifty years before, in the time of persecution. In 1740, a long and bitter dispute broke out when one of the elders was accused by the rest of the trivial offence of visiting another church and he was boycotted from the sacrament until, more than a year later, the area Presbytery decided in his favour and deposed the other elders from office. The fact that the congregation also took sides on this issue and that many of them were travelling to Glasgow to hear the ministers who had seceded from the national church, inevitably added to the minister's problems and must have driven him to more earnest prayer for the Lord to revive and restore love and unity to his divided fellowship.

The Preparation for the Revival.

On the positive side, however, M'Culloch must have been encouraged by news which had been reaching Scotland, since the mid-1730s, of the revival in New England, under the ministry of Jonathan Edwards, and then by the news of revival in Wales and England, through field preaching, after the conversion of Harris and Whitefield in 1735 and of the Wesleys in 1738. The minister was undoubtedly moved by these revival reports and made a practice of reading extracts of them to his congregation which, in turn, increased the number of meetings for prayer from three at the time he arrived in Cambuslang to twelve in 1742, the year of the revival. Generally, men met with men at these gatherings and women with women, and even children conducted their own meetings. Nearby Cambuslang, godly John Welsh, a great man of prayer, began to experience a deepening of his prayer life. He began interceding God for eight hours a day and often spending days and nights in fasting and prayer for revival. It was reported of him,

> On the coldest winter nights...he has been found lying on the ground weeping, and wrestling with the Lord... Overcharged with grief, he told his wife that he had that to press him which she knew not, the souls of three thousand to answer for, whilst he knew not how it was with many of them. [24]

Church authorities and individual ministers criticized these prayer societies as a threat to the local church but it was these societies, meeting regularly for prayer and Bible study in homes on weekdays, which kept the faith of God's people alive during the days of persecution and were an important preparation for

---

[24] Fawcett, Arthur, *The Cambuslang Revival*, p. 55

the forthcoming revival. It was said that people would often meet in some lonely cottage on the moor, accessible only by muddy roads or paths. When they met they hardly greeted each other, for they hadn't travelled a long way for socializing, but for earnest prayer and the serious searching of the Scriptures and discussion of points of doctrine, with the aim of personal holiness.

Apart from the benefit of these prayer societies, many Scottish people at this time, including the poorest, were able to read the Bible and the metrical psalms for themselves, as well as the best religious books available. Preachers like Whitefield commented on the love for the Bible in Scotland and on the rustling of pages made by congregations turning to his text, something he had never known before. Sermons were also taken down in various forms of shorthand for the benefit of those unable to attend. Years before, Daniel Defoe recorded the eagerness of the Scottish people to hear preaching. "It was as though", he said, "they wished to eat the words as they left the minister's mouth"! Family prayers too were almost a national habit, and people took their Bibles to their places of work and read and meditated on them when they could. In the year or two before the revival, however, it must have seemed to many as though the judgements of God were on the land. In 1739 there were, in places, the worst storms in living memory causing much damage, followed by the spoiling of the harvest in 1740, and widespread famine in which at least two thousand people died of hunger and cold. As a result, Presbyteries appointed days of solemn humiliation, fasting and prayer to be observed in all their churches.

M'Culloch had faithfully and personally witnessed to his parishioners about Christ from the first but, by the end of 1741, he was preaching with greater power and numbers were being converted. Throughout the winter of 1741, there was a growing spiritual expectancy in Cambuslang. One woman testified later that she was much and often taken up with praying for a revival of religion that she seemed in a greater measure to forget her own concerns and herself. Another parishioner had a dream of seeing, "a great multitude of people about the Cambuslang kirk". In the first week of January 1742, the various meetings for prayer in the district came together and there was a sense that they were about to experience a great work of the Spirit of God.

At the end of January, M'Culloch, in a sermon to his congregation, remarked on the signs of a greater concern about salvation that there was in the parish and he warned them against "a noisy and ostentatious religion". On the other hand, they were not to stifle any convictions they might feel. The following month he was pleading with them to go home and kneel before God and beg Him earnestly to change their hearts and natures, and to do so until they had received His salvation. At the same time there was a door-to-door petition to ask M'Culloch to preach a weekly lecture, as some of the prominent laymen felt that with the extraordinary concern about spiritual things, more teaching was needed.

Whitefield's Role in the Revival

In July 1741, Whitefield arrived in Scotland on his first visit and stayed for thirteen weeks, preaching several times each day to thousands and speaking personally with convicted people for most of the day. There were many who opposed his coming, as most of the descriptions of his ministry circulating in the various newspapers and periodicals were extremely derogatory and abusive, describing him as a rogue and a charlatan and interpreting his collecting for the Orphan House in Georgia as a means of squeezing the last penny from the poor to line his pockets. His preaching was described as a delusion of Satan and himself as a limb of Antichrist. At first, at the invitation of Ralph Erskine and the Seceders, Whitefield was invited to join their Presbytery and to preach in their churches, so long as he confined himself to them. He replied:

> I come only as an occasional preacher to preach the simple Gospel to all who are willing to hear me, of whatever denomination. It will be wrong in me to join in a reformation as to church government any further than I have light from above. If I am quite neuter as to that in my preaching. I cannot see how it can hinder or retard any design you may have on foot. My business seems to be to evangelize, to be a Presbyter at large. [25]

He also stated that he was of the Communion of the Church of England; and that none in that Communion could join him in the work they had pointed him to; neither did he mean to separate from that Communion till he was either cast out or excommunicated. Those who invited him then turned against him when he refused to support their particular view of church government. When he asked why they required him to confine his preaching to their churches, he was told that they were the Lord's people. Whitefield then asked:

> Whether there were no other Lord's people but themselves and, supposing all others were the devil's people, they certainly had more need to be preached to; and, therefore, I was more determined to go out into the highways and hedges; and that if the Pope himself would lend me his

---

[25] Tyerman, Luke, *Whitefield,* Vol. I, p. 505

pulpit, I would gladly proclaim the righteousness of Christ therein. [26]

The Seceders then vilified Whitefield, saying he was no minister of Christ, his practice was disorderly and his doctrine and success must be diabolical. They tried to prevent him preaching in Scottish pulpits and forbade their followers to hear him or to go to Cambuslang, unless they wanted to be possessed by the devil, or even to read or discuss the revival. Others, however, who had read his journals, were not influenced by these scurrilous reports.

By March 4th 1742, Whitefield had heard of the revival in Cambuslang and wrote to the minister that he rejoiced to hear of the great work begun in Scotland and that he was sure it would continue. The revival continued throughout the next few months and M'Culloch preached with results every day. In April, M'Culloch wrote to Whitefield informing him that, in less than three months, three hundred had been convicted and more than two hundred converted and that, on the previous two Sundays, nine or ten thousand had gathered in his small parish to hear the Gospel. He concluded by appealing to Whitefield to come and help in the work. Whitefield arrived in Scotland on June 3rd, when the revivals in Cambuslang and other districts were at their peak. He reached the village in June, and immediately preached morning and evening. The evening service attracted thousands and it went on until two a.m. The effects of his preaching were unforgettable. His graphic imagery evoked powerful visions in many minds of hell, or heaven, according to their spiritual condition, and some were so impressed they could later recall the whole of his messages. It was reported that, "there were scenes of uncontrollable distress, like a battlefield". Whitefield himself described the event:

---

[26] M' Kerrow, John, *The History of the Secession Church*, pp. 510, 511

Such a commotion was surely never heard of, especially about eleven o 'clock at night. It far outdid all that I ever saw in America. For about an hour and a half there was such weeping, so many falling into deep distress, and manifesting it in various ways, that description is impossible. The people seemed to be smitten by scores. They were carried off and brought into the house like wounded soldiers taken from a field of battle. The agonies and cries were deeply affecting. Mr. M'Culloch preached after I had done, till past one 'clock in the morning, and even then the people could scarcely be got to retire. Throughout the whole of the night the voice of prayer and praise might still be heard in the fields. [27]

Several days later he preached to twenty thousand people in services that went on well into the night, regardless of the weather. The most powerful and memorable sermon was on Isaiah 54:5, "Thy Maker is thy Husband". People who had been distraught by sermons on hell and eternal punishment were ready for one on the divine love of Christ for the sinner. They were overwhelmed by the sense of His love for them and the love they felt in return, so much so that they said they wished they could die on the spot and be with Him.

Much has been made of the part Whitefield played in the revival in Scotland but, although John Wesley was not as welcome as Whitefield, in view of his being known as an Arminian in doctrine, nevertheless his twenty-two visits to Scotland were significant, though he did not visit north of the border until 1751. His first visit was said to be one of consolidation, in face of the Arian and Socinian tendencies among the moderate leaders of the Church. He met with little success in establishing Methodist societies in Scotland and Whitefield was critical of his visits. In reference to Wesley's

---

[27] Duewel, Wesley, L., *Revival Fire*, p. 65

Arminianism he said that Wesley had no business in Scotland for his principles were so well known that if he had spoken like an angel, none would hear him and, if they did, he would have nothing to do but to dispute with one and another from morning to night. Wesley replied:

> If God sends me, people will hear. And I will give them no provocation to dispute, for I will studiously avoid all controverted points and keep to the fundamental truths of Christianity, and if any dispute, they may, but I will not dispute with them. [28].

Nevertheless, in spite of the prevalence of Calvinism in Scotland at that time, Wesley's impact on the national Church was permanent. Dugald Butler commented:

> If the John Wesley of Scottish history founded no extensive organization on Scottish soil, the John Wesley in Scottish religion has been an influence of the deepest and most pervading kind. In Scotland, assuredly, Wesley's work has been a victory; the spirit of his movement within the Church has been an expansive force. [29]

The Development of the Revival.

On February 14th 1742, the Cambuslang church was full, with many standing, and the minister preached again on, "Except a man be born again". Following the message, three sisters under conviction were taken to the manse, where one of them repeatedly cried out, "What shall I do?" The minister told her to believe on the Lord Jesus Christ and be saved but weeping

---

[28] Johnson, Henry, *Stories of Great Revivals*, p. 158

[29] Wood, A. Skevington, *The Inextinguishable Blaze*, p. 125

bitterly, she said her sins were so many He would not receive her. Between her hysterical outbursts, the minister kept assuring her of Christ's willingness to save and then, as she prayed, she said Christ was saying to her that He would never leave her or forsake her, and she repeated this over and over saying, "He is telling me He has cast all my sins behind His back". She then turned to several of her unconverted friends and began to commend Christ to them in a most moving way. This was the turning point in the revival, as though the floodgates of God's blessing were then opened. There was so much expression of joy from some, and weeping from others that the noise was heard a considerable distance away.

That week there were spontaneous meetings in the houses of Christians to which neighbours flocked. People came under conviction and the newly converted, many of whom had never spoken in public before, felt a compulsion to witness to the saving power of Christ. It was Thursday, February 18th, however, that proved to be the most memorable day in the parish for many years to come. The minister preached on Jeremiah 23:6, "The Lord our Righteousness". Many wept throughout the sermon and became so agitated that they couldn't sit still. After the service about fifty crowded into the manse for prayer and counselling. This went on throughout the night but only fifteen found peace with God at that time.

The reports and influence of the revival at Cambuslang spread throughout the country and soon the parishes around, such as Kilsyth, were also experiencing revival. As M'Culloch had been encouraged initially by the news of the revival in New England under Jonathan Edwards, so now Edwards was encouraged by the Cambuslang revival and, in 1743, the two men corresponded with each other and spurred one another on to believe for greater things. At M'Culloch's invitation, Whitefield returned to Cambuslang in July to share in the

Communion season. At one Communion service at this time, it was said that there were more than thirty thousand present, and some estimated as many as forty to fifty thousand, which was twice the population of Glasgow! Only three thousand were able to take communion while thousands of others were left longing to do so. Hundreds walked from places as far away as Edinburgh and Kilmarnock for this service and for Whitefield, whose life was spent in revival, it was the greatest service he had ever witnessed. He said:

> On the Sabbath, scarce ever was such a sight seen in Scotland. There was preaching all day by one and another; and in the evening, when the sacrament was over, at the request of the ministers, I preached to the congregation of upwards of twenty thousand persons. I preached for about an hour and a half. It was a time much to be remembered. On the Monday I preached again to near as many…Thousands were bathed in tears – some wringing their hands, others almost swooning, and others crying out and mourning over a pierced Saviour. [30]

In the afternoon, the concern was again very great. Much prayer had been previously put up to the Lord. All night, in different companies, persons were praying to God and praising Him. The children of God came from all quarters. It was described as like the Passover in Josiah's time.

---

[30]   Tyerman, Luke, *Whitefield*, Vo. II. pp. 6, 7

The Criticism of the Revival

When the news of these events became public, the work was immediately criticized in the press and in pamphlets and lectures, but it led to crowds of people flocking to Cambuslang in increasing numbers. M'Culloch and several neighbouring ministers preached sermons to them almost daily. Numbers of the most eminent ministers in Scotland also visited the village to see what was happening and, after seeing the remarkable change that had taken place in many who had previously led wicked lives, they testified that it was a marvellous outpouring of the Holy Spirit. Some who criticized the revival as being simply emotional, based on reports of the crying out and faintings, had a change of mind after visiting Cambuslang and attending the meetings themselves. One spoke of the profound reverence in the place and of the thousands in tears, many crying out in distress of soul and others, who had found peace, speaking of the preciousness of Christ and their faces were radiant when ministers spoke of His glory.

The Results of the Revival

M'Culloch did not emphasize the numbers of those converted. Over the next few years he interviewed and wrote an account of the experiences of the converts and only included about four hundred on his list, warning even those not to depend on being on his list, since Judas was included among the twelve apostles! This number was an under-estimate, however, considering the many converted from other places and, even in the village itself, it seems more came to faith than the cautious estimate of the minister. Ten years after the revival M'Culloch stated:

Setting aside all who have remarkably backslidden, there is a considerable number of such who were awakened in 1742, who appear to bring forth fruits of righteousness. I do not speak at random or loosely, but from a writing which I have now before me, dated 27th April 1751, which contains a list of about four hundred persons, who were awakened here in 1742, and from that time to the time of their death, or till now, have been able to behave in a good measure as becomes the Gospel. This I state on what I have myself observed, and on the best information I could obtain. [31]

Before the revival in 1742, there were four to five hundred communicants, the following year there were three thousand. The numbers declined in the next few years, but this was a common feature in all revivals. The fact is, many were added to the church that remained faithful all their lives. What was emphasized more was the remarkable change that took place in the community as a result of so many transformed lives. Those who had spent much of their time in pubs, drinking and playing cards until morning, now wanted to stay in their own homes with their families. Drunkards, who used to lie in bed late in the morning now got up at 3 or 4 a.m. to read their Bibles and other good books and pray and meditate until 7 or 8 a.m., when they called their wives and children together for family devotions.

There were many wonderful testimonies among these converts as to how God had transformed their lives, including their family relationships, forgiving all manner of sins and giving them a new holy nature, with a desire to please God in all things. People who had been worldly-minded and selfish now had a love for all men, and a zeal for personal evangelism and missionary work, and were giving sacrificially to God's

---

[31] Johnson, Henry, *Stories of Great Revivals*, pp. 153, 154

work. Others, already Christians, were given a much greater assurance and love for Christ. Also, with the converts, they used language to describe their desire for Christ in terms reminiscent of the Song of Solomon, and they spoke of death "as a message would be to a loving wife to come home to her husband".

There was also a link between the revival and the beginning of modern missionary work on an organized scale by William Carey and others, such as the Baptist Missionary Society being formed in 1792 and the Scottish Missionary Society in 1796. Two years after the revival, a number of Scottish ministers formed what was called a "Concert for Prayer", pledging them to pray on Saturday evenings or Sunday mornings, that God would revive true religion in all parts of the world. The practice spread and, in 1784, a group of Baptist ministers in Northamptonshire formed a similar group to pray for the spread of the Gospel, which was soon attended by William Carey, and it was from this group that Carey, in 1793, went out to India.

SECTION TWO

REVIVAL IN THE NINETEENTH CENTURY

Jeremiah Calvin Lanphier 1809-1898

The Noon Prayer Meeting
of the North Dutch Church
Fulton Street New York

The Fulton Street Prayer Meeting

James McQuilkin

CHAPTER FOUR
THE 1859 REVIVAL IN NORTHERN IRELAND

The beginnings of the 1858-9 revival in North America and later Britain, known as "The Prayer Revival", is usually traced to a small prayer meeting started in New York on September 23rd 1857. Jeremiah Lamphier, a recently appointed missionary in down-town New York, invited business people to join him that day for a weekly midday prayer meeting in Fulton Street. For the first half hour no one came then, one by one, people arrived until there were six. A fortnight later, on October 7th, the number had grown to forty and, coinciding with the time when the great financial panic of that year reached a crisis and paralyzed business even more, it was decided to hold the meeting daily. Significantly, that same week a revival broke out in Hamilton, Canada, news of which further stimulated prayer for a spiritual Awakening in the United States.

Within six months, ten thousand businessmen were meeting daily for prayer in New York and, during the course of the revival, an estimated fifty thousand conversions took place there amounting to over 6% of the population. Also, over the next two years, it is estimated that a total of some two million converts were added to the nation's churches. [32] There then followed an increasing number of local revivals in America and Canada towards the end of 1857 and the beginning of 1858 and, in the early months of 1858, the secular press began

---

[32] Edwards, Brian, H., *Revival, A people saturated with God*, p. 50

to notice that something unprecedented was happening. The influence of the revival was felt everywhere, affecting all parts of North America and all classes. The number of reported conversions in the United States reached fifty thousand a week, with average additions to church memberships of ten thousand a week for two years. In some neighbourhoods the whole adult population was influenced and many churches reported receiving between one hundred and two hundred converts.

In Northern Ireland, spiritual life before the revival was at a very low ebb. Ministers complained that their congregations were spiritually dead, formal, cold, prayer-less, worldly and stingy! Years of faithful preaching often failed to result in a single convert. Also, attempts to start prayer meetings generally failed and it was said that people were more concerned to win half-a-crown than to save their souls. Ministerial interest in the American revival, however, was such that at the General Assembly of the Presbyterian Synod in Dublin, in 1858, two sessions were set aside for addresses on revival. In addition, two leading ministers, William Gibson and William McClure, were sent to New York to investigate the revival and report back and their enthusiastic report, which they shared in meetings and in a book, increased the desire for revival in Ireland.

James McQuilkin and the preparatory prayer meetings

The person to whom generally the revival in Northern Ireland has been ultimately traced, humanly speaking, is James McQuilkin, who was brought to Christ in November 1856 through the witness of a Mrs. Colville, an English lady Missioner in Ballymena. This was in answer to her earnest prayer that God would give her just one soul and she would be content! McQuilkin then had his faith increased by a reading of George Muller's *The Life of Trust*; *The Life of Murray M'Cheyne* and Finney's *Lectures on Revival*. As a result, he began a weekly prayer meeting with three young friends, and then others, whom he had influenced, spiritually.

The prayer meeting took place in the schoolroom near Kells in the parish of Connor, County Antrim, in September 1857, at the same time as the beginning of the Fulton Street meeting in New York. On January 1st 1858, the young men saw their first convert and by the end of the year, there was an average attendance of fifty at the prayer meeting. Soon other prayer meetings, held each week, began in homes and by the end of 1858, there were about one hundred in the district, at which many were convicted of sin and their need of Christ. They prayed for an outpouring of the Holy Spirit upon themselves and the surrounding country. This was their one great object and burden of their prayers. They said they held right to the one thing and, though they were ridiculed for praying in that way, they kept on praying until the power came.

An eye witness gave a vivid account of one of these prayer meetings:

> For some time before the appointed hour, many of the younger converts assemble to sing together some favourite hymns. A little later the people pour in rapidly and soon every seat is occupied, men of business sitting beside their workers, all in their usual attire. A large proportion is made up of school children and of the lower classes, who were specially visited during the Awakening. Some seem very anxious and all are solemn. On the faces of the recent converts there is such a beaming gladness that even a stranger can tell their story at a look. The prayer which follows bears greatly on the three classes of worshippers, the converted, the anxious

and the unawakened, and contains earnest pleadings for the Spirit's presence for the spread of the revival work... [33]

Connor

During 1858, the revival movement was confined to the rural parish of Connor, in which it began, and where for years the Rev. John H. Moore, the Presbyterian minister, had faithfully preached, establishing Sunday schools and endeavouring to establish prayer meetings. He also read to his congregation accounts of revival in Wales under Daniel Rowlands and in America under Jonathan Edwards. These human efforts, however, bore little fruit at the time and the number of prayer meetings dwindled to one, with only two or three persons attending it. However, when the revival began he took a leading part in it, winning many to Christ, and the number of prayer meetings increased to more than one hundred!

Ahoghill

In March 1859, James McQuilkin and a friend held a meeting in the First Presbyterian church in Ahoghill, a village described as "the worst little place in the world". The savage population indulged in cock-fighting drinking bouts, fighting and blasphemy, even at funerals. Yet even here the crowd was so great that there were fears of fatal accidents as the galleries threatened to collapse under the alarming pressure, so the place was evacuated and three thousand people assembled outside. Despite a chilling rain, hundreds fell on their knees in the mud of the streets and others were prostrated under the conviction of sin as the Gospel was preached to them. Drunkards, blasphemers and savage, cruel men, were transformed and

---

[33] Paisley, Ian, *The Fifty Nine Revival*, p. 33

the churches overflowed with converts. People came under a deep conviction of sin, in the streets and fields. Children in schools were crying to God for mercy and trusting in Christ for salvation. For six weeks or so secular work stopped as people were unable to think of anything but concern for their souls.

It was at Ahoghill that the first physical manifestations of the revival were seen and described by an eye witness, the Rev. F. Buick of Ahoghill.

> Even strong men have staggered and fallen down under the wounds of their conscience. The whole frame trembles. Oh! It is a heartrending sight to witness. With wringing of hands, streams of tears, and a look of unutterable anguish, they confess their sins in tones of unmistakable sincerity and appeal to the Lord for mercy with a cry of piercing earnestness. I have seen the strong frame convulsed; I have witnessed every joint trembling; I have heard the cry, as I have never heard it before, "Lord Jesus, have mercy upon my sinful soul…oh, come and lift me from these flames of hell". These convictions vary in different individuals both in strength and duration. While some obtain peace in believing soon after their conviction, others do not attain it for several days. It is after many a conflict, with conviction often returning, with much prayer and reading of the Word, through which spiritual light makes progress in the mind, that a settled peace and holy joy takes possession of the soul. [34]

People came under a deep of sin, in the streets and in the fields, children in schools crying to God for mercy and trusting Christ as their Saviour. There were prostrations, convulsions and shrieks for mercy, which led to an initial critical distrust of the

---

[34] Johnson, Henry, *Stories of Great Revivals*, pp. 271, 272

movement in other parts of the United Kingdom. There were accusations of hysteria, hallucination and unholy excitement. The Irish Press accused ministers of "rascality" for "working it up" by unwarranted and artificial means. Some Irish ministers themselves at first attributed the manifestations to the influence of Satan, while others deplored the phenomena and wished the revival would go on quietly without these manifestations as it had started, but the change for the good in people and communities soon persuaded them that they were of God. Churches which had been formal and spiritually indifferent became spiritually alive, and towns and villages noted for ungodliness were transformed into sober, Bible loving districts and hundreds of ungodly homes became devoted to prayer and praise. Opinions were divided among ministers as to the cause of the physical manifestations. One minister said he thought they were as much for the benefit of others as for those who were the subjects of them and that every prostration was a sermon, a thrilling appeal to the profligate and a solemn warning to nominal Christians.

One minister criticized the manifestations, as reported in the Wrexham Advertiser, stating:

> After a good deal of actual examination, I have to state I believe that there is a dangerous physical malady abroad and that its seat is in the nervous system. It affects poor young girls who are working in factories all day with very insufficient food, and these girls I have seen myself suffering under the complaints I shall mention. I have known it to end in epilepsy. I have seen them in epilepsy. I have seen it in catalepsy. Will you find anything like it in the Bible? I deny it...[35]

---

[35] Edwards, Brian, H., A people saturated with God, pp. 201.202

The same paper reported a reply from another minister to this criticism a month later as follows,

> Many have looked upon these (manifestations) with wonder and perplexity and doubt. On this side of the channel they are commonly regarded as the results of mere animal excitement. This is a mistake. No one on the spot will ever dream of putting them down to such a cause. I never saw meetings more free from all display of mere feeling. A stranger going to any of these religious gatherings that now fill, evening after evening, almost all the Protestant places of worship in Ulster, would feel at once there is no rant here, no effort to get up any artificial feeling. An unwonted solemnity and earnestness of feeling shows itself in the faces of the people, but attempts to create any mere excitement there are none...I am quite sure that, with rare exceptions, there is no consistent way of explaining (the phenomena) except by confessing that they are the work of God. [36]

Another minister, in a lecture on the manifestations, reported in the Wrexham Advertiser said,

> I have heard some say, 'We do not like these bodily prostrations-we like all beside'. I do not think it is seemly to say to God what it is we like in his work and what we dislike. Is God to give an account of his doings? [37]

---

[36] Edwards, Brian, H., A people saturated with God. pp. 202,203

[37] Ibid., p. 204

Ballymena

The awakening at Ahoghill spread to Ballymena, a town of six thousand inhabitants, three miles from Ahoghill. It had one hundred and twenty public houses and was noted for its drunkenness and licentiousness. Yet one resident wrote that when the revival came, careless men were bowed in unaffected earnestness and sobbed like children. Drunkards and boasting blasphemers were awed in solemnity and silence. Languid believers were stirred to unusual Christian activity and ministers found themselves beset by inquirers and wholly unequal to the demands which were made.

Some, it is said, were suddenly pierced (with conviction) as with a sharp sword, and the whole town was affected with cries for mercy. Prayer or singing was also heard in the fields, streets and almost every house. Business was practically suspended and several crowds of people, all praying or praising, could be seen in the street at any one time. People sang in groups as they walked home from services marching four or five abreast as they sang. These singing bands became a common sight and they often walked the streets singing until dawn. United prayer meetings were held at all hours of the day and night. One large church was crowded to capacity for a prayer meeting on a Saturday, the day of the weekly market when, normally, hardly a dozen would have attended. Another church which usually had fifty attending a weekly prayer meeting, now had one thousand attending almost every day. At these prayer meetings the younger converts would meet before the appointed time to sing hymns. Then the people would pour in and every seat would be taken, many of them by children and working class people who were strangers to religious services. During a service there would be an unusual solemnity, and the most intense earnestness was seen on people's faces. Meetings went on long after the usual length of a service, with prayer, praise and exhortations. One minister reported:

> In this town at present, at public worship on Sabbath, the churches are thronged; pews, aisles and vestibules. The open-air services, whether in town or country, on any evening of the week are attended by thousands, and these services though so numerous are often not far from each other. Our congregational weekly prayer meeting was attended by some fifty persons ordinarily. During the past three months, whether held four or five times a week, it is attended by more than twenty times that number. The difficulty used to be to get people into the church, but the difficulty now is to get them out of it. One night and morning we had three services. The first of these lasted for three and a half hours. I pronounced the benediction intending to dismiss the people but no, they remained and only a few left. After some half an hour we engaged in prayer and praise again. I pronounced the benediction again intending to dismiss the people but no, they still remained, only a few left. [38]

Other meetings were held in kitchens, barns, schools, fields or on the streets. As elsewhere, business almost came to a standstill and people from all walks of life, the learned, the wealthy and upper classes, as well as labourers and the illiterate, crowded into the services under a conviction of sin. The churches themselves held services, which continued throughout the night, and ministers everywhere were being called to deal with those seeking salvation.

A description from the Ballymena Observer of a field meeting is an example of hundreds of similar meetings in Ulster in the summer and autumn of 1859:

---

[38] Paisley, Ian, *The Fifty Nine Revival*, p. 184

Row after row the people stretched upward from the speakers on a natural Amphitheatre of grass. There was perfect silence – no whispering or inattention. The multitude stood as if rooted to the ground…and now and then, as the service went on, the cloud of awe-striking influence seemed to come closer and a cry, an involuntary cry, broke the unearthly silence. Trembling and amazed, now a man, now a woman fell, sometimes softly imploring mercy and sometimes with shrieks to the Lord for deliverance. The person was quietly led away and the service continued…The benediction was pronounced and the vast multitude was about to slowly depart but a mysterious spirit held them. Suddenly one person then another fell to the ground, crying aloud. Friends surrounded those who had fallen, praying with them, singing psalms and pointing them to the Lamb of God. All the stricken ones poured out cries for mercy in agonized tones-once heard, never to be forgotten. [39]

Belfast

In May 1859, the revival reached Belfast, through a visit of the Connor converts. By June, most of the evangelical churches were crowded for weekday services which, as in other places, often went on until the early hours of the morning or daybreak. Ten thousand people are said to have been converted in the city at that time. That month, an estimated fifteen thousand people (some say forty thousand) gathered for a mass open-air prayer meeting in the Botanical Gardens when the crowd divided into small groups, some of ragged children, whose prayers greatly affected those who heard them. Children's prayer meetings were also held. One had three hundred present, a third of which were converted. A further meeting there in August attracted

---

[39] Johnson, Henry, *Great Stories of Revivals*, pp. 274, 275

twenty thousand. One of the most impressive results of the revival was the great freedom, eloquence and power in prayer shown by the new converts, as well as a hatred of sin and a love and zeal for the Saviour and unsaved souls. Prayer added a new dimension to the lives of many and there were outstanding answers to prayer, reported everywhere. What had been the favourite preoccupations of drinking and gambling were largely abandoned. The Maze Racecourse October Meeting only drew five hundred, instead of the usual thousand, and a large distillery, capable of producing a million gallons of whisky a year, was auctioned to be sold or dismantled.[40] Meetings for prayer and to hear converts and evangelists continued to be held throughout the autumn, with churches as full as ever, but the cases of prostration became rare.

Many of the forty thousand Roman Catholics in Belfast, a third of the population, were greatly disturbed by the Revival. At first they mocked it, but then became afraid and endeavoured to avoid all possible contact with Protestants, and their priests distributed holy water to safeguard them against the influence of the revival. Some priests also attributed the spiritual results of the revival to the evangelists carrying chloroform in their handkerchiefs!

Boroughshane

The Presbyterian minister of Boroughshane, when the revival began there in May 1859, said that the people had been praying for and expecting some such precious blessing but were taken by surprise, so sudden, powerful and extraordinary were the manifestations of the Spirit's presence. He thought about one thousand people were suddenly, sensibly and powerfully impressed and awakened. Workers in a spinning factory there

---

[40] Orr, Edwin, J., *The Second Evangelical Awakening in Britain*, p. 47

were seized by the Holy Spirit's conviction of sin and twenty or thirty people were prostrated on the ground. The factory had to be closed for two days while people prayed to be right with God and many, including notorious profligates, were converted. The first revival conversion there, however, took place in 1858. It was that of a drunkard who awakened his family in the night and said that he had had a dream. An angel came and told him to be up and busy praying for mercy for he would die at one o clock or, if not, certainly at four o clock. He dressed and gave himself to reading and prayer. His family thought that he was mad, but he refused all persuasion to take alcohol and went about crying for mercy until one a.m., when he went to bed and died happy at four a.m.

Comber

A minister in Comber, County Down, spoke of the whole neighbourhood being awakened. In a nearby quarry, where the workmen were noted for their vices, a preaching service was held and, as a result, out of ninety-six families represented, ninety started family worship. He stated:

> The whole town and neighbourhood were roused. Many did not retire to rest the first night at all and, for several days, great numbers were unable to attend their usual vocations but gave themselves almost unceasingly to the study of the Scriptures, singing and prayer and, for the first month, with about three exceptions, I did not get to bed till morning, such was the anxiety of the people for pastoral instruction and consolation.[41]

---

[41] Paisley, Ian, The Fifty-Nine Revival, p. 77

In another district every housewife was converted and these women formed a women's prayer meeting. In prayer meetings generally it is said that God's presence was so evident that the congregations were filled with awe and fear, then moved to tears and filled with an extraordinary love, as if the Lord had breathed on them.

Ballymoney, Ballycarry and Dundrod

Young and old of all denominations, even Roman Catholics, were eager to attend these meetings. The prayer meetings, which were sometimes led by laymen, attracted thousands. One area fair was turned into a prayer meeting with five thousand people attending. At Ballymoney, one of the first places to be affected, a hundred prayer meetings in the town and district were held and, at Ballycarry, after the revival began there, meetings continued for forty-two nights with prayers for the enquirers going on until daybreak. In Dundrod, the revival was said to spread with the rapidity of a prairie fire. People under conviction were unable to remain in the church there and, going out, fell prostrate in the graveyard. Some were in a trance, others crying for mercy. Some staggered for a while and then dropped to their knees to pray, or fell into the arms of friends as in a swoon, and a few rushed to the gates and fled in terror from the place.

Coleraine

Coleraine is said to have been more deeply stirred than any other town. The Rev. W. Arthur described an amazing spiritual Awakening in a large school there. One boy was so troubled about his soul that the schoolmaster sent him home to call upon the Lord in private. An older boy, a Christian, went with him and, before they had gone far, he led him to Christ. Returning to school with a beaming face the convert said to the master, "Oh I am so happy, I have the Lord Jesus in my heart". These simple words had a great effect on the rest of the boys. The report continued:

> The attention of the whole school was attracted. Boy after boy slipped out of the room. After a while the master… looked over the wall of the playground. There he saw a number of his boys ranged around the wall on their knees in earnest prayer, every one apart. The scene overcome him. Presently he turned to the pupil who had been a comfort to the one school fellow and said, "Do you think you can go and pray with those boys"? He went out and kneeling down among them began to implore the Lord to forgive their sins for the sake of Him who had borne them all on the cross. Their silent grief soon broke into a bitter cry… The girls' school was above, and the cry no sooner penetrated to their room, than apparently well knowing what mourning it was, and hearing it as a call to themselves, they too fell upon their knees and wept. Strange disorder for the school master and mistress to have to control. The united cry reached the adjoining streets, and soon every spot on the premises was filled with sinners seeking God. [42]

Neighbours and passers-by hearing the children's cry, flocked into the school and, as they entered the door, they came under the convicting power of the Holy Spirit. They all joined in the cry for mercy and, before long, every available space on the premises was crowded with people seeking God, and ministers were sent for to pray with those convicted. Dinner and tea were forgotten and it was not until eleven o' clock at night that

---

[42] Duewel, Wesley, L., *Revival Fire*, pp. 150

people left. Also, a New Town Hall had been built in the town and the mayor had planned a ball to celebrate its opening, but the spirit of repentance was so widespread, it had to be used for prayer. The courthouse of the town was filled too. Ministers prayed with anxious souls until they were exhausted. In many places there were so many converts that the churches could not hold them all. The churches witnessed hundreds of conversions, one experiencing eight hundred, and sometimes more than a hundred turned to Christ in a single night.

Castlederg

In Castlederg the congregation had begun singing the first verse of a hymn when suddenly a strong man fell to the ground. He was removed, and immediately there was an amazing manifestation of the presence of God. The whole church was filled with the glory of God. The singing had to stop and nothing was heard except sobbing and sighing, some crying for mercy and others rejoicing in God, who had forgiven their sins. Several hours later the minister could not get the people to go, although he pronounced the benediction six times! Eventually some left singing, others still crying for mercy, and some of these were so convicted they fell prostrate on the road. Those who had found peace immediately began to point to Christ others who were still under conviction of sin.

Many Roman Catholics were converted and discarded their beads and amulets and cried, "No priest but Jesus". Some were even convicted sitting in their chapels during Mass, but the priests denounced the revival as a contagious disease, newly invented by the devil and they blessed charms and consecrated water, which they sold as an antidote against the "contagion". One Roman Catholic servant paid a shilling for a bottle of holy water and, creeping into his master's room when he was praying, poured the water over him to prevent him 'catching the disease'! Many Catholic converts received threats and some, especially children, were brutally beaten by their families for their faith, but most remained steadfast despite severe persecution from the hands of relatives and priests. It is significant that the revival was most effective in the Protestant areas and, in Catholic areas, it was in inverse proportion to the size of the Catholic population.

The Results of the Revival

The whole of Northern Ireland was affected by the revival and the character of towns and villages was transformed. Sunday was observed as a day of rest, and reading the Bible became a habit for thousands who had previously neglected it. Family worship became the daily custom of thousands of households. One clergyman stated that, in 1857, only seven families in his parish had family worship but, during the revival, he had three hundred and fourteen requests for forms of family prayer. Another, whose congregation consisted of two hundred and nine families, had only two not observing family worship.

The courts and gaols were affected by a sudden decrease in crime. Profanity, drunkenness, vice, fraud and dishonesty, swearing, fighting, family feuds and litigation diminished, together with poverty, while savings increased. People became more courteous and considerate and, apart from a greater regard for the Bible, there was a new interest in sacred music, education, personal cleanliness and eliminating poverty. Public houses were closed or had only a few pence in takings and places of amusement became preaching stations. People were absorbed with prayer and carried Bibles wherever they went, even stopping their work in the fields or stopping on the road to read more of the Scriptures.

Also, before the revival there was the traditional animosity between Protestants and Roman Catholics but now, instead of Catholics being attacked with bricks and clubs, they were able to pass through the streets without even verbal abuse. Rather, leading Orangemen met to pray for Catholics and some with them. The members of the Orange Society in Dundrod were also changed by the revival and, as in other places, they kept the 12th of July anniversary of the Battle of the Boyne as never before, one girl commenting, "You wouldn't have known it was the 12th at all". The Orangemen requested their minister to hold a prayer meeting and afterwards, with Bibles in their hands, and with no music playing or flags flying, they walked peacefully to a field where hundreds met them and joined them in prayer and praise to God. Instead of extra police being employed, as usual on this anniversary, the only peace preserver was the usual night constable. People spent the day at work and prayer and preaching services took the place of demonstrations. Another result was the unity that existed between the churches. One Church of England minister said that to ask what denomination a convert belonged to would excite a smile of pity, and that it is now considered that there are only two sects in the world, the one for Christ and the other against him.

Before the revival, some people thought Ulster was the last place in the world where a revival would occur. The Protestant population, mostly of Scottish descent, was said to be shrewd, calculating and not susceptible to excitement. They were described as being trained to reason, cold in religion, dreading religious fervour, devoid of fanaticism and inclined to Unitarianism not enthusiasm, with wills remarkably unyielding. Up to the very week of the revival there appeared to be no general desire for it or sign of its coming. The Rev. John Moore, before the revival, said that what concerned him about his congregation was not only their disinclination to prayer meetings but their hostility to them. It was this congregation, however, which, through Moore's exhortations and his public reading of extracts of former revivals, was encouraged to pray and which became the vanguard of the revival.

There were, however, hindrances to the revival. One minister attributed them to constant visits to the homes of the poor converts by investigators from England and elsewhere, which interrupted people's work and, in some instances, caused converts pride in their experiences, as well as sects trying to "poach" converts. "The Rev. S.J. Moore of Ballymena commented:

> Consider a poor family that have to live by their industry, visited by twelve or fifteen parties every week. Then a gentleman or a lady from another land will sit down and, with pocket-book in hand, will take down their answers to the metaphysical, sometimes the very hard metaphysical questions, which they may be pleased to put to these poor unlearned people. "Oh, sir", said a woman to me, who had been converted, "if these people would only go home and look into their own hearts"! But also these visits have the effect of vanity among the people...A little child came to me and said, "Oh, sir, there has just been seven gentlemen visiting me, and they said I was the best case they ever saw"... Another matter is...almost all the strangers who have been among us have suggested the idea that we are to expect the work will cease. I ask you, is not this strong expectation of a thing one of the causes which might bring it about? We believe it is not for us to expect the Spirit of God will leave us. Why should we expect the Spirit of God to leave us? The Spirit is willing to abide with you, and why should you be the first to drive Him away? There is another point....

The spirit of peace has been disturbed during the last six weeks in my own town and neighbourhood, by the spirit of controversy. I refer to the distribution of tracts, and persons going from house to house, not for the purpose of winning lost souls to the Saviour but to win souls to a sect. [43]

Summary

It is estimated that at least a hundred thousand people were converted in the revival. All over Northern Ireland, ministers, who were the chief workers in the revival, eagerly told of the amazing work of God in their churches and districts and reported that none of those they believed had been truly converted had gone back on their profession of faith. No Mission workers were engaged in the early months but, when the revival was publicized, scores of ministers and evangelists from other parts of the United Kingdom went to see what was happening and helped in the work. Henry Grattan Guinness, later founder of the "Regions Beyond Missionary Union", and Brownlow North were among the most effective of these. Many who were also to be notable Christian leaders were converted at that time such as Dr. Barnado, as well as the Labour leader Keir Hardie, resulting in the foundation of many religious and social organizations such as the Salvation Army, The China Inland Mission and many other religious and social movements. It is impossible to adequately assess the religious and social effects of the revival but it transformed the whole province. Drunkenness considerably decreased. Magistrates and police testified to the remarkable decrease in criminal offences and disorderly conduct. The evil character of many towns and villages was transformed. Prayer meetings were established in places which had been spiritually dead, and reading the Bible

---

[43]   Johnson, Henry, *Stories of Great Revivals*, pp. 296, 297

and family-worship became a daily custom in many homes. Attendances at places of worship increased and there were many instances of crowded congregations, bringing about a zeal for evangelical Christianity and evangelism and a love for the Bible, perhaps unique in any country in the Western world, which has continued to the present day. Revival can only occur in the sovereign will of God but this revival, as others, humanly speaking, was undoubtedly due to the persistent prayer of a few dedicated men and women so moved by God.

Humphrey Jones

David Morgan

CHAPTER FIVE

THE 1859 REVIVAL IN WALES

Whilst a great deal has been written of the revival in Wales in 1904-5 comparatively little has been written, or is generally known, of the revival that took place in the principality in 1859. A rare book by Thomas Phillips, *The Welsh Revival Its Origin and Development,* published in 1860, was the first comprehensive account of the revival. This book, reprinted by the Banner of Truth Trust in 1995 and, *David Morgan The Revivalist, The 1859 Revival in Wales,* by J.J. Morgan, son of the revivalist David Morgan, published in Mold in 1909, and now out of print, are the main sources for this revival.

The Origins of the Revival

As in other revivals, this began with a conviction among God's people of the need of prayer for a spiritual Awakening. Following the great eighteenth century revival in Wales, a revival had taken place in some part of Wales in every decade in the second half of that century, and in the first half of the nineteenth century. During this period, in fact, Welsh churches expected God to build up his work by revivals, rather than by evangelistic campaigns. Also, in the early nineteenth century, the faithful ministry of notable preachers such as Christmas Evans, William Williams of Wern and John Elias had blessed Wales. By the early 1840s, however, these men had died and the churches were in decline, spiritually and morally. Preaching was still orthodox but lifeless, being generally in a polished, rhetorical style and concerned with being popular rather than with producing conviction and conversion. Principal T.C. Edwards of Bala, speaking of this time said:

> The churches were withering away in our country. A wave
> of spiritual apathy and practical infidelity had spread over
> Wales.[44]

From the mid-1850s, however, there were more hopeful signs. There were ministers who for years had been discouraged at the state of the churches and the poor results of their witness and who had prayed for a spiritual Awakening. Their preaching became increasingly more lively and earnest and their churches began to give more attention to prayer. Certain areas then experienced an outpouring of the Spirit, as happened in Trevecca Theological College in the winter of 1857. After some unforgettably powerful prayer meetings there, all the students experienced a filling of the Spirit and an overwhelming sense of the presence of God, which transformed their ministries and prepared them for the revival which followed. By early 1858, reports of the religious revival which was sweeping across the United States, as well as of numerous small local revivals in widely separated places in Wales, created a stir throughout the Welsh churches. In April, May and June 1858, the Calvinistic Methodists (Welsh Presbyterians), the Baptist and Congregational Association Meetings, respectively, discussed the reports of the American revival and called on their churches to pray for a national awakening in Wales and the churches responded. Then, on Sunday, August 1st 1858, churches throughout the southern counties of Wales united in prayer for the same purpose. People, in fact, began gathering for prayer all over the land. They met in special united prayer

---

[44]   Morgan, J.J. *David Morgan the Revivalist*, p. 3

meetings, as well as in the normal prayer meetings, and not only in churches and chapels, but also in drawing rooms, schoolrooms, town halls, tents and the open fields, and this devotion to fervent prayer for revival on the part of very many people was soon to be answered.

It was, however, the ministry of Humphrey Jones that is said to have been "the exciting and visible cause" of the revival. Jones, born in 1832, had emigrated to America in 1854 but returned to Wales in June 1858. He had worked as a missioner of the Episcopalian Methodists until 1856, when he became an independent preacher, being greatly influenced by the writings of Charles Finney, and soon became known as "Humphrey Jones the revivalist". Hundreds were converted under his ministry and he then decided to return to Wales to bring the revival to his native land. Arriving at his home village of Tre'r-ddol, ten miles north of Aberystwyth, he held a five-week mission in the area and daily exercised the same powerful, searching ministry there. His method was to awaken the local church before preaching to the unconverted and he challenged the churches with messages on texts such as Amos 6:1, "Woe to them that are at ease in Zion". There were amazing scenes and conversions in every service and witnesses described his meetings as "a second Pentecost". Sometimes, before he had finished his closing prayer, scores of people were praying aloud for mercy, drowning his voice. Someone commented:

> Only with the greatest difficulty was it possible to drive the carriage past the chapel, such was the crowd. The chapel was crammed full and the road in either direction past it, for about half a mile, was packed with people, young and old some worshipping, some praying, others praising, and everyone behaving orderly, with self-control. People congregated at the chapel at five in the morning, even on the busiest days of

harvest and the sound of praise could be heard in the houses and in the fields throughout the locality.[45]

Significantly, David Morgan, a Calvinistic minister of Ysbyty Ystwth, Cardiganshire, who was to be the principal human instrument in the revival, wrote in his Diary as early as 1855:

> It is a great thing for the Lord to revive his work. Whoever has the desire for this, it will compel him to do all in his power to revive the Lord's work. Reading Church History we realize that the great work of God fluctuates up and down, but whenever the Lord draws near to save there was among the godly an expectancy of His coming. Together with prayer we should also strive for the reviving of his work. This is how the godly have always done; they prayed and they worked.[46]

At the end of September 1858, Morgan heard Humphrey Jones for the first time at nearby Pont-rhyd-y-groes. Jones spoke to him about the spiritual dearth in the churches, about the need for persistent, earnest prayer and a greater endeavour by the ministers in their preaching and personal work among the people. Morgan, distrusting anything American or Wesleyan, was unhappy with Jones's suggestions and suspicious of his ministry until he heard him preach with convicting power, the next day, at Ysbyty Ystwth on Revelation 3:16, "So, because you are lukewarm,-neither hot nor cold-I am about to spit you out of my mouth". The whole congregation was moved by the message and Morgan became aware of the shortcomings in his own ministry in the light of the spiritual need around him. He had long prayed for a spiritual anointing and, three days later

---

[45] Evans, Eifion, *Fire in the Thatch*, p. 196

[46] Ibid, pp. 212, 213

at four a.m. he awoke, conscious that a new, mysterious change had come over him. He also began to preach with extraordinary power and was given a remarkable memory, whereby he was able to remember and pray for detailed individual needs of converts he had counselled and then, as suddenly, less than two years later as the revival was declining, the gift left him.

During this mission of Humphrey Jones in Ysbyty Ystwyth, the village churches of the two ministers, the Wesleyan and Calvinistic Methodists, had joint prayer meetings every night, alternately in their respective churches, and soon their churches were filled with returning backsliders and people who had never been to church for years. From this time, mainly under the ministry of these two men, the national revival began in Cardiganshire and then spread throughout the country as God used other ministers. It is significant that none of these men, Jones and Morgan included, were famous for their natural gifts but were exceptionally gifted by God for the work they were to do in the revival.

The Progress and Extent of the Revival.

The two ministers now travelled throughout Wales and revival broke out under their preaching wherever they went, growing from the summer of 1858, peaking in the second week of January 1860, during the annual Week of Prayer, declining thereafter and finishing towards the end of that year. Humphrey Jones, however, had burnt himself out by 1859 and, like Evan Roberts in the 1904-5 revival, he retired from public ministry and devoted himself to private prayer, though he returned to the ministry in later years. David Morgan then became the principal instrument of revival blessing under God from that time on, having several encounters with God, when he was anointed with extraordinary spiritual power. On the last day of 1858, he was travelling home from a preaching engagement over a lonely upland when he had an encounter with God like Jacob at Peniel.

> He was on this mountain for hours; whether in the body or whether out of the body, he hardly knew. Beyond a doubt he went through experiences unspeakable and full of glory... On this strange night on the hill he seemed to feel some mystical forces lifting him as it were body and soul from the earth. We cannot but think that One whose name is Wonderful came out of the darkness to meet him...When he let go the Divine Sojourner, and awoke to his terrestrial surroundings, his puzzled beast was standing by him. Giving it the reign, he arrived home with a countenance so strange, and garments so spoiled, that his people hardly recognized him. When questioned, he replied, "I have been wrestling for the blessing and I have received it.[47]

Throughout Wales, the services in the churches and chapels on weekdays and Sundays were crowded, and ministers reported that hundreds were being converted, including the worst characters in the district. It was common for churches of all denominations to have two hundred or more converts added to their membership. When he visited Aberystwyth, Morgan held six services daily, attended by all classes and four hundred were added to the Calvinistic Methodist church alone. Soldiers there also held a prayer meeting before their morning parade, as well as at midday and in the evening. Seamen, who had previously been a nuisance in the town, attended the revival meetings and were on fire for God. Seamen generally were particularly affected. The Rev. Prebendary Venn, going on a ship manned by Welshmen, found that nearly the entire crew

---

[47] Evans, Eifion, *Fire in the Thatch,* pp. 215

were Christians. Speaking to them one by one he was delighted to hear their testimony. On asking how they had become Christians he was told it was through the influence of a sailor who had joined them two years before, in 1858, and virtually the whole of the crew, who had then been utterly careless and ungodly, had been saved. One account said:

> All along the seacoast from Conway to St. David's, the seafaring people form a large proportion of the new disciples and that three quarters of the seamen are now professing Christians.[48]

The revival became the main subject of conversation among all classes of people and made a great impression on the nation in general. In many neighbourhoods there were very few people who had not made a profession of faith and there are recorded instances of the great joy when the last person in a community resisting the Gospel was converted! Workers in the coal and copper mines and slate quarries, proverbial at that time for their ungodliness and brutality, held prayer meetings before they began their shifts. At one mine, every miner was converted except one, for whom the rest were praying. The spiritual life of the churches themselves was transformed and young people particularly were affected. Children as young as eight years old held prayer meetings and prayed fervently for God to continue to pour out His Spirit upon them. In the Congregational church in Llanharan, Glamorganshire, there was a large influx of children aged eight to ten years, who had had powerful experiences and who showed unmistakable signs of a genuine conversion. The revival was not so powerful, it seems, in some English speaking parts of counties such as Monmouthshire, as it was in the Welsh speaking areas,

---

[48] Johnson, Henry, *Stories of Great Revivals*, pp. 256

particularly in Welsh speaking Cardiganshire and North Wales but, nevertheless, all parts and classes and denominations in the land were affected by it. Among the Welsh Congregational churches of Monmouth there was hardly a single church not affected.

As has been indicated, the revival was not confined to church services. At Ffestiniog, it broke out among quarrymen, while they were at work. Some young men came to work there from Bettws-y-coed who were under a deep conviction of sin, occasionally weeping on account of their lost condition before God. At lunchtime one day they were seen by the rest of the workmen going to the top of the nearby mountain, and the five hundred or so men from the quarry followed them, and they all held a prayer meeting there. As they prayed, the Holy Spirit came upon them all in a powerful way, and most of them wept aloud. The next day they were unable to work and spent the time in prayer on the mountain again and then met every night for prayer and praise in their respective churches. The following weekend, the workmen who lived at a distance from the quarry went home and took the revival fire to the surrounding churches and chapels. One minister was so impressed with the events that he reported that it may well be doubted whether anything had taken place in the 1859 revival in Ireland or in America, or in any part of the world since the Day of Pentecost, more truly wonderful than the revival at Ffestiniog.

The Features of the Revival.

There had been several revivals in Wales in the early nineteenth century, particularly in 1817, 1840 and 1848, but the old people said there was more of God in the 1859 revival than they ever saw in any previous one. It was characterized by a profound seriousness and it was different from former revivals in that there were comparatively few loud, dramatic expressions of feelings. It was rather marked by deep inward emotions expressed in tears, over an overwhelming sense of sin against God. One minister, William Griffiths of Llanharan, who was used in the revival said of the revival in his village:

> We have no cases of physical prostration; persons are not struck to the ground here as in Ireland and Scotland, but we have many cases of very sudden and powerful changes in those who have discovered their lost state, while following their several occupations on the mountains, and who on the spot were led to cry for mercy. Many of the old standard bearers of the Cross are led to seek pardoning grace. They now seem as though they were born over again; and the very sound of their voices moves the whole congregation into tears, and exclamations of 'Hallelujah!' universally burst forth. Now and then we witness persons, under the influence of saving grace, leaping in spiritual joy. We have converts whose ages vary from nine years to eighty, and both young and old give evidence of spiritual life. The new-born babes in Christ form themselves into various prayer meetings, and their supplications at the throne of grace are remarkably earnest and so earnest is the prayer that they will not leave the mercy seat until they prevail. [49]

---

[49]   Phillips, Thomas, *The Welsh Revival, Its Origin and Development*, p. 32

Many people who were initially critical of the emotion exhibited in the revival changed their attitude when they saw the complete change for the better in the workmen, friends and neighbours they knew. There were, however, some meetings of indescribable emotional intensity and an appearance of disorder, such as occurred in the 1904 revival, but these were not encouraged. The Rev. Thomas Phillips describes such a meeting in a large country chapel, which he thought would be an ordinary service, at which he was to give a Bible Society address.

For some time before the conclusion, strong deep emotions were felt and occasionally manifested. Efforts were made to repress the feelings but, during the last prayer, and more especially during the singing of the last hymn, the stifled emotions found vent... To give an adequate description of the scene is impossible. The hymns seemed to possess unusual unction and the prayers, by parties unused to speak and teach, possessed power, point and pathos, not unworthy of Baxter, Owen and Howe! It was an affecting sight, when strong men sank in their pews and on the floor and, pulling their hair, uttered cries of soul-distress; when young women, no longer able to sit or stand, first bowed on their knees and then prostrated on the ground; when from the gallery, as well as from the pews and benches below, the voice of prayer and praise, of grief and joy, commingled in every variety of tone and every degree of loudness. It is no discredit to the heads and hearts of the ministers present to say that they also were overpowered. The truth is there was neither time nor inclination for criticism, much less censure. If any questions at all were asked or thought of they were, "Is this a repetition of Pentecost?" [50]

Another feature of the revival was the earnest desire of those who had become Christians to win others for Christ. In fact it was they, perhaps, more than the preaching of the ministers from the pulpits, which spread the revival and won the great majority of converts through their prayers and zealous witness. One Sunday, three young men went with their Bibles to Hirwaen Common, in the Rhondda valley, where a crowd of men regularly met on that day to play "pitch and toss", and whom the police had previously been unable to disperse. At first the young converts were despised and laughed at but, after they had read a chapter from the Bible and prayed, the crowd broke up, leaving the game unfinished and the money behind, nor did they ever meet there again, numbers of them saying they intended going to the (adult) Sunday School. Meetings for prayer were also held in pubs and, wherever a place was thought to be indifferent to the Gospel, young people and others endeavoured to get permission to hold services there.

The revival was also characterized by heart-felt, inspired singing. At Llanwrtyd, in one weeknight prayer meeting in a remote house, the young people couldn't stop singing. They sang all the way home and, as some of the older people heard it, who had known previous revivals, they recognized the same spirit. When the singers reached their village, the feeling spread like wild fire and many of the people continued singing and praying throughout the night. Above all, people devoted themselves to prayer. Everywhere prayer meetings were full and often held every night. People, who a few weeks before the revival had had little or no desire for prayer meetings, now

---

[50] Phillips, Thomas, *The Welsh Revival Its Origin and Development*, pp. 140, 141

attended them in crowds and their sudden ability to pray as they did was remarkable. The children and young people began to hold prayer meetings from house to house, earnestly praying for their relatives and friends by name until they had the assurance that God had heard their prayer. A minister received a letter from Cwmcamlais saying that the old members were quite overcome with joy and the hearers flocked into the church. He was invited to come and give them two or three sermons. He was told that it did not matter what day he came, for every day was a Sabbath with them now and that the people couldn't think of doing anything but to feed their cattle and attend the prayer meetings. Prayer was, in fact, the principle means God used in carrying on the revival and, in some places, the first signs of it were through the prayers of children. This was not what Christian leaders at the time anticipated. A common comment was:

> We expected that the great outpouring of the Spirit would come by means of preaching. It was in former days; it may be so again, and it is now, to some extent. Thank God the ministry has not lost its power; but still, it is quite clear that the Holy Spirit's influence at present is communicated by means of prayer.[51]

In Maentwrog, people were encouraged by their minister to have a weekly prayer meeting to pray for an outpouring of the Spirit but, after a few meetings, they cooled off and became apathetic again. News of the revival in other places around them, however, made them afraid that God would pass them by and they determined to pray more earnestly and, before long, God blessed them too. This village was notorious for drunkenness and profanity, even the children using the foul

---

[51] Evans, Eifion, *When He is Come The 1859-60 Revival in Wales*, p. 109

language they had learned from their parents, but now these same children held prayer meetings together, reading the Bible and praying and singing for hours at a time. Young people too met in houses, barns and woods after the church prayer meeting was over, sometimes praying until three or four o'clock in the morning and women also had prayer meetings by themselves. It was not uncommon for people in crowded prayer meetings to spend six or eight hours in prayer and singing, sometimes praying until dawn, with the ministers' remarks occasionally being interrupted by cries to God for mercy. Prayer meetings in chapels also began at five a.m., before people went to work, and the workers continued in prayer during their lunch hour as well as in the church prayer meetings each night, so that the whole week was regarded as a continuous Sabbath.

The Results of the Revival.

There were few cases of prostration in this revival compared with the instances of them in Northern Ireland, but the power of conviction and the depth of feeling was just as great. It was common for the most notoriously wicked men and women in a place to be suddenly and gloriously transformed into earnest, godly Christians. The number of converts was impossible to count but it was commonly estimated to be about a hundred and ten thousand, 10% of the population, a large number of whom were under twenty years old. Many church members and attendants were also converted and backsliders restored. There were also very many cases of notorious drunkards and confirmed sceptics who had remarkable conversions, and who were then used by God to bring blessing to their neighbourhood and to many of their former unbelieving associates.

As in Northern Ireland, the revival also led to a widespread setting up of family worship, often brought about by converted children begging for family prayers. Converts were, however, expected to establish worship with their families at home, as evidence of the genuineness of their conversion. Inability and timidity were not accepted as excuses; they had to try! The revival also greatly strengthened the temperance cause. The efforts of the Total Abstinence Societies in the past had largely failed. Crowds of people who took the "pledge" went back to alcoholism but the revival transformed the situation. Its influence in some places was such that it was regarded almost as a temperance revival. Many pubs were closed because of a lack of business, others were virtually empty and drunkenness almost completely disappeared. One public house landlady closed her pub saying she had only drawn three half pints in a month. Other pubs were closed when the publicans were converted, as in Aberystwyth, where eight converted publicans became teetotallers and the alcohol was poured away!

Another effect of the revival was the new, remarkable unity that was shown among the various denominations. Bickering and bigotry disappeared, and ministers and members of all denominations met for fellowship, prayer and co-operation to win the unconverted to Christ, and these joint efforts did much to further the revival. Schoolrooms were often too small to hold these united prayer meetings and chapels too small to accommodate all the members at Holy Communion. The revival also restored an urgent evangelistic note in preaching and led to constant efforts for the conversion of others in Wales. Simple, direct and powerful preaching of the Gospel replaced the theoretical, oratorical style that was previously popular and the tendency to substitute liberal theology for orthodox doctrines was arrested. As in other revivals too, a great stimulus was given to missionary endeavours abroad.

The Rev. David Charles, Principal of Trevecca College, summarized the results of the revival by listing the three main characteristics of it. Firstly, an extraordinary spirit of prayer among the masses; secondly, a remarkable spirit of union among all denominations of Christians and thirdly, a powerful missionary effort for the conversion of others. Another revival report stated that what was amazing was that those meetings which were formerly attended by the fewest people, the prayer meetings, were those which were now predominant. In a real way, it was the spirit of prayer which was now poured out upon them. And yet another reported:

> The great fruit of the revival is prayer. It was preceded by prayer and it issues in prayer, which remains its chief agent. In previous revivals the ministry of the Word was the chief means…but the particular means of this present movement is prayer – everyone is coming to believe in the efficacy of prayer. [52]

Opposition to the Revival

In common with other spiritual Awakenings, however, this revival was severely criticized. Some criticized David Morgan's appeals to the unconverted after his sermon, giving them an opportunity of joining the church, saying he would fill the churches with "carnal men", although his appeal was given in a most searching and powerful way. It was also claimed that the revival was man-made, that there were no acknowledged leaders and that the ministers mostly used in it were of little significance, in terms of learning and ability, and were simply noted for their zeal and passion for evangelism! Also, that it was women and children who were mostly affected, and that the revival itself was mere excitement, and the disreputable

---

[52]   Evans, Eifion, *When He is Come, The 1859-60 Revival in Wales*, pp. 109

people who had changed their ways would soon return to their old habits.

Some objected to the noise and confusion in the revival services and the long and loud prayers, with apparently excessive emotion and extravagant language. But all this is understandable considering the radical change that had taken place in many lives, and the unusual power of the Spirit that was evident during the months when the revival was at its height. In any case, the spiritual life in these meetings resulted in a Christianity far more approximating to the New Testament ideal than the formal kind of worship and service common before the revival. Others, who hardened their hearts against the revival, said it would never make them change their ways and some tried to persecute their friends who had become Christians. In many cases, however, these people were seized with terrible conviction and, suffering mental agony, cried for mercy until at last they too found peace in believing.

In spite of criticisms to the contrary it was estimated that less than one in twenty converts relapsed and in some places none did. In one church of two hundred and fifty members, half of whom had been added through the revival, only one convert had to be disciplined, and that was for telling a lie. Churches were fully aware of the serious responsibility they had of providing teaching, guidance and pastoral care, especially in regard to alcoholism and immorality, which were common at the time. It was stressed that the Bible was the standard of religious practice as well as faith. Care was taken particularly to instruct people against resting in mere outward profession and it was emphasized that assurance was false if it was not accompanied by a hatred and renunciation of sin.

1355

1864

1891.

1872

1884

Charles Haddon Spurgeon "The Prince of Preachers"

© "The Pulpit to the Palm Branch" R. Shindler, Passmore & Alabaster, 1892.

CHAPTER SIX
THE 1859 REVIVAL IN ENGLAND AND SCOTLAND

Of all the major revivals in Britain, the 1859 revival in England and that in Scotland have been the least publicised. Apart from a few brief accounts, J. Edwin Orr's, *Second Evangelical Awakening in Britain* produced in 1949, and his *The Light of the Nations*, published in 1965, are perhaps the best known documented accounts of this remarkable movement of God. Fortunately, the weekly evangelical paper, *The Revival*, now *The Christian*, gave an extensive contemporary coverage of the movement through-out the United Kingdom and Orr made full use of this invaluable record, among others. One reason, perhaps, why there has been the general neglect of this revival is that the revival in England, at least, was generally unlike that in other parts of the United Kingdom at this time. The influence of the revival in America, Northern Ireland and Wales resulted, especially in the later stages at least, in a nation-wide endeavour by the churches and individuals to reach the unsaved everywhere in the country with the Gospel, by innumerable crusades. God, however, blessed this evangelistic preaching in a way unparalleled in British history, equalling perhaps the results of the eighteenth century revival.

The Revival in England.

Before the outbreak of the revival, there were multitudes of people in the growing industrial cities and towns who had no connection with the churches and who were described as more ignorant of the Gospel than the natives of Africa. The revival in America and other parts of the United Kingdom then challenged the churches in England to earnest prayer and a greater concern for these un-churched multitudes. In fact, the characteristic of the revival in England, as elsewhere, was the priority given to prayer and, considering the disinclination of even Christians to attend prayer meetings, the rapid growth of these meetings was in itself an evidence of the reviving power of the Holy Spirit.

In 1858, a great number of daily and weekly united prayer meetings for revival were held throughout London, and these attracted huge numbers of people simply to pray for revival. These meetings were then followed by innumerable evangelistic campaigns in the largest buildings in the city, in parks, on commons and in other public places. This endeavour to bring the Gospel to the masses was led by C. H. Spurgeon and many other notable evangelists, and these years were described at the time as a time of glorious spiritual harvest. An indication of the desire of many for a personal blessing, in the spiritual Awakening in the capital at this time, is seen in a well-known hymn written in 1860 by a London lady, Elizabeth Codner.

> Lord I hear of showers of blessing, Thou art scattering full and free,
> Showers the thirsty land refreshing, Let Thy blessing fall on me
> Even me, even me. Let Thy blessing fall on me.

William Booth, 1829-1912, first General

Revival in Southern England.

At the beginning of 1860, numerous well-known London theatres, such as the Garrick and the Sadler's Wells theatres, were opened for Sunday evening services for the un-churched masses and attracted an aggregate nightly attendance of twenty thousand, and an aggregate of two hundred and fifty thousand each winter to hear sermons from both Anglican and Nonconformist ministers. This caused a great concern for some religious people. It was regarded as a serious and objectionable innovation. Viscount Dungannon commented that the appearance of clergymen on the stages of theatres was unparalleled, as extraordinary as the appearance of comedians in the pulpits of parish churches! He moved a resolution in the House of Lords condemning these services as:

> Highly irregular, inconsistent with order, calculated to injure rather than advance the progress of sound religious principles and would end in materially undermining the foundations of the Church of England. [53]

The services were strongly defended, however, by the Archbishop of Canterbury and Lord Shaftesbury, as well as by several of the Lords and Bishops, and the resolution was withdrawn. Shaftesbury commented that it was not the locality which would desecrate the Word of God but the Word of God which could consecrate the locality. Special services were also arranged for the middle classes in St Paul's Cathedral and Westminster Abbey, when "vast but orderly" crowds attended. An estimated fifty thousand unchurched people, at least, were reached each week by these services or a million aggregate each season, during the revival years. Independently,

---

[53]   Orr, J. Edwin, *The Second Evangelical Awakening in Britain*, p. 97

evangelists held services in the Victoria theatre, Waterloo, with an attendance of over eight hundred and fifty thousand during four winter seasons in the early 1860s. Thousands of children were converted and there were many cases of deep conviction of sin. Often these children were then the means of convicting their parents and grandparents. In July 1859, there was an outbreak of revival in the George Muller Homes in Bristol and, in one school of one hundred and twenty girls, more than half were converted. In early 1860, a further hundred and forty-four were regarded as converted there, with fifty-three about whom there was some uncertainty, making a total of almost two hundred and sixty within a year.

Revival in Cornwall

Instances of spontaneous revivals took place in various parts of Cornwall but the most effective work was through the ministry of William and Catherine Booth, who held campaigns in various towns for eighteen months from August 1861, and seven thousand people were converted during that time. Their mission began in Hayle and the whole neighbourhood was moved, especially the men. Great crowds were unable to get into the services and were ministered to by other clergymen while Booth was preaching. Two thousand attended the final meetings and five hundred were converted, most being added to the various churches. Many of these converts then visited St. Ives and testified of their experience. A further mission in St Ives by the Booths resulted in over a thousand being converted there and added to the churches, not only from St. Ives but also from other parts of the county. In St. Just, when again the various churches co-operated in a mission lasting four months, there were more than two thousand conversions. This was followed by a mission in Lelant, where hundreds couldn't get near the Wesleyan chapel, where the mission was held, because of the crowds there, and a further two hundred were converted. The Booths then visited Penzance where again the Methodist chapel was crowded and it was said that, "a most blessed and glorious work was accomplished", beginning with a deepening of the spiritual life of Christians and followed by the conviction and conversion of outsiders on a scale as elsewhere. Two thirds of those wanting to attend the final service in Penzance were unable to do so. In Redruth too, there were more than a thousand conversions and a similar number in Cambourne.

A Methodist minister reported to the *Wesleyan Times* that Booth's ministry was

> A commanding oratory we have never heard excelled, climaxing in the preacher's voice being drowned in the shouts of the saints, the prayers of the people and the cries of the penitents. The chapel was packed out, with every space on the stairs and pulpit taken up and there were no children among the penitents, rather sturdy men and matronly women. [54]

Also, the *Wesleyan Times* reported on the Booth Cornwall mission, stressing the remarkable conversion of sinners, the reviving of churches and the perseverance of the converts and yet, in spite of Booth's ministry adding over four thousand new members to Wesleyan churches in Cornwall, in June 1862 the Methodist New Connexion accepted William Booth's resignation, disapproving of his revivalism. The next month at Cambourne, the Wesleyan Conference instructed its superintendents not to allow the use of their chapels for continuous services by outsiders, no doubt the result of ministerial jealousy of the success of a layman.

---

[54] *Wesleyan Times*, 4 June 1862

Revival in East Anglia and the Midlands.

In Lowestoft, in East Anglia, no buildings were able to accommodate the crowds that attended the revival ministry of Reginald Radcliffe there. The railway goods depot was hired and an audience of three thousand attended, one third of the population. The next morning, the Town Hall was filled to overflowing, with people anxious about their spiritual condition. Within a few weeks five hundred converts had been registered, including people reclaimed from drunkenness, profanity and immorality and the Methodist membership almost doubled. In Norwich, also, a railway goods depot had to be used to accommodate a crowd of about three thousand, and one thousand two hundred inquirers remained behind to receive Christ.

In Oxfordshire towns and villages the revival was even more spectacular and was traced to a daily prayer meeting, which began in September 1859. The phenomena of the Ulster revival were seen here, with sinners being prostrated and others crying out in deep distress. Ministers and church members didn't know what to do and sat paralyzed by surprise. Oxford and Cambridge Universities were also moved by the revival. A University Prayer Union began in 1858 and a mission to Oxford University was held in 1861. Three years later it was said that "a sort of evangelical revival amongst undergraduates had taken place"! In April 1861 in Leek, North Staffordshire, four thousand attended the meetings of the evangelist Richard Weaver, and five hundred converts were registered in the first six days including, "some of the most intelligent as well as the vilest in Leek". The following year, two hundred young male converts held there a celebration of their being saved from drunkenness and vice. Also, in 1863, Dr. and Mrs. Walter Palmer, who had been in the initial outbreak of revival in North America in 1857, and William and Catherine Booth, visited Walsall in South Staffordshire. Thousands were attracted to open-air meetings, and hundreds were converted, most of whom were working-class men. Numerous notoriously wicked characters were converted, such as pickpockets, prize fighters, bear wrestlers and train robbers! One of them was a former drunken, gambling, prize fighting hooligan, who had previously needed six policemen to take him to gaol! These converts then formed themselves into the "Hallelujah Band" and toured the Midlands singing and testifying to their faith in Christ. William Booth wrote of them:

> They are just of the stamp to grapple with this (working) class, chiefly of their own order, talking to them in their own language, regarding themselves as illustrations of the power of the Gospel.[55]

Revival in Northern England.

An awakening occurred in Newcastle in the summer of 1859 through the ministry of the Palmers. Daily midday prayer meetings were held, as well as afternoon meetings for exhortation and prayer and similar meetings in the evenings. Services were crowded and many were filled with the Holy Spirit. In one church alone, one thousand four hundred were converted by the end of the year, as were a "vast number of young people belonging to the senior classes of the Sunday Schools". Five years later, it was reported that the movement was "going on gloriously among our working men". In Sunderland, after hearing of the revival in America and elsewhere, ministers decided, from September 1859, to hold simultaneous prayer

---

[55] Orr, J. Edwin, *The Second Evangelical Awakening in Britain*, p. 137

meetings in all the churches "morning, noon and night". These also led to an awakening under the Palmers later in the year, in which three thousand five hundred people joined the local Methodist societies. Also, a remarkable spiritual work went on among young people, with scores weeping in conviction. In Gateshead, in 1860, a further five hundred were converted and, years later, the movement was still powerful and chapels in the district were crowded. In Whitehaven, in Cumberland, some prostrations occurred among the scores of people who were convicted in the meetings. It was significant, however, that these services were conducted by Ulster evangelists who regarded prostration as an evidence of revival and encouraged it as such. Even the remote areas of Cumberland and Westmorland were affected, although local clergy disapproved. Near Windermere, two workingmen began to pray and all the people around them were constrained to join them. Though there was no preaching there were many conversions. It was said that it had been all prayer, prayer, and more prayer, and that the work had continued to increase without any human instrumentality or sectarianism, with no preachers and nothing but prayer. On the Isle of Man too, a spiritual Awakening followed daily prayer meetings. In 1862 the Palmers visited Douglas and preached in halls crowded to capacity. Many were saved, backsliders were restored and lukewarm Christians stirred up.

In early 1861, Richard Weaver held a mission in the Methodist church in Macclesfield, which was crowded, and there were amazing results. Some of the vilest characters were converted and, in all, over one thousand two hundred converts registered their names with the church leaders. Publicans complained of the lack of customers and closed their pubs while policemen and magistrates testified to the transformation that had taken place in the morals of the town. In the summer of 1861 the Palmers visited Liverpool for a rest, and were immediately involved in an extraordinary work of the Holy Spirit with converts numbered in the thousands, including hundreds of young men. So many sought spiritual help that there was an acute shortage of personal workers. In Bolton, the preaching of Charles Finney, the famous American revivalist, led to two thousand conversions, four hundred in one week. Many remarkable cases of conviction and restitution were recorded and, before the end of Finney's campaign, the movement had affected every family in the town. A report described Finney's ministry as follows:

> The Rev. C.G. Finney, by whom these services are conducted…is close upon seventy years of age. His style of Address is singularly direct. There is a total absence of display, and a complete forgetfulness, on most occasions at least, of the graces of elocution. There is the most rigid exactness of statement, the severest simplicity, the closest reasoning, and the discourse proceeds step by step, the judgement of the hearer forced along with it until the end.[56]

In Manchester, among every Christian denomination, there had been an earnest longing for revival from early autumn 1859, and united prayer meetings were densely crowded. They were still continuing three years later and campaign after campaign was blessed with conversions. Previously powerful infidel organizations dwindled away and their lecture hall was taken over by religious charities. Many criminals here were won for Christ through the distribution of cards inviting them to teas, to which only thieves, etc., would be admitted! Through one invitation to thieves, three hundred came to hear the Gospel and a number remained to receive Christ and change their way of life. Thousands of pounds were restored to their rightful

---

[56] Orr, J. Edwin, *The Second Evangelical Awakening in Britain*, p. 158

owners, varying from a few shillings to hundreds of pounds and many drunkards became teetotallers.

In the Leeds district, some of the most abandoned characters were converted. Also, one well-known secularist, J.H. Gordon, was converted and wrote to the ministers saying that he was no longer opposed to them and asking to be regarded as a Christian brother. He also resigned as Lecturer of the Leeds Secular Society and made a public recantation of his former infidel views. During the revival a quarter of the two hundred thousand population of Leeds gathered to see the public hanging of two murderers. Evangelists, including the famous evangelist Henry Moorhouse, took the opportunity of this occasion to preach the Gospel to the vast crowds.

Denominational Attitudes to the Revival.

The attitude of the Wesleyan Methodist Church has been mentioned and that of the Anglican Church was as varied as its many schools of thought. The High Church party was generally opposed to the movement, because it was against uniting with Nonconformists; extemporary prayer in prayer meetings; open-air services and services being held in theatres. Broad churchmen sometimes supported it and sometimes ignored it, and many were indifferent because it seemed alien to their own religious life style and limited experience. Attitudes among evangelical Anglicans were also mixed. Some enthusiastically welcomed the revival while others regarded it with caution. It seems Anglicanism had not learned the lesson of its opposition to the eighteenth century revival. Dr. Eugene Stock wrote that if the clergy had more heartily welcomed the revival, its effect within the Church of England would have been much greater.

Roman Catholics and Unitarians strongly opposed the revival and received little or no benefit from it. Baptists, apparently without exception, supported the movement and, of the two hundred and fifty thousand members of Baptist churches in England and Wales in 1865, one hundred thousand had been added as a result of it, eighty thousands of them in England. Presbyterians also made gains, as did the Plymouth Brethren who, in proportion to their existing membership, probably gained more than any other religious body. Congregationalists too wholeheartedly supported the Awakening and one hundred and thirty-five thousand members were added to their churches in England and Wales, two thirds of them in England. There were prominent lay Methodists who opposed the movement, being wealthy brewers, but generally there was limited Methodist opposition and an estimated two hundred thousand members were gained through the revival, in all the branches of the Methodist Church.

The Revival in Scotland.

The revival in Scotland was more remarkable and less localized than that in England due, perhaps, to the greater preparation for it. Unlike England, there had been significant spiritual Awakenings in Scotland during the first half of the nineteenth century. First, there was the evangelistic work of the Haldane brothers, under whom thousands were converted. Then in 1839 at Kilsyth, Dundee, Perth and other places, revival broke out under the ministry of Robert Murray M'Cheyne and W.C. Burns, which influenced Scotland for many years. Later, the preaching of Duncan Matheson and a number of other godly evangelists, whose ministry God greatly blessed, contributed to the preparation for the revival. There was, however, by no means a universal acceptance of the revival by the churches at this time. In Scotland, Anglicanism was less evangelical than established Presbyterianism, and it was less enthusiastic about the spiritual Awakening. Also, in spite of the results, many Presbyterian parish ministers disassociated themselves from it because of their distaste for the itinerant revivalists and evangelists.

The priority of prayer in the Revival.

From 1858, at least, when Scottish Christians heard the news of the great revival in America and of outbreaks of blessing in parts of the United Kingdom, they began to pray for and expect a similar outpouring of the Spirit on their own land. Then, by 1860, the three main branches of the Presbyterian Church, representing 70% of the population, declared Scotland was experiencing a revival of religion as striking as that in Northern Ireland and that their churches had gained 33% more members as a result of it. The American and Ulster pattern of united daily midday prayer meetings was followed. More than one thousand two hundred were held in the various cities and towns all over Scotland and these led to morning, afternoon and all-night prayer meetings and preaching services. People from all walks of life also began prayer meetings in their homes and at work, in fact wherever they could meet together. Sunday school teachers had prayer meetings in which they earnestly wrestled in prayer for their scholars, and children also were eager to have their own prayer meetings. Many remarkable answers to prayer were soon seen as people prayed for individuals in the circle of their family, friends and neighbours. These prayer meetings continued for several years and produced praying converts who regarded private and public prayer as all-important to their spiritual life.

The nature of the revival in Scotland

Churches and halls were crowded and hundreds waited for hours through the night to receive spiritual counselling. In the shops too, customers were asking the way of salvation after they had made their purchases. It was quite common to see people reading their Bibles in railway carriages and even on the streets. God used many ministers and evangelists at this time, especially men like Reginald Radcliffe and Brownlow North who, with other evangelists, held missions in Scotland in 1858, beginning in Aberdeen. Thousands of all ages and from all classes were converted and added to the churches. A remarkable work began exceeding in depth and intensity anything the evangelists had previously witnessed.

Irish visitors found the same phenomena they had known in Northern Ireland, such as bodily prostration, although the instances were not as numerous as in Northern Ireland. In some cases, after they were struck down, people lay for long periods on the floor, but these incidents decreased as the revival progressed. Prostitutes came under great conviction and cried out for mercy in the meetings, with piercing and heart-rending cries. Meetings went on into the early hours of the morning and those who had come into peace and assurance immediately began to plead with those who were still unconverted to come to Christ as they had, testifying to what Christ had just done for them.

The dominant feature of this revival was an overwhelming sense of sin. In one meeting, as soon as the minister gave out his text, everyone in the meeting broke down. People of all ages were sobbing as if their hearts would break in agony of soul under a conviction of sin. The noise was so loud that it was impossible for the minister to preach his sermon. The feeling of solemnity was almost overpowering and the realization of the presence of the Holy Spirit was such that Christian workers began speaking in whispers as they pointed people to Christ. People had a new sensitivity with regard to the things of God and there were many sudden conversions, sometimes accompanied by extraordinary physical phenomena. One minister said, "In 1859, we were all Simon Peters falling at Jesus' feet and crying, 'Depart from me, for I am a sinful man O Lord'". The feeling of solemnity pervaded whole towns and cities as if people realized they were in direct contact with God and the world to come.

The revival in Scotland came at a time when many were saying that Christianity was dead and then, suddenly, thousands were converted, who testified to their new life in Christ. The usual features of genuine revival were seen everywhere. There was a great concern for the unsaved and converts showed a boldness in confessing Christ and what He had done for them. There was also a deep love between Christians of all denominations and there was a great respect for ministers and much prayer for their ministry. Everywhere people were anxious to hear the Gospel and to learn more of the Christian Faith, and the "three R's" were the leading truths of every address: Ruin by the Fall; Righteousness by Christ and Regeneration only by the Holy Spirit.

Revival around the Firth of Clyde.

In July 1859, evangelists who had been in the Ulster revival visited Rothesay and urged people to repent. Scores of people responded and a spiritual movement began which spread throughout the county of Bute. Moving west, the revival affected towns north and south of the Firth of Clyde. First Helensburgh and then Dumbarton experienced a spiritual Awakening and, as in Ulster, people wouldn't leave meetings even though ministers had brought them to a close several times. United prayer meetings were held every night and churches were filled. People of all ages cried out under conviction of sin. In Dumbarton, one boy was heard speaking to a number of children, who were afterward found in groups by the roadside praying that they might be saved. The whole town seemed awe-stricken with the sense of the presence of God.

In the summer of 1859, the revival became sudden news in the religious and secular press when it spread to Port Glasgow. Newspapers reported the increased numbers in prayer meetings, the large number of converts and the crowded revival services. A man came from Coleraine, Northern Ireland, and witnessed to what had happened there and the place of his meetings was crammed with more than two thousand people and some of the worst characters of the town were saved and transformed. Men were so moved they were in an agony of conviction, lying prostrate on the floor yet soon, having been assured of forgiveness, they were said to be the picture of joy. Others were so convicted of their sins they were carried out in great distress of mind and some even ran out of the meeting in fear. After one meeting was closed a great many remained, as well as crowds outside who wanted to hear more of the Gospel. The meeting continued until ten p.m. and even then they were unwilling to go away.

Revival in Glasgow and district.

By August 1859, revival had broken out in Glasgow and was attracting the attention of the religious and the secular press. One report that month stated that twenty thousand were packed on Glasgow Green, pushing to hear the speakers, and it referred to the increased attendances at prayer meetings and the large number of conversions. Also, more people now sought admission into membership of the churches than at any other period in Scottish history, and it was not uncommon for a church to have a few hundred applications for membership. One Glasgow newspaper wrote:

> The wonderful change that is perceptible on the very surface of society is now frequently the subject of remark. In the family party, in the bus or railway carriage, on board the steamer, in the street, it is no longer "a strange thing" to hear people as Christians able to, "give a reason for the hope that is in them", or...as earnest inquirers more or less audibly demanding, "What must we do to be saved?" [57]

Richard Weaver, preaching in Glasgow, encountered the phenomenon of bodily prostration. The Holy Spirit came upon the people there in such power that they were struck down and lay on the floor as if dead, seemingly unconscious of everything around them. A year later Glasgow was still experiencing revival when crowds, as large as previously, were gathering on Glasgow Green and enquirers were filling an adjacent theatre. Famous evangelists, including Robert Cunningham, Reginald Radcliffe and Richard Weaver addressed the vast crowd and some of the preachers collapsed with fatigue, because they worked so hard dealing with the great number of enquirers. Every Sunday evening an open-air service was held outside the Bridegate Church, which upwards of seven thousand people attended. At the close, an invitation was given to those wishing to make a decision to attend the prayer meeting in the church. Within minutes the church, seating nine hundred, was packed with over one thousand one hundred people, and the meeting went on until almost midnight. The influence of the Glasgow revival

---

[57] Orr, J. Edwin, *The Second Evangelical Awakening in Britain*, p. 61

was felt throughout the neighbouring county of Lanarkshire, in fact every part of south-west Scotland was affected.

In Dunlop, south of Glasgow, the wife and daughter of a publican attended meetings of the evangelist Richard Weaver. They were converted and returning home began to sing the hymn, "Christ for me". The husband was deeply moved by the truths of the hymn and so convicted of his own spiritual need that he "fell on the floor as if dead". When he became conscious his first words were those that had been imprinted on his heart and mind, "Christ for me". He had the sign of his public house taken down and closed the pub, making it known that he had chosen to follow Christ. Another publican heard the news and laughed saying, "Yes, it is Christ for him and all the customers for me". One night men and women passed his pub singing the same hymn. He decided to go out and hear the singing but the Holy Spirit convicted him and he fell on his knees, crying out, "What must I do to be saved" and he too became a Christian. His pub sign was also taken down and, for some time, the place was without a public house.

Revival in the Western Isles.

In 1860 the revival swept further north affecting the whole of Skye and also the Outer Hebrides. Young people and children flocked to the prayer meetings and, for several months, some walked twenty miles to the Sunday meetings and up to seven miles to weekday services, generally in groups, which read and sang as they walked. Their desire to read the Scriptures in the daytime and pray in barns in the evening then led to the awakening of the adults.

Revival in the Highlands, Orkneys and Shetlands.

In the northern Highlands the news of the Irish revival had drawn hundreds to pray and whole communities were changed. Soon the physical phenomena seen in Ireland were also experienced but they gave way to quieter behaviour as the weeks passed. In Lybster, revival broke out when a group of revived fishermen, whose boats had been blown off course, marched in a body to the market-place, Bibles in hand, and zealously exhorted the local fishermen to seek the Lord. In John o' Groats, it was reported that certain fishing crews held worship services in their boats in the harbour, singing hymns and psalms, in contrast to their former drunken ways. The revival then spread to the Orkneys. Someone from the Orkneys said:

> There is a most marvellous, miraculous work of God's Spirit going on here...I believe that the whole character of this end of the island is changed.[58]

At the end of 1859, the seaport of Cullen was moved as by an earthquake under the ministry of Duncan Matheson. People attended church who hadn't been there for many years and worldly people began to talk about how they might become right with God. Stories of many remarkable conversions were recorded. A typical conversion story was that told by a woman who, meeting Duncan Matheson one day said, "I am happier than I was on my wedding day". She had been converted some time previously but her husband was a drunkard and sceptic and was furious that she had been converted. She was almost killed by his constant beatings but she endured the brutal treatment without complaint, praying constantly for

---

[58] Orr, J. Edwin, *The Light of the Nations*, p. 136

his conversion. Her prayers were answered and her husband was transformed. He began to hold family worship and did everything he could to please his wife! The Shetlands too were affected in the early 1860s when special prayer meetings were held and people crowded the churches night after night to hear the Gospel. On some small islands, half the population was converted and none was known to have backslidden.

Revival on the East Coast.

In Aberdeen, after special and united prayer by the churches for an outpouring of the Holy Spirit, the spiritual results were said to be similar to those of the labours of Wesley and Whitefield. Hundreds were saved of all ages and classes of society. The whole of the east coast was similarly affected. London religious papers were informed that there was scarcely a town or village between Inverness and Aberdeen that had not been visited by the quickening power of the Spirit. A woman living with her mother and sister in an Aberdeenshire village was converted and was so fired with enthusiasm that she went from door to door, pleading with people to let the Lord Jesus into their hearts. The local minister stated:

> The mother and sister had a consultation, and they came to the sad conclusion that Mary was mad. The village doctor was called in, and also the doctor of a neighbouring village. They consulted, and expressed the same opinion. They thereupon signed the schedule for Mary's admission to a lunatic asylum, simply because she besought one and all of those whom she loved to come to Christ. On the night preceding the day arranged for her conveyance to the asylum, the sister and the mother had strange thoughts and, on meeting in the morning, the mother said to her daughter, "Do you know,

I have been wondering all night whether it is Mary who is mad, or we". "Well, mother", the daughter answered, "it is strange that I have been wondering the same thing". They thought and reflected and searched their hearts until they decided that it was not Mary but they themselves who were mad… The whole family and relatives, twenty-three in all, through Mary's pleading were then led to Christ.[59]

Open-air revival meetings attracted thousands. In Dundee also, the revival continued for over a year from the autumn of 1859 and, among others, hundreds of young mill-workers were converted. Almost every parish in Perthshire was revived during those years and local ministers reported, "all the country around is on fire". In the fishing town of Celladyke, south of St Andrews, hundreds of fishermen became burdened by sin and sent for the ministers. Stormy weather kept the crews on shore for a week, during which meetings were crowded to suffocation and three hundred adult inquirers were dealt with out of a population of one thousand eight hundred, and the place was changed beyond recognition.

In Edinburgh, revival did not break out until the autumn of 1859. Charles Finney, the famous American revivalist, held meetings there in November that year and many were saved. Independently, scores were being converted in other missions, including numerous prostitutes. Other well-known English evangelists, such as Radcliffe and Weaver, could not get a place large enough for their meetings. On one occasion, one thousand eight hundred crowded into a chapel while thousands more packed the street outside. Weaver and Radcliffe had to walk on men's shoulders to alternate with each other from ministering inside the church to preaching to the crowds outside. Hundreds stayed behind to be counselled, even though the preaching

---

[59] Johnson, *Henry, Stories of Great Revivals*, pp. 235, 236

service had gone on from 7 to 11 p.m. Similar scenes as these were seen along the whole of the east coast. One minister reported:

> It is indeed a most wondrous work of the Lord and is passing along this whole coast like a mighty wave, having assumed a character identical with the work in Northern Ireland. [60]

The Results of the revival.

Five years after the outbreak of revival, one report of the General Assembly of the Free Church of Scotland stated that the Awakening had continued through the intervening years, and had been the beginning of the spread of a revitalized Christianity. All classes were influenced and the instruments were laymen as well as clergy. Many future Christian leaders were saved or had life changing experiences in the revival, such as the famous preacher, Rev. Alexander Whyte; missionaries, James Chalmers (New Guinea); James Gilmour (Mongolia); scientist, Professor A.T. Simpson and theologian Professor James Orr. No attempt was made to count the number of converts of the revival in Scotland, but it was estimated that three hundred thousand were converted, representing 10% of the population, and that church membership increased by one third. Also, in 1865, *The Revival* paper, now *The Christian,* summed up the revival's effect on Scotland

> The wave of Divine blessing came to us apparently from Ireland four or five years ago. It struck first the west coast of Scotland, then spread over a great part of the country. It was a very blessed season, perhaps the most extensive in its operation that we have ever known among us. But

---

[60] Orr, J. Edwin, *The Light of the Nations*, p. 136

it has, in a great measure, passed away. Still, fruit remains – living, active, consistent Christians who keep together, cherishing the memory of the time, blessing and praying for its return…The number of students entering our divinity halls this season will be double or triple that of former years; this is the blessed fruit of the Revival. Such men are likely to be of the right stamp…[61]

In total, the gains in membership in United Kingdom churches from this revival exceeded one million, the equivalent to ratio of population of almost three million today and, in England, it included four hundred thousand additions to the Nonconformists and two hundred and fifty thousand to the Anglicans. One important feature of the revival as a whole was that it produced no division among Christians, unlike that of the eighteenth century. Only the Salvation Army was formed as a separate religious body and that made no claim to be a Church. It might be said, in fact, that the revival marked the beginning of a movement towards church unity. It also assumed the form of a great Home Mission, because what had begun as a mighty turning to God in prayer became a great movement for evangelizing the country, and an innumerable number of evangelistic and philanthropic organizations were created. The doctrine of the Second Coming of Christ came to the forefront of Christian thought again and these organizations were formed to fulfil the Great Commission by bringing the Gospel to every creature before the Second Advent.

---

[61] *The Revival*, 19th January 1865

SECTION
THREE

REVIVAL IN THE
TWENTIETH CENTURY

Dr. F. B. MEYER

Rev. SETH JOSHUA

Rev. JOSEPH JENKINS

© Dr. Meyer from "Preachers I have heard", A. Gammie. Pickering & Inglis, 1945.

CHAPTER SEVEN
THE 1904-5
REVIVAL IN WALES

Pre-Revival Preparations and Blessings.

The Welsh Revival of 1904-5 has been referred to as "The Evan Roberts Revival" but, while it is true that he was the central figure in that revival, there were many others who played a major role in preparing for it and furthering it once it had begun. The Rev. Robert Ellis wrote of these men in his book, *Living Echoes,* as did B.P. Jones in his book, *The King's Champions.* They included ministers such as Rev. W.S. Jones; Rev. W.W. Lewis; Rev. Keri Evans; Rev. Joseph Jenkins; Rev. W. Nantlais Williams and Rev. R.B. Jones, through whom revival came to North Wales, and who was the most powerful and influential preacher in Wales for almost three decades after the revival. Moreover, for at least two or three years before the national revival broke out, numbers of Christians in Wales prayed in earnest for an outpouring of the Spirit, and several churches began to experience unusual blessing with overwhelming manifestations of God's presence and constant conversions. Numbers of church members were also filled with the Holy Spirit.

At the end of 1903 after feelings of failure and discouragement, Joseph Jenkins, minister of the Calvinistic Methodist church in New Quay, Pembrokeshire, began to pray for a greater spiritual vitality in himself and the church and particu-

Rev. R.B. Jones

larly in the young people. The following February he preached a searching sermon on 1 John 5:4 and a young girl, Florrie Evans, was convicted and led into blessing by him. At the next youth meeting she stood up and said, "Oh, I love Jesus Christ with all my heart". The effect was startling and an overwhelming sense of God's presence solemnized the whole congregation and set the other young people on fire. From that time they were used to spread a spiritual Awakening in meetings in the surrounding area, including one at Newcastle Emlyn, which proved to be a turning point in Evan Roberts' life. Churches throughout the country held weeks of prayer for revival and, in August 1904, at the second "Keswick in Wales" Convention at Llandrindod, people prayed for God to raise up someone through whom a national revival would come to Wales. Prior to that Seth Joshua had prayed for four years that:

> God would take a lad from the coal mine or from the field, even as he took Elijah from the plough to revive his work, someone not from the universities and colleges, which would feed pride and intellectualism. [62]

The prayer was answered in the call of Evan Roberts. Also, some of the ministers mentioned above, who were to be influential in the revival, attended those meetings at the Llandrindod Convention very conscious of their need of a greater spiritual power. They consulted the famous Dr. F. B. Meyer who had been converted in the 1859 revival, and God blessed his ministry to them, and that of Mrs. Penn-Lewis, resulting in their experiencing an anointing of the Holy Spirit that transformed their lives and ministry and equipped them to be effective leaders in the revival. R.B. Jones commented later:

---

[62] Adams, Kevin, *A Diary of Revival, The Outbreak of the 1904-1905 Welsh Awakening,* p .57

It was on Friday that F.B. Meyer came to us according to his promise. He said to each one of us, "What is it that you want?" I told him, "I don't know for certain but one thing I do know, I want the Holy Spirit". Then he said, "You want the Spirit; well then, take hold of Him. I see you are like the Jews waiting for a sign. Yet all you need to do is to take hold of the Spirit whom He has given to you." A new world opened up for me. Now I saw it. I went home next day and took the service as usual on the Sunday without telling anyone. Next Sunday I still said nothing, yet they somehow knew that there was a new man in the pulpit.[63]

The Role of Evan Roberts.

God had been preparing Roberts for years before the revival. Born in 1878, he began work at the age of twelve as a door-boy in the local mine, opening and closing the doors underground for the trams to pass. He became a spiritual influence in the mine and then, after twelve years as a miner, he had a job for a short time as an apprentice Blacksmith with his uncle. As a teenager he spent many hours in prayer and reading the Scriptures. He was also challenged as a thirteen year-old boy by the remark of an elder in his church in Loughor, South Wales. The elder said to him:

> Remember to be faithful; what if the Spirit descended and you were absent, remember Thomas and the loss he sustained. [64]

From that time he resolved to pray to be filled with the Spirit and to be faithful to the means of grace. For ten or eleven years

63 Jones, B.P. *Voices from the Welsh Revival, 1904-1905*, p. 15
64 Ellis, Robert, *Living Echoes*, p. 23

Evan Roberts

© *A pictorial History of Revival, K. Adams & E. Jones, 1904 Ltd., pub. CWR 2004.*

he also prayed for revival, often rising in the middle of the night to do so. He attended five church meetings in the week besides the Sunday services and spent hours, including every spare moment in the mine, studying the Bible and learning verses. At the end of 1903 he applied to train for the ministry at the ministerial preparatory school in Newcastle Emlyn. Then, in the spring of 1904, he had a remarkable experience of God, when he spoke of the privilege of speaking face to face with God:

> During the spring of 1904, on a Friday night, while on my knees, I was swept into space oblivious of time and place;

it was communion with God. Prior to that experience my God was distant. I had a fright that night but never afterwards. Such was my trembling that the bed shook and my brother woke. After that I was awakened each night after one o'clock. This was remarkable because I usually slept like a rock. After awakening I had three or four hours of communion with God then, after five, I could sleep until nine. There followed divine communion until twelve or one o'clock. This lasted for about three months. My one fear when I went to the Grammar school in September 1904, (the ministerial preparatory school) was the losing of this experience. I endeavoured hard to keep up with the work of the school but the divine visitations became irresistible.[65]

That month, on Sunday the 18th, the evangelist Seth Joshua began a week's mission in New Quay and found "a remarkable revival spirit there", due to the blessing Joseph Jenkins and his young people had already received. Joshua commented that he had never seen the power of the Holy Spirit so powerfully manifested among the people at that place. The revival was breaking out there in greater power: the young were receiving the greatest measure of blessing and they broke out into prayer, praise and testimony in a wonderful way. The people seemed to have an insatiable appetite for spiritual things and became oblivious in the meetings of time and the need to eat and sleep. Though Joshua closed meetings several times they would start up again and go on into the early morning. The following Sunday he began a week's mission in Newcastle Emlyn, where he gave an account of the Awakening at New Quay.

It was the time when students returned to the preparatory school and, on the Tuesday of that week, Roberts attended Seth Joshua's mission and the following day went with other

---

[65] Ibid., p. 24

young people to a two-day conference at Blaenannerch, arranged for young people, and at which W.W. Lewis spoke. On the Thursday Seth Joshua attended the conference, as a substitute second speaker. In the first meeting that day Joshua prayed, "Lord bend us" and God spoke to Roberts that that was his need. Roberts' own prayer in the second meeting that the Lord would bend him was referred to by Joshua in his diary as "remarkable". Roberts said he felt so ablaze with a desire to go through Wales with the Gospel that, if it were possible, he would have paid God for the privilege. He had several visions, in one of which he saw an arm stretched out to the world and in the hand a piece of paper with the number one hundred thousand written on it. God was promising him that one hundred thousand people would be converted in the coming revival, a vision which was to be fulfilled.

Throughout the latter part of October he expressed his concern for his home church at Loughor, and especially for the young people. On Sunday, October 30th, he also had a vision of himself speaking to rows of his friends and companions there. He tried to shake the vision off but he heard a voice saying, "Go and speak to these people" and, after agreeing to go, the whole chapel where he was sitting was filled with light and the glory of God. The following day he obtained permission to leave the school and to hold a meeting for the youth that evening. He was assured of the victory God was going to give to the church in Wales and of the many souls that were going to be saved. His family, however, were surprised to see him and were sceptical of his intention to hold young people's meetings, and they were also puzzled with his talk of his baptism in the Holy Spirit. They even thought he had become mentally ill seeing his tears as he thought of the need in Wales, and hearing his laughter when he thought of God's promise of revival.

In the meeting with the young people, however, he saw them as he had seen them in his vision and he told them of God's blessing at Newcastle Emlyn and his vision for Wales. Seventeen were present and, by the end of the meeting, all of them had responded to his request to confess Christ as their Saviour. More conversions took place in the further meetings that week and numbers also grew. Old as well as young were now attending and the meetings went on until the early hours of the morning. The news of the revival was then a stimulus for many more churches in Wales to pray for a similar Awakening and the revival phenomena began attracting public attention.

The Form of the Revival Meetings.

The usual pattern to be followed in Roberts' meetings now began to emerge. This was for a series of informal prayer meetings, in which young people invariably took a prominent part, until the blessing increased to the point that the meetings went beyond human control. Also, at first, Roberts invariably explained in a brief challenging exhortation about the four following essential points on which he believed the revival depended. Roberts' clarifying remarks are in parenthesis:

1. The past must be clear, every sin confessed to God, any wrong to men must be put right. (Have you forgiven everybody – everybody? If not don't expect forgiveness for your sins. Better offend ten thousand friends than grieve the Spirit of God or quench Him).

2. Everything doubtful must be removed once and for all out of our lives. (Is there anything in your life that you cannot decide whether it is good or evil? Away with it.

There must not be a trace of a cloud between you and God).

3. Obedience, prompt, implicit, unquestioning to the Spirit of God. (At whatever cost, do what the Holy Spirit prompts you to do without hesitation or fear).

4. Public confession of Christ as your Saviour. (Multitudes are guilty of long and loud profession. There is a vast difference between profession and confession. We also forget there is a Trinity of Persons in the Godhead and that the Three Persons are of absolute equality...Is not He, the Holy Spirit, ignored entirely in hundreds of churches? Hear the Word of God, "Quench not the Spirit, (1 Thessalonians 5:19). That is the way of revival).[66]

Another essential ingredient in the meetings was the praying of a simple set prayer for the Holy Spirit-"Send the Spirit now, for Jesus Christ's sake, Amen". This was to be prayed by everyone present. Roberts' first week's meetings in Loughor ended in a powerful Sunday evening service when, by midnight, the whole congregation was overwhelmed with tears. Roberts then told the sixty or so remaining to each pray the prayer for the Holy Spirit. He began, then the prayer went from seat to seat until some cried out for mercy, lying prostrate on the floor in an agony of conviction. Others were so blessed that they called out, "No more, Lord Jesus or I die". Roberts eventually closed the meeting in the early hours of the morning.

From the beginning of the memorable second week of meetings, the Loughor chapel was crowded. The measure of blessing increased during this week and meetings went on

---

[66] Brown, Larry, V., "Evan Roberts, Welsh Revivalist", in *The World Revival, 1900-1910*, p. 9

for up to eight hours, with scenes of wild jubilation. People were shouting, singing, praying and numbers were being baptized with the Holy Spirit, including young children of twelve or thirteen years of age. Shopkeepers were now closing early to get a place in the chapel, and many men came from work in their working clothes and some with the following day's packed lunch! Everyone was talking about Evan Roberts and the powers he possessed. The presence of God pervaded everywhere and eternity seemed inescapably real and near. In one meeting many heard a powerful sound in the distance and then it seemed that God's presence entered and filled the building. People prayed in great distress for themselves or others who were unsaved and Roberts again asked that each person stand and pray the prayer they had prayed previously. The prayer chain was then repeated two or three times until the Spirit came irresistibly upon the people and the meeting went on until three a.m. On the Wednesday, because of the crowds, one of the larger churches had to be used. Miners, as soon as they left work, ran to the chapel as they were afraid there would be no room for them.

The meeting on the Thursday night was reported in the *Western Mail,* which stated that everything was left to the spontaneous impulse of the preacher who walked up and down the aisles, Bible in hand, exhorting one, encouraging another and kneeling to pray with a third. A young woman gave out a hymn and, while it was being sung, several people dropped down in their seats as if they had been struck and began crying for pardon. A young man then read a passage of Scripture. Finally, Mr. Roberts announced there would be further meetings and, at 4.25 a.m., the gathering dispersed. Even then the people stood about the road discussing what was now the chief subject of their lives.

On the Friday night the crowd was larger than ever, with people from all denominations present. The meeting was characterized by the intensity of conviction in it. Scores of church members and unbelievers were on their knees overcome by guilt, some unable to speak and others crying for mercy, making the most remarkable confessions of sin. Roberts then asked people to repeat the following prayer chain:

> Send the Spirit now. Send the Spirit powerfully now, for Jesus Christ's sake. Send the Spirit more powerfully now, for Jesus Christ's sake. Send the Spirit still more powerfully now, for Jesus Christ's sake".[67]

He believed the success of a meeting in saving souls was in proportion to the amount of fervent prayer. Many homes in the area held all-day prayer meetings. Young people held open-air services outside public houses and, when the drinkers came out, many were convicted and saved. The meetings were now held in two Loughor churches, but still the crowds were so great that people could not push in or out. Services sometimes went on until 6 a.m., since people lost all sense of time and desire to eat or sleep, as in New Quay previously.

Soon Roberts was known throughout the country and, realizing that he could not go back to the school, he visited many towns and villages in South Wales before the end of 1904, with similar results to those in Loughor. When he accepted an invitation he usually stayed in the place for three days but sometimes only for a day. Five female singers from Loughor often accompanied him, as well as other young helpers. Sometimes some of these stayed behind and held further meetings after he had left. As many as four services were held daily, at 7.30 a.m., 10 a.m., 2 p.m. and 7 p.m. At

---

[67] Jones, B.P., *An instrument of Revival*, p. 38

times hundreds stood outside chapels unable to get in and some walked the streets singing hymns. People travelled many miles to attend these services and then returned with the revival fire to their own towns and villages. People who came to market towns where Roberts was holding services would be convicted and, forgetting their business, they became absorbed in the services. When he left a place the blessing continued, and the churches continued to be crowded every night and many were converted.

The meetings were open for anyone to take part and new converts prayed and spoke with such power and eloquence that their ministers were amazed. Campbell Morgan commented that there was none of the things churches normally depend on: no hymnbooks, no choirs, no organs, no collections and no advertising. Someone would start up a hymn and everyone would join in. The unsaved broke down and wept as one after another of them received Christ and the conversion would then be announced publicly, when people would break out in praise. Roberts had no methods in conducting a meeting. He gave only a brief exhortation and, if prayer or praise interrupted him, he would immediately give way. The theme of his comments was usually on the sufferings of Christ and the love of God. He didn't talk about hell or future punishment and didn't, at this time, denounce individuals or particular groups, but would emphasize the need to forgive others in order to be forgiven. He stressed that it was the Spirit who controlled the meetings and defended his frequent non-intervention in meetings saying,

> Why should I teach when the Spirit is teaching and why should I control the meetings when the meetings control themselves, or rather the Spirit that is in them controls them? What need have these people to be told they are sinners?

What they need is salvation. Do they not know it? It is not knowledge they lack but decision – action. And why should I control the meetings? The meetings control themselves, or rather the Spirit that is in them.[68]

However, as Brian Edwards commented in his book, *Revival a people saturated with God,* that the weakest part of Evan Roberts' ministry was the freedom he gave to the meetings and the lack of preaching in them. Also, under the nervous strain of those days, he often sat silent in the pulpit and took little part in the meetings other than in quiet prayer. As mentioned, in the years following the revival, R.B. Jones dominated the religious scene in Wales by his powerful preaching and did all he could to address this lack of teaching, as did other of the leaders named above.However they could not altogether avoid the consequences of many falling away in the following months and years due to Roberts' undue emphasis on experiences, rather than grounding converts in the Faith. He emphasized that public confession was important, more so than preaching. He depended, in fact, on public testimonies as one of the proofs of a change of heart. He would invite those who had been forgiven to stand up or raise their hand, to go forward or to testify, and these brief testimonies became a characteristic of the revival. Often when one church was packed, the overflow would meet in a neighbouring church and a spontaneous service would begin there. People sang and prayed everywhere and the services were mostly taken up with singing. Some days all compartments on a train were filled with people singing hymns. If the train stopped and people saw a crowd around a church, they would leave the train and join the service! Some mines closed temporarily to allow workers to attend the meetings and, although the most intense excitement followed

---

[68] Ellis, Robert, *Living Echoes of the Welsh Revival 1904-1905*, p. 25

Evan Roberts, the revival movement went on at the same time throughout Wales and many came from other parts of Britain and overseas to witness it.

At Bethesda near Bangor, in November 1904, Joseph Jenkins' ministry produced results resembling those at Pentecost and by the following month the village was transformed. The public houses were practically empty, the streets quiet and swearing rarely heard. People were unable to restrain themselves from dancing. Some found themselves laughing for hours and one minister said he felt he could pray by laughing! At young people's prayer meetings the noise of agonized prayer, with many praying simultaneously, weeping and shouting, was said to be deafening and yet harmonious. Children met frequently for prayer and used the playtime at school for prayer. Also in North Wales, in the second week of November, at the same time that revival was breaking out in Loughor, a notable Awakening took place in Rhos when R.B. Jones held a series of meetings there. He relates the events of the Rhos revival, and that of a most amazing service later in Anglesey when Pentecost was repeated, in his book *Rent Heavens: The Revival of 1904*.

He stated:

> The memory of that meeting, even after a quarter of a century, is well-nigh overwhelming. It was easily the greatest meeting the writer was ever in. The theme of the message was Isaiah chapter six. The light of God's holiness was turned upon the hearts and lives of those present. Conviction of sin and of its terrible consequences was so crushing that a feeling almost of despair grew over all hearts...Could God forgive and cleanse? Then came the word about the altar, the tongs and the living coal touching the confessedly vile lips, and the gracious and complete removal of their vileness. After

all, there was hope! God was forgiving and he had cleansing for the worst. When the rapt listeners realized all this the effect was-well "electrifying" is far too weak a word; it was absolutely beyond any metaphor to describe it. As one man, first with a sigh of relief, and then with a delirious shout of joy, the whole huge audience sprang to their feet. The vision had completely overwhelmed them and one is not ashamed to say they were beside themselves with heavenly joy. The speaker never experienced anything like it anywhere. The whole place at that moment was so awful with the glory of God; one uses the word "Awful" deliberately; the presence of God was so manifested that the speaker himself was overwhelmed; the pulpit where he stood was so filled with the light of God that he had to withdraw.[69]

An experience similar to that experienced by Jews on the Day of Pentecost occurred when one monolingual Englishman, the Rev. B S. Fidler, who later became the Principal of the South Wales Bible College, heard R.B. Jones preaching in Welsh in that service and understood every word! Thousands were converted during the revival in Rhos and it was said that it seemed as though the whole town was going to church! Many drunkards were afraid to come out of their houses or to go into the public houses, which were forced to close throughout 1905 because of a lack of customers. The presence of God was such that all entering the town were conscious of it and the effects of the revival were felt in the area for many years.

The Awakening then spread to the Welsh churches in London, which had held prayer meetings for revival when they heard of the blessing in the principality. Six Welsh students held a campaign in one Welsh church there and saw seven hundred and twenty converts. During November and

---

[69] Jones, R.B., *Rent Heavens, The Revival of 1904,* pp. 42, 43

December 1904 the revival was in its purest phase. Roberts seemed to be inspired and the deepest and most lasting work was done among the people, and the excesses were most effectively restrained. Those most affected were the miners. Their managers claimed that they became better workmen and attended work more regularly and trade union disputes were changed for the better. Prayer meetings and short services were also held down the mines before the shifts began, which were as sincere and emotional as the revival meetings themselves. By the end of November 1904 revival had swept the mining valleys of South Wales independently of Roberts being present. At Tylorstown two hundred converts were registered before Roberts reached there and, at Morriston, one thousand two hundred converts had been registered before he arrived at the end of December.

W.T. Stead, the journalist, who attended many of the revival meetings, commented on a typical one in Maerdy which lasted for over two hours, three quarters of which was taken up with singing, all without a hymn book, besides a lot of preliminary singing while the congregation was assembling. It was absolutely without human direction or leadership. The last person to control the meeting was Evan Roberts and, after a scripture passage was read, the meeting was open to anyone to participate as they were led. People prayed and praised, gave a testimony and exhorted as the Spirit led them. Stead concluded: "The thousand or fifteen hundred people present merged into one myriad-headed but single-soul personality".

The Welsh nature of the revival was also evident in a meeting in Briton Ferry, near Neath, which was reported by the *Llanelly & County Guardian*, by one of its reporters who was present.

> The most prominent feature of the service is, of course, the
> singing, and the rendering of the old Welsh minor tunes is

very fine and soul-stirring. The singing also serves another useful, and sometimes necessary purpose when a brother, (or sister), becomes prosy and unduly lengthy, he is very promptly and effectively silenced by a sudden outburst of song. This is generally done with good judgement but sometimes the interruption is untimely, as on one occasion a lady got up to speak (in English) after they had been singing, "I need Thee, oh, I need Thee…" and although speaking very well indeed, and very much to the point on the words of the hymn, she was completely silenced by a sudden outburst of "Diolch Iddo – Thanks to Him"….However, one address by a working man in the gallery was much appreciated and evoked a storm of enthusiastic approval and, though lengthy, was not sung down being in Welsh. It was the cold, unemotional English that was generally silenced in song![70]

Criticisms of the revival.

A turning point in Evan Roberts' experience came with the publication of a strong criticism of the revival by a Congregational minister in Dowlais, the Rev. Peter Price, which appeared in the *Western Mail* on January 31st 1905, and which began a long and heated public debate. Price's objections were against Roberts' claim to an immediate, sustained control by the Holy Spirit, and he also dismissed the physical manifestations as sheer exhibitionism. He maintained that he thought he could claim to have had as good an opportunity as most people to understand what was really going on in South Wales; and he had come to the conclusion that there were two so-called revivals going on. The one, undoubtedly from above – Divine, real, intense in its nature, it was of God and its fire heavenly. This had been in progress for two years, in which his

---

[70] Jones, Brynmor, P., *Voices From The Welsh Revival 1904-1905*, p. 82

own church had been blessed with an increase of hundreds of converts in the previous five or six months. The other, the Evan Roberts revival, was "the bogus revival", "a sham... a mockery, a blasphemous travesty of the real thing and was of man and its fire false and fleshly". Roberts did not join in the debate but, from this time, he seemed to depend more and more on direct Spirit-inspired perception as to the conduct of the meetings and the content of his messages. Roberts was psychologically affected by the criticism and, thereafter, seemed to detect an obstacle of some sort in every meeting, and located the obstacles and even named the hinderers. This was particularly the case in his three-week mission in Liverpool at the beginning of 1905. In early February 1905, he was obliged on doctor's orders to take a rest "in consequence of an attack of nervous exhaustion".

Some questioned the public ministry of women in the revival as unscriptural and also the emphasis on the Keswick teaching and the pre-millennial interpretation of the Second Coming of Christ, as being not according to the traditional theology of the Welsh Calvinistic Church. Another criticism was that an estimated 20% of the converts fell away in the first few years after the revival, but this number apparently represents the total of those who were lost to the main denominations and includes those who defected to Pentecostal groups and mission halls. As mentioned, the defection of all these was attributed to the lack of adequate teaching of the new converts and an undue emphasis on experiences, which was later deplored by many Welsh ministers. Whenever Roberts saw signs of brokenness he would dispense with teaching, believing its purpose had been achieved, and he also curtailed the exposition of Scripture to allow more time for prayer. The emergence of Pentecostal groups was partly due to the emphasis by Roberts on the baptism of the Spirit, and his teaching that the primary condition for revival is for believers to experience the baptism.

Also, this revival was compared unfavourably with that in 1859, in which more care was given to assessing experience, whereas in 1904 the criteria was superficial and subjective, accepting experience at its face value. Critics affirmed that in 1904/5 no account was given of a person's knowledge of the Faith or reasons for his Christian hope, and prominence was given to emotion in praying, singing and testimony, rather than to Christian doctrine and character.

The Spread of the Revival.

The simultaneous outbreak of revival, north and south, revealed that the Awakening was not dependent upon any one person or any combined effort. Nor was it due to psychological techniques or publicity methods, but was evidently due to the sovereign power of God. As the revival progressed it was reported in the British and foreign press, the Cardiff *Evening Express* printing one hundred and twenty thousand copies of a revival edition every Monday. People then came from various parts of the world to observe the revival, including many well-known Christian leaders, and prayer requests too, came from many countries.

In England the revival mostly affected Cornwall, presumably through the contact of Welsh miners working there. Other parts of England were influenced to a lesser extent. Glasgow and the Orkneys also experienced a movement of the Spirit and there were good results in missions in Belfast during this period. Between 1905 and 1907 the impact of the revival was felt too among Welsh exiles in various parts of the world, such as Patagonia in Argentina and on mission fields served by Welsh missionaries, such as Madagascar and India. Welsh churches in North America were also revived. The revival phenomena there were as powerful as those experienced in Wales, and the Awakening spread beyond the Welsh settlements. Most of the countries in Western Europe experienced some local revival blessing, often through the ministry or reports of those who had visited Wales. Parts of Africa, Australasia and China were affected, but the most notable outbreaks were in parts of India and in Korea, where the revival was also as intense as it was in Wales. The revival in Korea resulted in crowded churches and a continuous religious awakening affecting the whole nation. There were many conversions and it was described as a "spreading fire", leading to further outbreaks of blessing, up to the ongoing revival in South Korea today. In the Khassia hills in Northern India, the mission field of the Welsh Calvinistic Methodists, and in southwest India, among the Tamils of Dohnavor, the mission field of Amy Carmichael, all the phenomena and spiritual results of the Welsh revival were repeated. In all, the Welsh revival made an impact on the Church worldwide and contributed significantly to the task of evangelizing the world.

The Effects of the Revival.

The most significant feature of the revival, as in others, was the overwhelming sense of the presence of God which seemed inescapable. People of all ages were gripped by the Holy Spirit not only in churches and prayer meetings but on the streets, on the trains and in public houses. Public houses, in fact, were virtually empty and some went bankrupt, while others were used for public worship. According to R.B. Jones:

> A sense of the Lord's presence was everywhere. It pervaded, nay it created the spiritual atmosphere. It mattered not where one went the consciousness of the reality and nearness of God followed. It was felt, of course, in the Revival

gatherings, but it was by no means confined to them. It was also felt in the homes, on the streets, in the mines and factories, in the schools and even in the theatres and public houses. The strange result was that wherever people gathered became a place of awe, and places of entertainment and carousal were practically emptied. Many were the instances of men entering a public house, ordering drinks, and then turning on their heels leaving their drinks on the counter untouched. Public houses, in fact, were virtually empty and some went bankrupt while others were used for public worship. The sense of the Lord's presence was such as practically to paralyze the arm that would raise the glass to their lips. Football teams and the like were disbanded, their members finding greater joy in testimony to the Lord's grace than in games. The mine pit-bottoms and galleries became places of praise and prayer, where miners gathered to worship before they dispersed to their various stalls...Indeed the cloud of God's presence hung over much of Wales for months. The land was covered by a canopy of prayer and people everywhere hungered for more of God's presence and power.[71]

Due to the huge increase in demand, shops ran out of stocks of Bibles and New Testaments. In one month alone a colporteur in Denbigh sold one thousand six hundred and thirty-five copies of them! Churches were filled and many new ones were built or enlarged. New life was infused into services and prayer meetings and new ones were started. It was also usual for the converts, even those who had never prayed before, to set up family worship. Men formerly addicted to drinking and gambling and notorious blasphemers were transformed and took an active part in extending the revival, quoting Scripture

---

[71] Duewel, Wesley, L., *Revival Fire*, pp. 183, 184

in open-air meetings with remarkable insight and power. Whole towns, where drunkenness and other vices had caused constant havoc, were now characterized by the sober, religious habits of the people. In one church of the two hundred men converted, half had been drunkards. Coal mines became places where God's name was honoured and praised and even pit ponies used to oaths and curses had to be restrained by gentler methods. One mine was visited by a reporter on the *Western Mail* and he wrote:

> The workmen on the night shift had gone down half an hour earlier than the usual time so as not to interfere with the operations of the pit... Seventy yards from the bottom of the shaft, in the stables, we came to the prayer meeting. One of the workmen was reading the sixth chapter of Matthew to about eighty comrades. He stood erect, reading in a dim... light...and around the impressive figure the colliers grouped themselves...earnest men, all of them, faces that bore the scars of the underground toiler...[72]

Long-standing quarrels were settled and outstanding debts paid. Interest in concerts and Eisteddfodau declined. Theatres only had a tenth of their normal takings and these too were used as revival venues. Magistrates found themselves out of a job as so few cases were coming before the courts. N.S.P.C.C. inspectors also had little to do. Footballs were burnt and teams disbanded as people lost interest in playing or watching the game. Men sold their racing dogs in which, up to then, they had had the greatest pride and infidel and gambling books were burnt.

Many who had no belief in God or desire to attend church were converted but the majority of converts were those who

---

[72] Edwards, Brian, H., *Revival A people saturated with God*, pp. 125, 126

had some regard for Christianity and had attended a church or chapel. In Wales, by the end of 1904, thirty-two thousand converts had been counted, most of whom were in the south and, by March 1905, over eighty thousand people were known to have been converted. By 1906, the Calvinistic Methodists had had twenty-four thousand added to their membership, the Wesleyans over four thousand, the Congregationalists twenty-six thousand and the Anglicans and Baptists together almost fifty thousand, making a total of over one hundred thousand. It was chiefly these converts, in the period of decline following the First World War, who maintained the spiritual life of the churches in Wales. Also, as a result of the revival, two Bible Colleges in Wales were formed, training men and women for Christian service at home and overseas and many revival converts went out as ministers and missionaries into all parts of the world. It is impossible, in fact, to put into words the transformation that was made by the revival in the churches, the community and tens of thousands of individual lives.

Rev A Douglas Brown   Rev Hugh Ferguson

London Road Baptist Church 1921

CHAPTER EIGHT
THE 1921 REVIVAL IN
SOUTH-EAST ENGLAND

The background to the Revival

It is strange that the most recent revival in England is also the least known, but that is so with regard to the revival which broke out in East Anglia in 1921. The human instrument used by God was the Rev. A. Douglas Brown, minister of the Ramsden Road Baptist Church, Balham, South London, and son of the famous nineteenth century evangelist, the Rev. Archibald Brown, formerly of the East London Tabernacle. This was the result of Douglas Brown being invited to conduct a week's mission in the London Road Baptist Church in Lowestoft by the minister, the Rev. Hugh P.E. Ferguson, who began his ministry in that church in 1917. Mr. Ferguson was concerned at the lack of converts in the church and, though the church had well attended services and prayer meetings, as well as a large number of young people attending the services and Bible classes, he felt the need to call the church members to pray specifically for revival.

Lowestoft had a prosperous fishing industry at the beginning of the century but, after the First World War it had declined, and there were many people unemployed, resulting in a general depression and disillusionment. There was, however, spiritual life in the town. As well as the strong London Road Baptist church, where the mission began, there were several evangelical Anglican churches, a lively Primitive Methodist church and a number of mission halls, All these churches were well attended and some, at least, had strong Bible classes and prayer meetings.

With the arrival of the new minister in 1917, the Baptist church abandoned sales of work, bazaars and concerts as a means of raising money and relied on direct giving. Also, after Mr. Ferguson's call for prayer, the weekly prayer meeting on Monday evenings, including Bank Holidays, was attended by almost a hundred people, who prayed fervently for two years before the revival for an outpouring of the Holy Spirit. The church then felt the time was right to hold special preaching services and, in the autumn of 1920, the minister went to Balham to ask Douglas Brown to conduct them, initially for one week, which he agreed to do in the spring of 1921.

The Preparation of the Revivalist.

Douglas Brown had had times of blessing in his own church but, when the invitation to hold the mission came, he did not feel he was yet ready for the work God intended him to do in Lowestoft, feeling there was something missing in his spiritual life, nevertheless he reluctantly agreed to the invitation. Preaching later at the Keswick Convention on 2 Chronicles 7:14, "If my people, who are called by my name, will humble themselves and pray and seek my face and turn from their wicked ways, then I will hear from heaven and will forgive their sin and will heal their land", he said it had taken four months for that truth to come home to him, even though he had been a minister for twenty-six years. He then went on to describe the experience that prepared him to be the instrument of the revival in Lowestoft, soon after the visit of the Lowestoft minister.

God laid hold of me in the midst of a Sunday evening service, and He nearly broke my heart while I was preaching. I went back to my vestry and locked the door and threw myself down on the hearthrug broken-hearted. Why? I do not know. My church was filled. I loved my people, and I believe my people loved me. I do not say they ought to, but they did. I was as happy there as I could be. I had never known a Sunday there for fifteen years without conversions. That night I went home and went straight up to my study…I had no supper that night. Christ laid his hand on a proud minister and told him that he had not gone far enough, that there were reservations in his surrender, and that He wanted me to do a piece of work (as an itinerant evangelist) that he had been trying to evade. I knew what He meant. All November that struggle went on, but I would not give way. I knew God was right, and I knew I was wrong. I knew what it would mean for me, and I was not prepared to pay the price. Then Christmas came and all the joy round about seemed to mock me…The struggle went on, and I said to the Lord, "You know that is not my work. I will pray for someone else who does it, but please do not give it to me, it will kill me. I cannot get into the pulpit and plead with people. It is against my temperament, and you made me…" [73]

Before the crisis came the struggle within him continued for four months, until February 1921. Finally, he wrote out his resignation to his church, feeling that he could not go on preaching while he had a contention with God. But then, in the early hours of one morning, he had an experience of the love of God which transformed him. He said he found himself in the loving embrace of Christ for ever and ever; and all power and joy and blessedness rolled in like a deluge Then he prayed,

[73] Griffin, Stanley, *A forgotten Revival*, pp.17, 18

"Lord, Jesus, I know what you want. You want me to go into mission work. I love you more than I dislike that". God, in his own time, had prepared his man to do his work in his way. He soon saw a greater blessing on his ministry. That month ninety-six people came to faith in his church.

However, as is so often the case, the power of God through human weakness was seen in this instance in that, when Douglas Brown arrived in Lowestoft on Monday, March 7th 1921, he was still feeling unwell after being ill with influenza for almost two weeks. As a result, he had arranged for another minister to go with him, because he was afraid he would not be strong enough to carry out his engagements for that week. He was, however, able to preach with power that night and at hundreds of other meetings in the following months.

The Revival in Lowestoft

In the meantime, the members of the Lowestoft Baptist Church began to be afraid that they would not attract enough people to the week's meetings to make Douglas Brown's visit worthwhile, but their fears proved unfounded. The building, seating seven hundred and fifty was filled on the first evening and there was a spirit of expectancy among the congregation. Special prayer meetings were held in the mornings with Bible readings in the afternoons. Nothing spectacular happened on the first two days, but the power of the Holy Spirit was felt increasingly as the week went by in all these meetings, with the prayer meetings being described as "wonderful". A fifteen year old boy attended the meetings that week and, almost seventy years later, commented:

> At the end of the Wednesday evening, Douglas Brown had been preaching to a packed church and he announced the

closing hymn: "I hear thy welcome voice that calls me Lord to thee…" with the chorus: "I am coming Lord, coming now to thee…" I cannot recall what he had been preaching about, and there was nothing emotional or sensational, but he gave an appeal for people to come forward who were seeking Christ… we were conscious that people were moving from all over the large building. By the end of the hymn the aisles were full; we were taken to the school-room, which was soon filled up. In describing the atmosphere of that meeting I can only speak of a peculiar movement, something extraordinary…[74]

Other accounts speak of scores who tried to crowd into the vestry and schoolroom in order to surrender themselves to the Lord Jesus Christ, including sixty to seventy teenagers, for whom the church had been praying for years. Mr. Ferguson announced that there were so many people in the street outside wanting to get in that he would like those who were Christians to leave their seats and go to the school-room to pray, and he walked up and down the aisles encouraging people to do so. The young people, however, kept their seats as they didn't want to miss anything! The minister said later, "We had been praying for 'showers' that night and God gave us a 'cloud-burst' instead". The enquiry room continued to be so packed each night that, once they were in, people could not move. The situation was described as being like an auction room with people crying to God in their distress and ministers standing on forms trying to point them to Christ.

The next day news was spread that God was moving in an unusual way and more room was needed to accommodate the crowds, who were flocking in from the surrounding neighbourhood. Some people were sitting on the floor and

---

[74] Edwards, Brian H., *Revival A people saturated with God*, p. 249

it was clear that other churches would have to be used. Also, the ministers of the town decided they would have to scrap their arrangements and do as the Spirit of God led them. In the prayer meetings, numerous tearful requests for prayer for the salvation of relatives, friends and neighbours were read out and, at the same time, prayer for an outpouring of the Spirit in Lowestoft was being made in churches in London and elsewhere.

Douglas Brown had only been booked for a week's mission and he returned to London for the weekend, as he had to preach in his own church on the Sunday. Before he left, however, he promised he would return on Monday for a further week in the light of what had happened. The meetings then moved to the Parish church as the largest building in the town, and as at this time all the other churches were supporting the mission. Even non-church goers in the town were asking each other, "Have you heard Douglas Brown?" He also preached all over East Anglia with remarkable results, with scores of hardened fishermen being gripped with the fear of God. In Great Yarmouth as well as Lowestoft, strong fishermen were literally thrown to the ground under conviction and one eye witness reported: "the ground around me was like a battlefield, with souls crying to God for mercy".[75]

At an Anglican church in Yarmouth, many fishermen were converted and, in the parish church in Oulton, hundreds knelt at the altar in full commitment to Christ. Though the revival was comparatively short-lived, there were long term results. There were increased numbers in prayer meetings and a new endeavour to evangelize the villages with teams of lay preachers, many young people being introduced to preaching in this way, and some entered the ministry or became missionaries. Young people also held weekly open-air meetings. Almost

---

[75] Richie, Jackie, *Floods upon the Dry Ground*, p. 30

seventy years after the revival one man recalled three marks of it, common to other revivals: a coming together of spiritually minded people, irrespective of denominations; a renunciation of what was offensive to God's law and a sincere following of the Scriptures.

The outstanding characteristic of the revival in Lowestoft was the powerful, searching preaching of the Word of God to Christian and non-Christian alike. There was hardly any advertising, no sensational methods and no hysterical appeals. The original five-day mission now went on for a month. The evangelist spoke simply on the basic truths of the Christian Faith, with the Cross central in every message. The truth of the Second Coming was also emphasized and particularly the Judgement Seat of Christ and the believer's accountability and need of faithfulness in serving the Lord. It was said that the messages came like bombshells and there was an awesome sense of the presence of God in the meetings, followed by a deep sense of repentance among Christians and unbelievers alike. Meetings were held whenever work was finished and went on until the early hours of the morning. Due to bad weather, boats were often tied up and the unoccupied fishermen would gather together eagerly and take the further opportunity of attending the services. There wasn't the musical support there usually is in modern evangelistic crusades but the singing was memorable. It was said:

> On the Denes (Dunes) where most of the curing yards were, and across the river at Gorleston in the yards there, the songs of Zion were sung. Far out at sea, as the boats lay at their nets, the singing of men who were redeemed wafted over the waves.[76]

---

[76] Richie, Jackie, *Floods upon the Dry Ground*, p. 32

Many exciting stories of conversions were recorded, some of respectable professional people, others of prostitutes, drunkards and criminals. Tough burly fishermen, newly converted, testified as to how God had dealt with them and, as they told how and when they were saved, the atmosphere was charged with the presence of God. And conversions took place not only in the churches but also in the lanes around the town where people knelt, on the road, under the conviction of sin. One publican and his wife were converted at Somerleyton, a village a few miles from Lowestoft, and they closed the pub and tipped the barrels of beer into the marshes!

The number of converts was small, compared with other revivals covering a larger area, but more than five hundred were recorded. Many of these subsequently entered Christian service at home and abroad, and it was also estimated that there were many more converts of whom the churches had not heard. The chief results, however, were among those who had been nominal Christians, who now fully gave their lives to Christ. Ministers too re-dedicated themselves to Christ and resolved to faithfully shepherd the converts and train them for Christian service.

Douglas Brown returned again to Lowestoft in Whitsun week 1921 for further meetings, which were reported in *The Christian* as even more remarkable than the ones in March and, on the following Sunday, the churches in the town and neighbourhood experienced another moving of the Holy Spirit with further conversions. Before this took place Brown, who was staying at a Lowestoft rectory, was awakened in the early hours of the morning by a voice saying, "You will see greater things than these". He went downstairs and met the rector, who had also been awakened by the same message!

The Revival was the result of prayer, prayer and more prayer

This was so evident that towards the end of 1921 even the secular newspaper, the *Yarmouth and Gorleston Times* reported, "God has become very near and the secret of it all can be summed up in one word – prayer." [77] It was right, after a time of spiritual decline, for six months before the outpouring of the Holy Spirit in February 1921, about sixty members of the London Road Baptist Church had met every Monday evening to pray for nothing but the revival.

The Revival spreads to Scotland.

In the autumn of 1921, as every autumn, thousands of Scots involved in the fishing industry, fishermen, wives, sweethearts and sisters, moved to the East Anglian ports for the herring season. They were soon influenced by the revival preaching of the evangelist Jock Troup, himself a former fisherman and later superintendent of the famous Tent Hall, Glasgow, as well as by the ministry of Douglas Brown who had returned to the area. The revival then spread to Scotland when these fishermen and their families went home to their Scottish ports, and whole communities were changed. A newspaper reported that in Cairnbulg, a small town with a population of one thousand five hundred, six hundred were converted in two weeks.

While Jock Troup was ministering in Yarmouth he saw a vision of a man at Fraserburgh calling on God to send him to that town. As a result, to the surprise of his friends, Jock Troup left preaching at Yarmouth and went to Fraserburgh. The blessing continued in Yarmouth, however, with powerful, crowded prayer meetings preceding the evening meetings.

---

[77] Edwards, Brian, H., *A people saturated with God*, p. 82

Fisher-folk prayed publicly for their relatives and friends and whole families and boat crews were saved. When the herring season was over the Scottish boats left for home, but the news of the revival had already reached Scotland and families eagerly awaited their return.

Soon after Jock Troup arrived in Fraserburgh, he went and preached in the market-place where a crowd of people gathered, and he began to preach to them. Jackie Richie described what followed;

> Because of the intense cold Jock Troup suggested they find a church in which they could continue the meeting. Being a stranger in the town he had no idea where the churches were and the crowd suggested the Baptist Church. They arrived at the church to be met by the minister and his elders, who had just concluded a special meeting at which it had been decided to send an invitation to Jock Troup to come and conduct an evangelistic mission. Amongst the group of elders Troup recognized the face of the man in his vision! [78]

They all entered the church and, as Jock Troup started the meeting, unsaved people began weeping in their conviction of sin and in their prayers to Christ for forgiveness. There is evidence that there was a movement of the Holy Spirit in northeast Scotland earlier that year, before the fishing fleet sailed for East Anglia, but it was not until it returned that the revival proper broke out. Now it spread, as converts went everywhere preaching the Gospel, and thousands were saved. In Peterhead there were six hundred seekers registered and the Wick Salvation Army Corps alone received at least five hundred enquirers. Large numbers of Christians were revived and almost all denominations received new spiritual life. There

---

78 Edwards, Brian, H., *Revival A people saturated with God*, p. 211

were many other towns and villages in Scotland including Dundee, Aberdeen and Glasgow which were affected by the revival in 1921-1922, and meetings often went on in these places into the night. Under Jock Troup's preaching, as in East Anglia, strong fishermen were thrown to the ground and cried to God for mercy and, in the next few weeks, hundreds were converted in his meetings. Sometimes the fisher-girls also were too distressed to continue their work, or even to go to work, and Jock Troup had to be sent for to counsel them. Also, some men were saved out at sea on the fishing grounds. In November, in the providence of God, the blessing increased at a time when crews were free to attend the Gospel meetings, due to the weather being unusually bad and they were unable to put to sea. The atmosphere and effects of the revival continued for many years and, sixty years later, people could testify to the great things God had done at that time.

The Aftermath of the Revival

The revival gave an impetus to evangelistic outreach, not only in East Anglia and Scotland but also throughout Britain. Lionel Fletcher, later British Empire evangelist with "The Movement for World Evangelism", held highly successful campaigns in Ipswich in 1921 and 1923, which he describes in his book, *Mighty Moments*, when thousands attended open-air meetings and hundreds were converted. The revival also stimulated other campaigns in many towns and cities, such as those run by the National Young Life Campaign, founded by Arthur and Frederick Wood, and again hundreds were converted by those means. In Scotland, the revival helped and encouraged the work of the "Faith Mission", whose results that year were greater than any in the previous twenty years. Also, every year until the Second World War, the Scottish fishermen brought a breath of revival when they visited East Anglia for the autumn fishing.

Why did the Revival not spread throughout Britain?

At the time of the East Anglian and North-East Scotland revival, God was also using the Rev. W.P. Nicholson in revival in Northern Ireland, where he held missions all over the province. There was there, in 1921, the now familiar political unrest and sectarian violence, but whole communities were affected by the revival and hundreds were converted. Enormous crowds filled the largest halls to overflowing and the usual results of revival were seen. Bad debts were paid off, public houses were closed and church memberships increased greatly.

Understandably the evangelists, Brown, Troup, Nicholson and others, were expecting the revival to spread to other parts of Britain, but this did not happen. At Keswick and elsewhere Douglas Brown warned against the terrible indifference; worldly-mindedness; defective consecration among Christians; the sin of disunity and the evil of modernist theology, as well as the danger of trying to organize the revival. Others believed the revival was quenched when the preaching missions of Douglas Brown were actually taken over by a committee and he was no longer as free to be led by the Holy Spirit. One person hearing of it said, "This is the end". Brown himself, like Evan Roberts before him, suffered a breakdown in health and was ordered to rest and, in later years, he lacked the spiritual power he had once had, which he sadly confessed himself.

Criticisms of the Revival

There were criticisms of this revival, from people inside the church as well as from the world, as there have been of all revivals. Dr. Carlisle, president of the Baptist Union in 1921, although expressing his despair of organized religion and the need of people in the church to be converted, spoke of it as "an emotional wave produced by a hypnotic preacher". At the same time, however, he spoke of Douglas Brown as his friend! There was, however, no emotionalism in the revival, only the emotion of people weeping under a conviction of sin. Nor was there any pressure put on those who responded to the preaching of the Gospel, and the follow-up of converts was mostly left to the local ministers and their experienced members. The revival was small and not so intense in comparison with some other revivals, but it resulted in solid converts who proved as genuine and faithful for the rest of their lives as those produced in any other revival.

Lowestoft had known something of revival blessing in former years. It had been affected by the 1859 revival, although that spiritual Awakening did not reach the town until 1860. All the usual fruits of revival were seen then, as in 1921; a decline in drunkenness and crime, backsliders being restored, churches filled and a greater unity among God's people. As a result there was, subsequently, the desire and prayer in the area that God would "do it again". Someone has said that it is easy to light a fire on a warm hearth and, while revival only occurs according to the sovereign will of God nevertheless, in his time and way, he honours the heartfelt prayers of his people, when they seek him according to such Bible promises as 2 Chronicles 7:14. In fact, 1 John 5:15 teaches that such prayers may be taken as an indication that God is going to work.

Duncan Campbell, Hebrides Revival 1949-1957

CHAPTER NINE
THE HEBRIDES REVIVAL, 1949-1957.

Since the Isle of Lewis revival is the most recent major spiritual Awakening in Great Britain, a study of this revival is particularly significant and most challenging, and should provoke us to a greater preparation of heart and more earnest prayer. In the years immediately following the revival in the Hebrides little appears to have been written on it, apart from the brief accounts that were published as a small part of books or booklets on revival generally. Even Duncan Campbell's, *The Lewis Awakening, 1949-1953*, amounts to less than twenty small pages in Colin Peckham's, *Heritage of Revival*. Moreover, these brief accounts were not always consistent and sometimes vague or confusing as to when and where the various events occurred. However, Duncan Campbell's brief account was enlarged in his book, *Revival in the Hebrides, 1949-1952,* being an anthology of his sermons, an account of his conversion and testimonies of converts of the revival. This book, with Colin and Mary Peckham's book, *Sounds from Heaven, The Revival on the Isle of Lewis,* are now among the main sources for the revival.

The island of Lewis and Harris.

The island of Lewis, is about eighty miles in length and has a population of only twenty-five thousand, three thousand seven hundred of whom are in Stornaway, the island's only large town. Some of the rest of the population live in very lonely places, but most of these places are in more or less small compact villages, several being so near to each other as to form a large community within the radius of a few miles. Most people are employed in small scale farming or crofting and weaving, making the well-known Harris Tweed. In the 1940s and 1950s many of the islanders lived in thatched cottages and Gaelic was universally spoken. People were traditionally religious and most homes still observed family worship and held the doctrines of the Faith, nominally at least, and in most churches the Gospel was faithfully preached. The island had known revival in the past but, as in other parts of the United Kingdom, in the post-war period of the late 1940s and early 1950s, its spiritual condition was at a low ebb. Few attended services or the prayer meetings in the village churches and most of the young people spent their time instead in drinking, dancing and cinema going. The Free Church Presbytery of Lewis expressed its concern about this situation in a declaration, which was read in every parish and published in the *Stornoway Gazette and West Coast Advertiser*, on December 9th 1949. Taking into consideration the low state of religion on the island and throughout the land generally, it stated:

> The Presbytery of Lewis, having taken into consideration the low state of vital religion within their own bounds, and through the land generally, call upon their faithful people in all their congregations to take a serious view of the...divine displeasure manifested, not only in the chaotic conditions of international politics and morality, but also... in the lack of spiritual power from Gospel ordinances, and to realize that these things plainly indicate that the Most High has a controversy with the nation. They note especially the grow-

ing carelessness toward Sabbath observance and public worship, and the light regard of solemn vows and obligations…
and the spreading abroad of the spirit of pleasure among
the younger generation, that all regard for anything higher
appears with very few exceptions to have been utterly dismissed from their thoughts.[79]

The report went on to say that the Presbytery affectionately
pleaded with their people, especially the youth of the church,
to take these matters to heart and to seriously inquire as to
what the result would be if there was no repentance, and they
called on every individual to examine his or her life before God.
Especially they warned their young people against the cinema
and the public house, which they called the devil's man-traps!

Duncan Campbell, the Revivalist.

The name of the Rev. Duncan Campbell will always be
remembered in connection with the revival in the Hebrides,
which began in December 1949. As in the case of other men
whom God used in revival, Campbell himself had to have a
spiritual experience which would prepare him for his special
task. During the First World War Campbell was shot from his
horse and seriously injured in one of the last cavalry charges of
the war. He was carried on horseback to the casualty clearing
station and, in this critical condition, he reviewed his Christian
life and he saw how empty it had been. He quoted Psalm 103
in his native Gaelic and prayed the well-known prayer of the
Scottish saint, Robert Murray M'Cheyne, "Lord make me
as holy as a saved sinner can be". His life was spared and he
was filled with the Holy Spirit, and experienced the presence

---

[79] Campbell, Duncan, "The Lewis Awakening 1949-1953", in Peckham,
Colin, *Heritage of Revival*, pp. 162

of God to such a degree that he felt he was going straight to heaven. The presence of God was so real on that occasion that other wounded soldiers were conscious of it and seven were converted and, one by one, they began to testify to the experience they had received. As a result, from that time, his mind was set on eternal realities. Campbell himself, having experienced the supernatural power of Holy Spirit, from that time had his mind set on eternal realities and had an all-consuming desire for God, revival and further manifestations of God's power.

After the war, when he was fully recovered, he began a Christian witness in Argyllshire, visiting house to house, reading the Scriptures and testifying and praying with people. He also trained to be an evangelist with the Faith Mission Bible College in Edinburgh and, in one class there, he rose to testify that Jesus was his dearest Friend and God's power fell on the class. After he graduated Campbell preached to people all over Scotland, wherever he found them, winning them for Christ and experiencing foretastes of the revival that was to come, with God's power falling on his meetings and resulting in many conversions. However, he had a time later when he lost the sense of the presence of God he had had previously. Then there was an occasion when, on his face in his study at 5 a.m., he came to know the recovering power of the blood of Christ after spending seventeen years in a spiritual wilderness, frustrated in his Christian work and witness. He spoke of suddenly coming to realize the provision God had made for a holy life and, he said, in a small way the revival on Lewis was related to that experience of cleansing and of the Holy Spirit.

Before Campbell went to the Hebrides he had been a Presbyterian minister in a lowland industrial community. Then, out of concern for the Gaelic-speaking people of the highlands, he re-joined the Faith Mission in January 1949, having been in similar work from October 1919 as well as his twenty-five years in the ministry of the United Free Church of Scotland. After re-joining the Mission, he felt led to go to Skye and had a number of missions there with much blessing, but it was on Lewis that he was to see God work in a remarkable way. In October 1949, he had an urgent message from the praying people of Barvas on the island of Lewis and Harris to go there, through their minister, the Rev. James Murray MacKay.

The Lewis Revival., 1949 – c. 1951

Revival in Barvas.

Before he thought of engaging the services of Campbell the Rev. MacKay, having begun his ministry in Barvas in 1949, had decided to spend several nights a week, from 10 p.m. to 4 or 5 a.m., in prayer for an outpouring of the Spirit. That autumn, for three months or so, he and his church elders, seven of them in all, met to pray in a barn. They made a solemn covenant with God, in accordance with Isaiah 62:6, 7, that they would not cease to pray until he had sent revival to the Hebrides. Also it seems unknown to them two godly sisters, Peggy and Christine Smith, had had a similar burden. Living in a small cottage at the other end of the village, Peggy was eighty-four and blind and Christine was eighty-two and almost bent double with arthritis. Unable to attend church, for months they spent three nights a week bowed in earnest prayer for the young people of the island and for the people in each cottage in the village. They pleaded the promise God had given them, in Isaiah 43:3, a promise they said, made by a covenant-keeping God, who must be true to his Word. They had such a burden in prayer that they felt that God must answer them.

For the men praying in the barn, time passed and nothing apparently happened until, one night, one young man read Psalm 24:3-5, "Who may ascend the hill of the Lord? Who may stand in his holy place? He who has clean hands and a pure heart...he will receive the blessing of the Lord..." He said to the others, "Brethren, is it not so much sentimental humbug to be waiting in this way night after night if we ourselves are not right with God". He then cried, "Oh God! Are my hands clean? Is my heart pure?" He immediately fell prostrated on the floor and an awesome sense of the presence of God filled the barn and the holiness of God and the sinfulness of their hearts was revealed to them as never before. They poured out their hearts in confession and then, suddenly, the glory and joy of the Lord swept over them. Duncan Campbell commented later that at that moment, a moment that will always be remembered on the island of Lewis, something happened. God swept into that prayer group and, at that wonderful moment, the seven elders discovered what they evidently had not realized before, that revival must be related to holiness. They discovered things about themselves that they had not suspected. But the blood of Calvary heals and cleanses. Then similar events followed all over the island as recorded by Duncan Campbell as follows:

> Here is a scene witnessed during the early days of the movement: a crowded church, the service is over, the congregation, reluctant to disperse stand outside the church in a silence that is intense. Suddenly a cry is heard from within the church: a young man, burdened for the souls of his fellow men, is pouring out his soul in intercession. He prays until he falls into a trance and lies prostrate on the floor of the church. But his prayer is heard and the congregation, moved by a power they could not resist, came back into the church and a wave of conviction of sin

swept over the gathering, moving strong men to cry to God for mercy. This service continued until the early hours of the morning, but so great was the distress and so deep the hunger which gripped men and women that they refused to go home and already were assembling in another part of the parish. An interesting and amazing feature of this early morning visitation was the number who made their way to the church moved by a power they had not experienced before: others were deeply convicted of their sin and were crying for mercy in their homes before ever coming near the church... Within a matter of days the whole parish was in the grip of a spiritual Awakening. Churches became crowded with services continuing until three o' clock in the morning. Work was largely put aside as young and old were made to face eternal realities. Soon the fire of blessing spread to the neighbouring parishes.[80]

When people returned to their homes, they found virtually everyone in the village up and gathered at the police station, which was next door to the sisters' cottage. They discovered that at the very time they were prostrated in the barn, the Holy Spirit had fallen on practically everyone in the village. Some were unable to sleep and, with others awakened from sleep, were convicted of their lost condition. These people dressed and gathered together, trying to find out how to be saved and before dawn broke many experienced forgiveness. The same day Peggy Smith had a vision of churches crowded with people, including many young people, and hundreds being brought into the kingdom of God. She also saw the Lamb of God on the throne with the keys of heaven in his hand. She then sent

---

[80] Campbell, Duncan "The Lewis Awakening 1949-1953" in Peckham, Colin N., *Heritage of Revival*, pp. 167, 168

a message to the minister that God had shown her that he was going to send a great revival.

It was then, as mentioned, that the minister was led to invite Duncan Campbell to conduct a ten-day mission. This was confirmed when one of the praying group had a vision not only that revival was coming, but also that Campbell was to be the human instrument. He arrived in December 1949, and his first meeting was ordinary, with about three hundred attending and, after it, Campbell suggested a night of prayer. This had already been planned. It started at 10 p.m. with thirty present but, by 3 a.m., two hundred were outside, mostly unsaved who, unable to rest, had come seeking the Lord. That evening for the second meeting the church was crowded, with people standing on the pulpit steps. Over fourteen thirty-two seater buses had come from ten different centres, one even from Leverburgh, at the other end of the island. In addition a butcher's van brought seven young men, all of whom were saved. Campbell had to stop his message on the doom of the damned because of the cries of the people and the meeting went on until 4 a.m. and one hundred were converted. As he left the church Campbell saw people prostrate on the ground almost every yard of the way and people everywhere, men and women, were crying out, "God be merciful to me". Normal business stopped and the whole island gave itself to seeking God, and it is said that Campbell preached the following day from noon until 3 a.m. the next day.

Campbell's method was not to preach on the love of God but on sin, judgement and hell during the service and to reserve preaching the way of salvation until the after-meeting, to those who were under conviction and genuinely seeking Christ. As a result there was an entire absence of superficial emotion. He emphasized repeatedly that the revival was not dependent upon him and his going to Lewis, but that it had already begun, in the sovereignty of God, before he arrived. One night he preached from Matthew chapter twenty-five on "The Wise Virgins", and he rebuked a young woman who had the Bible in one hand and *The People's Friend* in another. The next night she went to the meeting with four friends and she said to them, "There are five of us and he will preach on the five Foolish Virgins tonight, being terrified that he would. He did, and the five young women were saved. At the close of that meeting, when he went outside, he found all the congregation standing there under conviction as if they were rooted to the spot. Others, under deep spiritual distress, also felt irresistibly drawn from their homes to the church as by an unseen hand, and Campbell invited them all back into the church.

The presence of God was so profound that even Christians felt a deep conviction of their sinfulness, while the unsaved groaned or cried for mercy as they repented of their sins, and then, one after another, they received the assurance of salvation. The next day the minister told the Smith sisters what had happened. They replied that the previous night in prayer they had overcome the opposition of Satan, putting the blood of the Lamb between Satan and themselves and that, before morning, they knew a spiritual victory had been won. News of the revival soon spread across the island and, the next night, buses from various places came filled with people anxious to meet with God. Work was stopped throughout the area as people prayed for themselves and their friends and neighbours. Many experienced salvation or new blessing in their homes, barns and fields, by the roadside or wherever they went to seek God. The revival then spread to other villages and calls to help came from other churches.

A strong sense of the presence of God now seemed to pervade the area, wherever people were they were aware of it, as were visitors to the island, some of whom were gripped by the

Spirit of God before they landed. Christians were led by the Spirit to go to homes where unconverted people were seeking God and, when people met on the road, a common greeting was, "Have you done business with God today?" There were also extraordinary spiritual experiences. One man, who had been resisting God for years, was frightened when he heard of the revival in Barvas and refused to attend Duncan Campbell's meetings. Eventually he went and was so burdened at the end that he rushed out to the evangelist crying, "I am lost, really lost" but, as he prayed for forgiveness, he instantly received assurance and seemed to see on the floor the locks and chains of sin which bound him. Going home with an elder a circle of light seemed to surround them and, looking up, he found himself gazing into the face of the Saviour.

Revival in Ness.

What happened in Barvas spread to Ness and then to other areas. Campbell went to Ness with some other ministers in the early hours of the morning and found the church packed. He was told there were three hundred in a field praying, unable to get into the church. Meetings were held there for a week, in the afternoons and evenings and frequently into the early morning, and buildings of all kinds were used to accommodate the people seeking God. Communities were revolutionized. Some had five prayer meetings and three half nights of prayer every week. Pubs were closed and boarded up and there was hardly a house where everyone wasn't converted and where there wasn't family worship morning and evening.

Revival in Arnol.

When Campbell went to the village of Arnol, in May 1950, he met with an unresponsive attitude. Although many attended from other areas very few locals did so, because the parish minister organized a meeting to oppose the mission since he believed the evangelist's theology was not sound, nor his teaching about the baptism of the Spirit as an experience subsequent to conversion. A night of prayer and waiting on God to overcome this negative attitude was arranged in a nearby farm and about thirty men met together, including four other ministers. About midnight Campbell felt led to ask a young blacksmith to pray. In the middle of his prayer the man paused and said, "O God, you made a promise to pour water upon him that is thirsty and floods upon the dry ground and Lord it is not happening". The blacksmith paused again and said, "Lord, if I know anything about my own heart, I stand before thee as an empty vessel thirsting for thee and for a manifestation of thy power". He stopped again and then after a tense silence he said, "O God, your honour is at stake, and I now challenge you to fulfil your covenant engagement and do what you have promised to do". Duncan Campbell described what happened following that prayer:

> Before midnight God came down…and a wave of revival swept the village. Opposition and spiritual death fled before the presence of the Lord of life. Here was demonstrated the power of prevailing prayer and that nothing lies beyond the reach of prayer except that which lies outside the will of God. There are those in Arnol today who will bear witness to the fact that, while a brother prayed, the very house shook. I could only stand in silence as wave after wave of divine power swept through the house, and in a matter of minutes

following this heaven-sent visitation, men and women were
on their faces in distress of soul...[81]

At the same time that the granite farmhouse shook and the
dishes rattled on the sideboard, God's power fell on all who
were in the building. Some thought it was an earthquake
but Campbell remembered that a similar visitation of divine
power followed the Day of Pentecost, as recorded in Acts 4:31.
He ended the meeting about 2 a.m. and, as the people went
outside, they found that the power of God had fallen on the
village and the whole community was aware of the presence of
God. People came carrying chairs and stools and asked if there
was room for them in the church and many were saved in that
area in the following days. People couldn't sleep and walked
the streets under conviction. Within two days every young
person between twelve and twenty years old was converted, the
drinking house* was closed and fourteen of the worst drunkards
were saved. When Campbell visited the village years later the
drinking house was still closed and the former drunkards were
in the prayer meeting.

One night the meetings in Arnol went on until the early
hours of the morning and, as the people were leaving, someone
came with a message that revival had broken out in another
church several miles away. Campbell and about two hundred
people then set out to go there, taking a short cut across the
fields. As they went they all heard the sound of angelic singing
filling the sky and they fell on their knees in the field, some
being converted as they knelt there. The Awakening at Arnol
illustrated the sovereignty of God in revival. It was said that

---

[81] Campbell, Duncan, "The Lewis Awakening 1949-1953" in Peckham,
      Colin, *Heritage of Revival*, p. 170

*   A place where men met to drink alcohol they had bought elsewhere, as
     the only licensed premises were in Stornoway.

a place as hard as the rocks and barren as the wilderness had become a garden of the Lord. Other places, however, where there was opposition to the revival, were not blessed.

Revival in Uig.

This part of the island is sparsely populated with villages far apart and with no public transport. When Campbell visited the parish, however, people came in Lorries and vans from the scattered communities and here, too, an indescribable consciousness of the presence of God came over the congregation. A second service was held in a neighbouring parish, and again Lorries and vans conveyed the people to the meeting place while many walked from miles away across moors and over hills. As a result the churches were filled with zealous new Christians, eager to worship and witness to their faith in Christ.

Revival in Lochs.

One man from the parish of Lochs was so burdened for others that night after night, for two years, he transported people who were seeking Christ to revival meetings, many of whom were converted, including members of his own family. In Lochs, too, an awakening took place and meetings went on until two or three a.m. and remarkable scenes were witnessed. In the little church of Habost, in Lochs, long before the service began, buses and vans brought a crowd from a nearby parish who filled the church and the regular congregation had to sit in their vehicles!

Revival in Tarbert and Leverburgh.

The awakening in Lewis was also felt in Harris in the southern part of the island. Revival also broke out in Tarbert and Leverburgh and here too, wave after wave of deep conviction swept over the congregations before they found peace in believing. As in other places, the outstanding feature of the revival in this area was the awe-inspiring sense of the presence of God. Meetings were held during the day and throughout the night in churches, homes and in the open. Every time people met it became an occasion of seeking God and of worship. Many village churches also were now crowded where only two or three attended previously. One young man said, "We didn't know what church-going was. Now the prayer meeting is the weekly attraction and the worship of God in his house is our chief delight". The revival affected every part of life and gave a new hunger for spiritual things. The whole island was aware of the awesome presence of God, so much so that many were terrified of being converted. Some refused to go to the meetings, but God met them in the fields. Others sat near the church door to make a fast escape, but they were still converted! Coupled with the preaching was the congregational singing of the unaccompanied metrical psalms in Gaelic. People commented that they had never heard, before or since, singing such as they heard in the revival. The presence of God was often closer then than at any other time. Many were converted during the singing.

1952. A Second Wave of Revival.

Revival in Berneray Island.

On Easter Monday 1952, Campbell was about to preach at The Faith Mission Convention in Bangor, Northern Ireland, when he sensed that God was telling him to go to Berneray, a small island off the south coast of Harris. He did not know anyone on the island, nor had any invitation to go there, but he left immediately, to the consternation of the chairman! When he reached the island he met an elder who told him he was expected. When Campbell asked him how he knew he was coming, he replied that three days before he spent most of the day in prayer, and he was impressed with the fact that God would visit the island with revival and would send Campbell as his instrument of blessing. He was so certain that God would send him in three days' time that he sent notices all around the island announcing that a service would be conducted by the Missioner at 9 p.m. that evening.

The spiritual life of the place was low with a growing disregard for public worship, especially by the youth. The first few church services which were held were ordinary, with no spiritual response, but the elder insisted that God was going to send revival. One night, when the congregation had left the building they were arrested by the power of God and a tremendous sense of the presence of God. The elder called Campbell to the door and said, "Mr. Campbell, see what's happening! He has come! He has come!" About six hundred people were gathered outside, including those who had been in the meeting, whom the Holy Spirit had so convicted as they left the chapel that they could not move any further, and they were groaning under the burden of their sin. Campbell called them all into the chapel and another spiritual Awakening began affecting the whole island.

Campbell, however, encountered some resistance to his ministry when he went to Bernera Island in Lewis. He sent for certain men from Barvas, noted as intercessors, to come and help in prayer. Among these helpers was a teenage boy named Donald Smith, who had been converted under Campbell at Barvas at the beginning of the revival. He was particularly effective in prayer and soul winning, having brought scores to Christ. Even his presence struck deep conviction into the hearts of the unconverted, and he was called "the Evan Roberts of Lewis".

One night, during 1949, Campbell was having difficulty in preaching in a meeting on the Isle of Lewis because of a hard atmosphere He stopped and asked Donald to pray and later described what happened:

> The lad rose to his feet and in his prayer made reference to the fourth chapter of Revelation, which he had been reading that morning. He then prayed, "O God, I seem to be gazing through the open door. I see the Lamb in the midst of the throne, with the keys of death and hell at his girdle. He began to sob, then lifting his eyes toward heaven, cried: O God, there is power there, let it loose". With the force of a hurricane the Spirit of God swept into the building and the floodgates of heaven opened. The church resembled a battlefield. On the one side many were prostrated over the seats, weeping and sighing; on the other side some were affected by throwing their arms in the air in a rigid posture. (The power of) God) had come.[82]

---

[82] Woolsey, Andrew, *Duncan Campbell: a biography: the sound of Battle*, pp. 134, 135

The Spirit of God swept over the village and there was a new sense of the presence of God throughout the island and a new sense of liberty in witness and worship. Wherever people were, at home or even fishing in the bay, they were gripped by a conviction of sin, including atheists, drunkards and indifferent business people. They then felt a compulsion to go to the church as though drawn by a magnet and, though it was midnight, the hills were filled with people streaming to the church from all directions, many from miles away. The Spirit of God seemed to sweep in among the people on the road like a wind, so that they gripped each other in fear. In agony of soul they trembled before God and fell to the ground under conviction.

Wherever Campbell went at this time meetings continued day and night and, one day, he preached eight times, five times in crowded churches, twice to crowds in a field and once by the seashore. As he went from one service to another he would leave behind hundreds crying out for mercy. After he left one church the elders sent to call him to a field where several hundred people were waiting, some prostrate on the ground asking God for mercy. Such prostrations were a feature of the revival and difficult to explain, but Campbell didn't encourage them. He preached to the newly converted that they were to make a full surrender of their lives to God and to receive the fullness of the Spirit. It was because they grasped that truth, he said later, that there was practically no backsliding among the converts. A good number went into Christian service in Scotland or abroad and, three years after the revival began, out of the hundreds converted only four, one man and three women, were known to have gone back on their profession of faith.

1957 A Third Wave of Blessing

Revival on the island of North Uist.

In December 1957, revival came again to the Hebrides. The island of Uist had never known revival before but God graciously worked in the village of Lochmaddy and then the movement spread to a neighbouring parish. People walked miles over roads and fields to the places where services were being held and the meetings were crowded every night with people seeking God. After the revival Duncan Campbell said that in some villages everyone was converted and whole families came to Christ. Public houses were closed and communities were completely revolutionized. It was doubtful if there was a house in the area affected by the revival where there wasn't family worship morning and evening. Perhaps the most significant factor was that, of the hundreds who came to Christ in these three visitations, the Holy Spirit converted 75% of them directly before they came to the meetings.

Duncan Campbell's Later Years.

The presence of God also accompanied Campbell in the following years, as he ministered in various places at home and overseas, before his death on March 28th 1972. Wherever he went people became aware of the glory of the Lord and the nearness of the spiritual realm. From 1958-1966 he became the principal of The Faith Mission Bible College in Edinburgh. Students said that there was something sacred about the way he used God's name. They felt they were on holy ground when he simply said "Jesus", and a heavenly atmosphere filled the place. In March 1960, during a college prayer meeting conducted by Campbell, God's power was so present that many wept. Some were so conscious of God's presence that they believed that if they looked up they would see God! Wave after wave of God's power passed over the meeting and suddenly all in the room heard heavenly music in the skies! In another service, taken by Campbell in Aberdare, South Wales, six young men were so conscious of God's presence that they fell on the floor weeping and began to repent and confess and get right with God and one another.

Duncan Campbell's message to Christians was that, if they wanted revival, they must not soft pedal the Gospel, because people needed a profoundly disturbing message, not one that made them feel all nice inside. He said Christians had been far too afraid of disturbing people, but the Holy Spirit would have nothing to do with those who were afraid of disturbing people. Also, he emphasized that there must be sacrifice and self-renunciation. A favourite theme of his was the account in 1 Kings 18, of the sacrifice on Mount Carmel, where we read that the fire fell when the last piece of the sacrifice was put on the altar. Campbell asked his congregations the challenging question, "Have you put the last piece on the altar, or are you holding things back from God?" There must be, he said, a true longing for God, absolute purity and obedience and absolute confidence in the promises of God. Quoting Hudson Taylor, he would say, "God gives his Spirit not to those who long for him, or those who desire to be filled, but to those who obey". The reality of that truth in Campbell's own life was evident to those who listened to him as his face shone when he spoke of the love of Christ and God's welcome to returning sinners.

Finally, the outstanding features of the revival were summarised by Campbell as follows:

> Three (features) stand out clearly. First an awareness of God.
> To be fully realized this has to be felt. A rector of the Church

of England, referring to his visit to Lewis said, "What I felt, apart from what I saw convinced me at once that this was no ordinary movement". I have known men out on the fields, others at their weaving looms, so overcome by this sense of God that they were found prostrate on the ground... I have no hesitation in saying that this awareness of God is the crying need of the church today. The second main feature has been deep conviction of sin, at times leading almost to despair. I have known occasions when it was necessary to stop preaching because of the distress manifested by the anxious. Thirdly, physical manifestations and prostrations have been a further feature. I find it somewhat difficult to explain this aspect, indeed I cannot; but this I will say, that the person who would associate this with satanic influence is coming perilously near committing the unpardonable sin. Lady Huntingdon on one occasion wrote to George Whitefield respecting cases of crying out and falling down in meetings. She said, "You are making a great mistake. Don't be wiser than God. Let them cry out; it will do a great deal more good than your preaching".[83]

Campbell concluded that he regretted that from the beginning there were those who opposed the revival and quoted someone who had been mightily used of God in the revival, but who had been bitterly opposed by leaders in the church, and this man said, "I verily believe revival would have come to...if prayerful sympathy, instead if carnal criticism, had been shown". That criticism Campbell said was based on hearsay, and if only those who opposed the revival had gone to see and hear for themselves, how different the story of it would have been.

---

[83] Campbell, Duncan, "The Lewis Awakening" 1949-1953 in Peckham, Colin, *The Heritage of Revival*, pp. 178, 179

SECTION FOUR

REVIVAL AND REVIVALISM IN THE NINETEENTH AND TWENTIETH CENTURY

HUGH BOURNE, 1772-1852.
JOHN PETTY, *d.* 1868.
PETER PHILLIPS.

JOHN FLESHER, *d.* 1874.
HUGH GILMORE.
DR. ANTLIFF, *d.* 1884.

WM. CLOWES, 1780-1851.
C. C. McKECHNIE, *d.* 1896.
LORENZO DOW.

CHAPTER TEN
EARLY PRIMITIVE METHODIST CAMP MEETINGS AND LATER REVIVALISM

The American Precedents to the English Revivalist Camp Meetings.

As revivals in the past two hundred and fifty years have almost invariably begun in America and then moved to Britain, so has the practice of "revivalism", a word not used in Britain until the early 1820s. Also, in the late eighteenth and early nineteenth centuries, the term "revival" came to mean something very different in America from what it had meant previously. Rather than an occasional and unpredictable supernatural event, the term was used to describe organized religious meetings. This change came about during the Second Great Awakening in America. The First Great Awakening was localized and comparatively short in duration, consisting of a revival in Northampton, under the preaching of the Rev. Jonathan Edwards in the winter of 1734-1735. Then, a further Awakening in Boston and Northampton began in 1740, largely through the ministry of George Whitefield. This continued for about four years, not only in New England but also in New York, New Jersey and Pennsylvania, as well as in Maryland and Virginia. The Second Great Awakening, however, was not only more extensive but also lasted much longer. There is no general agreement as to how long it lasted but there were spiritual Awakenings from about 1798 and, in 1832, W.B. Sprague, in his major work *Lectures on Revivals*, described the revival as still continuing.

Generally, the religious situation in the 1790s in America was discouraging. Bishop Madison of Virginia expressed the view that the Church was too far-gone to be revived, while the Bishop Provost of New York felt the situation was hopeless and simply gave up any further effort to improve it. At that time the colleges were hotbeds of infidelity and immorality but, imperceptibly at first, a handful of students here and there began tentatively to pray together. By the turn of the century a spiritual Awakening was sweeping through the colleges and, in 1802, one third of the students of Yale made a public profession of conversion. This movement was then continued in the following years. Out of the college spiritual awakenings grew the whole modern American missionary movement, a generation of evangelical ministers was produced and the spread of infidelity was halted. Also, numerous theological seminaries, religious societies and philanthropic organizations were begun.

In none of these college spiritual Awakenings was any extravagance reported, but a different response occurred in frontier settlements such as in Logan County, Kentucky, under the Rev. James McCready. The area was notorious for escaped murderers, counterfeiters, highwaymen and horse thieves who settled there, and was known as "Rogues Harbour". McCready's ministry was so powerful that it attracted greater crowds than any church building could contain, so meetings were held in the open air and, as there were few houses there, multitudes camped for days to listen to the preaching. This movement then spread to nearby counties and, at Cane Ridge, in Bourbon

County, crowds estimated at between ten and twenty-five thousand attended the preaching of dozens of ministers, who ministered at the same time to different sections of the crowd. The meetings went on for several days and, it was said, about a thousand people were converted. This was the beginning of the Camp Meeting movement. It grew and, by 1811, the number of such meetings had increased to four hundred. The term "Camp Meeting" first appears in the journals of Francis Asbury, the first Methodist bishop in America. He said:

> We must attend to camp meetings, they make our harvest time…I hear and see the great affects produced by them. [84]

The preaching in the Camp Meetings was adapted to frontier conditions. It was simple and emotional and was intended to achieve sudden conversions. Sometimes, thirty to forty thousand people gathered, mostly illiterate pioneer settlers and extraordinary emotional excesses were witnessed. Meetings were characterized by a solemn chanting of hymns, and then a fiery exhortation and earnest prayers, followed by fainting, convulsions and prostrations, sobbing and shrieks and shouts from individuals under an intense agitation of mind. Scores were suddenly seized with spasms and unexpectedly fell to the ground. It all caused a terrific general interest and worked up people's feelings to a high pitch of excitement, but it also caused inevitable criticism. Untold good was done nevertheless. A godly awe pervaded the country, a thorough reform of behaviour took place and many thousands were added to the churches. Camp Meetings then became a feature of American life and denominations used the great summer gatherings as evangelistic and devotional rallies. Significantly, as people

---

[84] Murray, Iain, H., *Revival and Revivalism The Making and Marring of American Evangelicalism* 1750-1858, p. 183

became more literate the excesses declined and, later, similar meetings were called, "old-time religion".

British Revivalism.

Revivalism was also present in British Wesleyanism in the 1790s and probably began in November 1792, in Dewsbury, West Riding. William Bramwell was used to awaken the Methodist society there and to overcome indifference and disunity in it, and brought in a handloom weaver named Cutler to work in the circuit. The revivalism soon spread through the West, East and North Ridings and was said that by 1794 it had reached almost every Wesleyan society. It also flourished in Cornwall. By the turn of the century, Wesleyan leaders were concerned about the indiscipline in revivalism and, although it appeared in Wesleyan circuits throughout the next two decades, in the main the fervour was confined to the Bible Christians, the Primitive Methodists and other breakaway groups. As an example of the new revivalism one minister was holding a love feast[85] when he was approached by a local preacher who thought the meeting was very dull. He asked the minister permission to "set the chapel on fire". He then set about doing that by working the people up and soon they became highly excited, some praying for pardon and others for holiness

Lorenzo Dow, 1777-1834

News of the American Camp Meetings soon came to the attention of British Methodists, particularly through three visits to Britain, at the end of the eighteenth century and in the early nineteenth century, of an eccentric American

---

[85] A simple meal at which hymns are sung, the Scriptures read and testimonies and stories of faith are shared

THE CAMP-MEETING.

LORENZO DOW, the eccentric evangelist.   PEGGY DOW, his wife.

AN OLD-TIME ITINERANT.
(From old engravings.)

Methodist preacher, Lorenzo Dow. His most significant visit was in December 1805, when he came under the aegis of the Methodist New Connexion and stayed for three years. His style was completely different from anything conservative church-goers had ever seen before and his eloquence and unusual mannerisms; shouting, screaming, story-telling and humour drew immense crowds. Though he began his ministry as a probationer lay-preacher in Methodist churches, because of his peculiar style of preaching the American Methodist Conference refused to authorize him, and the English Wesleyan Methodist leaders also disowned him and threatened to have him arrested, but when churches were closed to him he preached anywhere he could: in halls, barns and fields.

He remained in Britain until April 1807, preaching and circulating tracts describing the American Camp Meeting system and held his farewell services at Congleton, where the future British revivalists, Hugh Bourne and William Clowes heard him. He also brought a revivalist hymnbook from America, editions of which were published in England from 1806 and adapted later by Bourne. Dow was anxious to see similar meetings established in Britain that had taken place in America, because he believed the new outburst of religious life, begun in the American Camp Meetings, would sweep through the whole Protestant world.

Dow offered a particular revivalist style, which appealed to people who were tired of the formal Anglicanism of that time. Accordingly, the English Camp Meetings, which began in 1807, reflected the desire of many of the poorer people to set up a religious society of their own, more suited to their own social class and culture. Dow's criticisms of the Wesleyan ministry also appealed to the democratic would-be revivalists, who resented the formalities imposed after Wesley's death in 1791, and which led to the formation of the Methodist

New Connexion in 1797. In spite of being rejected by the official Methodist bodies, Dow was perhaps the most popular preacher of his time, and a pivotal figure in the British Camp Meetings movement, as well contributing to the Second Great Awakening. He was also a popular writer, and it was said that his autobiography at one time sold more copies than any other book in America apart from the Bible.

The Social Conditions in England at the time of the introduction of Camp Meetings.

In the second decade of the nineteenth century, when the number of Camp Meetings was increasing, the poor were suffering great hardships. There was heavy taxation as a result of the Napoleonic War and there were many disabled soldiers and discharged veterans who were unable to get work, as well as widows and orphans who were left unsupported. In addition, there was a succession of bad harvests and the price of bread soared, causing widespread starvation. The misery these conditions created led to discontent and violence. New machinery in the manufacturing districts of the Midlands was reducing the need for labour and was, therefore, seen as the enemy of the working class. Luddites and Levellers went around destroying machinery and committing arson and other acts of sabotage. The government reacted mercilessly and promptly hanged anyone found to be connected with these crimes.

It was at this critical time for law and order that the "Ranter" preachers of the Camp Meetings proved more effective than the government measures in restraining the violence of the Levellers. The effects of the eighteenth century revival had largely passed away and England was in need of a new spiritual Awakening. The churches were concerned with missionary work overseas but, generally, had neglected evangelizing and thereby improving the morality of the masses at home. Kendall, the historian of the Primitive Methodist churches, records an incident in 1817 of how the preaching of one of the Ranter preachers averted a local tragedy.

> In Countesthorpe, a village eight miles south-east of Leicester, where workingmen had joined the Levellers, arms were stored and nightly drillings went on. Work was neglected until many stood on the verge of starvation. In anticipation of a popular uprising, timed to take place on June 9th 1817, which was to usher in the era of lawlessness, a man took his revenge on one who had wronged him by maiming his sheep. While the sheep maimer was awaiting the sentence of death, his brother resolved to waylay the principal witness against the condemned man. But before he could effect his purpose a "Ranter" preacher entered the village and began to preach the Gospel there. The would-be assassin, along with a number of his fellow Levellers was seized with conviction and converted. In the absence of the preacher he convened a meeting for prayer but there was no one present who could lead the devotions. So he took a family prayer book and undertook the duty of a prayer leader and the singing and praying went on by turns. For many years that man maintained a consistent Christian life and the barn which had been an armoury for the Levellers was turned into the village preaching room.[86]

---

[86]   Kendall, H.B., *History of the Primitive Methodist Church*, pp. 8, 9

Hugh Bourne (1772-1852), Leader of the "Camp Meeting Methodists".

Bourne grew up in Bucknall, a few miles north of Stoke-on-Trent, and later moved to the village of Bemersley, where he trained to be a wheelwright. He was converted in 1799 and then joined the local Methodist society in Burslem and, after a time of Bible study, he became a Methodist lay-preacher while continuing his work as a wheelwright. In 1800 he moved a short distance to the mining village of Harriseahead. The inhabitants were mostly colliers and irreligious and Bourne was appalled at the moral state of the place which was noted for its profanity and ungodliness. In those days it was dangerous for a stranger to pass through such a village, as he was likely to be stoned or have the dogs set on him! The annual Wakes and "Feasts" were also times of excess and violence, when many were injured. In 1801, soon after his conversion, Bourne led two local colliers to Christ and a revival took place through the personal witness of the three men and cottage prayer meetings, and a great reformation took place in the neighbourhood. The Wesleyan authorities, however, disliked the movement as it was without the direction and oversight of the officers of the circuit. This attitude, in turn, led to a series of reactions against a growing Wesleyan formalism and ecclesiastical rigidity. Bourne then formed a society in the village which, from 1802, was only slightly attached to official Methodism and was marked by personal witness and "noisy" cottage prayer meetings rather than formal pulpit preaching. Critics, used to traditional services, complained that in these meetings the people repeatedly invoked the name of Jesus and indulged in rapturous exclamations with such a clamour as if they would open heaven by their prayers. They were also accused of being far from the spirit of humility, sober-mindedness and

213

the humble adoration that befits sinful men in prayers to the throne of Grace!

Bourne also introduced a class meeting and helped to finance and build a chapel. He taught a school in the chapel on weekdays and Sundays, and also learned to pray and speak in public. He was then stirred by the accounts of the Second Great Awakening in America, which appeared in the Wesleyan Methodist Magazine, from 1802 to 1806. As indicated, there had been revivalist activity in England before Dow's arrival. Apart from William Bramwell's revivalist preaching as early as 1792 there were revivalists in Macclesfield in 1802-3 and another group in Manchester in 1806. The Methodist leader, Jabez Bunting, who believed that revivalism if not checked would gradually ruin genuine Methodism, took steps to stop it. Of particular interest to Bourne and his little devout group, however, were Dow's experiences and descriptions of the early Camp Meetings and the fact that they went on for several days. Bourne also bought Dow's tracts on the Camp Meetings and began to consider how to introduce such meetings in North Staffordshire. He had already considered having an open air meeting on Mow Cop, a nearby high ridge of land which divides Staffordshire from Cheshire, and was convinced from what he had heard from Dow that Camp Meetings were the best way forward to evangelize the unconverted.

The Early Camp Meetings at Mow Cop and the surrounding district.

The first took place on May 31st 1807, and Bourne took the leading part in preparing for it. Spectators and participants arrived from Congleton, Knutsford, Warrington, Burslem, Tunstall and elsewhere. A flag was erected to mark the site and volunteers exhorted, led hymns, prayed, preached and testified

Mow Cop, where the famous camp-meeting was held.
Extract from Bourne's Journal.
Early Class-tickets of the Primitive Methodist Connexion.

© *A New History of Methodism as above.*

as they saw fit. Bourne estimated two to four thousand people were present, attracted partly by the interest and curiosity created by Dow on a recent tour in Lancashire and Cheshire. Many were reported to have been converted. William Clowes described the event in his Journal.

> The first day's praying on Mow-hill presented at this period a most magnificent and sublime spectacle. Four preachers were simultaneously crying to sinners to flee from the wrath to come; thousands were listening... many in deep distress and others pleading with Heaven on their behalf. Some were praising God aloud... whilst others were rejoicing... that their sins, which were many, had been all forgiven. The Camp Meeting continued full of glory and converting power. About four o' clock in the afternoon the number of people was prodigiously large but, after this time many began to retire homewards, yet the power of the Highest continued with undiminished force and effect until the very last. Towards the conclusion, the services were principally carried on by praying companies and, at the close, which took place about half past eight o'clock, several souls (including children) were set at liberty...Much of the good remains. [87]

Clowes went on to say that at the end of the day he was exhausted as he had laboured from first thing in the morning until eight in the evening with hardly a break, but that the glory that had filled his soul far exceeded his ability to explain. He said that much good that was done in that great meeting still remained but that the full account of it only eternity would reveal and that myriads would everlastingly praise God for that day's praying on Mow-hill

---

[87] Kendall, H.B., *History of the Primitive Methodist Church*, pp. 15, 16

Bourne also immediately printed a tract recounting the day's events and advertising two future Camp Meetings. After this was circulated, the Wesleyan ministers in the Burslem and Macclesfield circuits, reacted against Dow and revivalism, and were also concerned about the possibility of another split in Methodism. They distributed handbills denouncing the meetings and kept many of their members away from them. At this time Napoleon was at the height of his power, and the Government suspected large popular meetings. In spite of Bourne being non-political, his opponents stated that he was "disaffected towards his majesty's government" and that these meetings were got up for political purposes. In 1807, the Conventicle Act and the Five Mile Act had not been repealed and, under the former, an unlicensed preacher could be fined twenty pounds and his hearers five shillings each. Bourne, therefore, obtained a licence to preach and also erected a wooden "Tabernacle" and three tents on Mow Cop, so that the site could be registered as a Protestant place of worship.

The second Camp Meeting on Mow Cop, on July 19th 1807, attracted people from up to forty miles away and sixty people were registered as being converted. From this time, these meetings were also organized to end what was seen to be the wickedness of the Wakes at that time and the unrestrained violence of the traditional football matches between adjacent villages, when the villages were the respective goals and all the villagers the teams. The meetings also provided a focus for revivalist activities, and attracted support from groups of people associated with the revivalist sects outside mainstream Methodism. On the other hand, many converts, made at the Camp Meetings joined Wesleyan Methodism.

The third Camp Meeting was at Norton-in-the-Moors, on Sunday, August 23rd 1807, and continued until the following Tuesday. The first two meetings had been held in the name of Methodism but, to the Methodist leaders, they were examples of the spread of "revivalism". This took various forms in different places and was known by different names such as, "Tent Methodists" in Bristol, "Band Room Methodists" in Manchester and "Independent Methodists" in Warrington. Many sympathized with this more fervent type of Methodism, which sought to revive the spirit and methods of early Methodism and to do more than was being done to reach the un-evangelized masses. The significance of the third Camp Meeting was that it was held after the Methodist Conference in Liverpool had voted, in July 1807, against these meetings, although the decision to hold the Camp Meeting was taken beforehand. The Conference was suspicious of those enthusiastic for Camp Meetings, however, and feared they would give the government an excuse for invoking the old Conventicle Act against them. Conference disowned them, therefore, and those who persisted in supporting the Camp Meetings were expelled from the denomination. It was also decided that no stranger from America or elsewhere was to be allowed to preach in any of their chapels unless he was fully accredited. The Conference decision stated:

> It is our judgement that, even supposing such meetings to be allowable in America, they are highly improper in England, and likely to be productive of considerable mischief; and we disclaim all connexion with them.[88]

Bourne was then deserted by several who were going to help him in ministry but who now stood aloof, intimidated by the Wesleyan Methodist authorities. A Dr. Paul Johnson from Ireland arrived, however, and he saved the day by preaching

---

[88] Kendall, H.B., *The Origin and History of the Primitive Methodist Church*, Vol.1, p. 77

"with power" from morning until night. The success of this third meeting ensured that Camp Meetings would continue for years to come. Bourne held one on the Wrekin in Shropshire, in May 1808, at the time the local inhabitants caroused at a major pagan festival, intending the practice to be replaced by a Christian celebration. After three further meetings, on June 27th 1808, Bourne was expelled from the Wesleyan Methodist Church under the terms of the 1807 Conference, "because he had a tendency to set up other than ordinary worship", that is, unauthorized Camp Meetings. Bourne didn't complain and, for two years, he and his helpers still regarded themselves as Wesleyan Methodists and he urged his converts to join the Methodists. Matters came to a head, however, when the circuit authorities refused to take over a society raised by Bourne at Stanley, unless it promised to have nothing to do with Camp Meeting Methodists. Bourne's group felt not only that they had to get men converted but also to provide pastoral care for them so, about May 1810, the unattached Camp Methodists became a small but distinct fellowship, with Bourne as its leader.

Although Bourne adopted the so-called Camp Meeting system as an open air meeting method, there were no "camps", as usually understood, for few could have been free for several days to attend one. These English meetings were usually only on Sundays, lasting from dawn to dusk and often rounded off with a love feast in a convenient chapel. This was a Christian fellowship meal recalling the meals Jesus shared with his disciples, when small pieces of bread were taken around, with water. In these "camps" there were a number of preaching stands, usually wagons, which provided pulpits for a variety of speakers, as Bourne didn't believe in depending on the personality of a single speaker and they also gave a greater opportunity for people to hear the gospel more clearly. After the speakers teams of men held prayer meetings for the next hour, concentrating on those affected by the preaching. Sometimes, instead of preaching, there were "reading services", when the speaker read a religious biography with an obituary, containing a triumphant deathbed account. There was also singing, interspersed with the prayers and readings. The meetings reached a crisis between 1816 and 1819, however, and Bourne states that they degenerated to a monotonous programme of tedious sermons, many more than an hour long. The praying services had been dropped, so the Camp Meetings became nothing more than one sermon after another.

William Clowes, 1780-1851.

Clowes, a potter, related to the Wedgwood family, was born in Burslem and, after living for pleasure, was converted in a revivalist meeting in Tunstall on January 20th 1805. He then became active in tract distribution, and a class leader, exhorter and "flaming evangelist" on the circuit plan of the Wesleyan Methodists. He was, however, expelled in September 1810 for his participation in Camp Meetings. He recorded in his journals:

> In the June quarter of 1810, my name was omitted from the preacher's plan...At the September visitation, my quarterly ticket as a member of the society was withheld...Mr. A., the travelling preacher calling over the class names passed by my name as the class leader and, in speaking to the people, he rebuked them for their liveliness in their way of worshipping and praising God and remarked he supposed they acted as they had been taught (by me). I was then told my name was left off their plan because I attended Camp Meetings contrary to Methodist discipline, and that I could not be a preacher or leader among them unless I promised not

to attend such meetings any more. I told the members of the meeting that I would attend all the means of grace and ordinances of the church, but to promise not to attend any more Camp Meetings, that I could not conscientiously do. God had greatly blessed me in these meetings, which were calculated for great usefulness, and my motive for assisting in them was simply to glorify God and to bring sinners to the knowledge of the truth as it is in Jesus. I was then told that I was no longer with them; that the matter was closed. I therefore immediately delivered up my class papers to the meeting and became unchurched.[89]

He and Bourne and their followers then met in the home of an elderly Methodist named Joseph Smith in Tunstall and, on May 30th 1811, they formed an organization with two hundred members and opened a chapel on July 13th that year. Almost three years later, Bourne reluctantly agreed to be General Superintendent. The founders shared a revivalist evangelical fervour and unconventional spirituality and, accordingly, broke from the restraints imposed on them by official Wesleyan Methodist policy, forming a Connexion, which gave scope for lay participation in church government. This was not a split in the sense that the Methodist New Connexion had been in 1797, rather it was a new revivalist movement, which had had only loose links with the Methodist parent body. The name "Primitive Methodist Church", which was adopted in February 1812, was taken from one of the last addresses of Wesley, in which he said, "I still remain a Primitive Methodist". By that time they had two dozen preachers and three dozen preaching places. Later, as a working-class Church, it spread and flourished in working class areas throughout England and Wales through revivalist Camp Meetings, in which female itinerants and local

---

[89]   Clowes, William, *Journals*, pp. 83-85

preachers played an important part. Within fifty years they had one hundred and fifty thousand members and as many Sunday school children, half the totals of the Methodist body that expelled them. The characteristics of Bourne's group and the Clowesites were fervent prayer meetings under a shared leadership, open air preaching and large-scale participation in worship, as well as personal evangelism and these features were continued in the new Primitive Methodist Connexion. There is little doubt that genuine revivals occurred in these Primitive Methodist circles but revivalist excesses often marred them.

The Primitive Methodist local preachers were mostly humble day-labourers who, in the early years, were abominably treated everywhere and persecuted in every way, as Wesley and his lay preachers had been. One cannot help but be impressed by these earnest men who endangered their lives, day after day, by faithfully and fearlessly preaching the Gospel. They were cursed and pelted with stones, rotten eggs and all kinds of filth and, sometimes, were so badly beaten that they nearly died. At a Camp Meeting at Witney, forty horns were blown at once to drown the preachers' words. Elsewhere, bells were rung and dogfights were started and bulls set on the congregation. Clergy and landlords worked together against these local preachers and some received notice to quit their smallholdings, and those who opened their homes for preaching or hospitality for the preachers were evicted. Sometimes the local clergyman would go around his parish and order his parishioners to stay indoors and shut their doors and windows, so that they would not hear the message of the revivalists. Numerous local preachers were imprisoned with hard labour for open-air preaching, including the potter Wedgewood, but when they were released, they cheerfully made their way to the place where they were arrested and began another service! Their travelling from place to place was almost entirely on foot. When John Petty, the movement's historian, was told to work for the Connexion in Haverfordwest, he walked there all the way from Tunstall, preaching here and there as he went. It is estimated that, in twenty-one years, he travelled nearly forty thousand miles and preached over six thousand sermons. William Clowes also walked up to thirty-five miles in a day, preaching five times either without food or with simply bread and water.

In 1818-1819 Lorenzo Dow returned to Britain for his third and final visit, and he contacted the Primitive Methodists and visited thirty to forty of their chapels. He held an open-air meeting in Bingham, Nottinghamshire and, after his address, he invited the people to draw back and form a circle and then invited the penitents to come forward and receive the blessing of pardon. Soon the whole space was filled and not less than two hundred were on their knees seeking forgiveness. He then began to pray and his voice was lost amidst the groans and cries for mercy. In less than half an hour about a hundred were, as he said, "brought to liberty". Such Camp Meetings at this time were described, as consisting of praying, singing and exhortation. The praying was sometimes conducted by individuals who took the lead alternately and, at other times, all the more active members were engaged together, working upon each other's enthusiasm and presenting to astonished passers-by, a cacophony of cries, groans and shrieks. The meetings had a tendency to be confused rather than ordered. Some of their preachers, even women, openly spoke of their former sins, and the people were wound up to such a frenzy that their gestures and actions were said to be more like the orgies of the heathen than to the dignified behaviour of devout Christian worshippers. Also, the principal speakers would work themselves up to a state of the utmost frenzy. At the close of the evening, a number of enthusiasts would begin to loudly harangue at the same time, resulting in confusion defying description.

A similar situation took place in the 1830s in a revivalist mission in a crowded chapel in Sheffield, when scores professed to be converted each night. One preacher shouted with all his might and another also sang and ranted at the top of his voice. They jumped over forms, climbed over pews to kneel down and pray with those they believed to be penitents, shouting threats of eternal wrath and damnation at those they thought were not convicted. Scores of people joined together to excite the people to the highest pitch. It was said that the screams, shouts, moaning or groaning, jarring songs, disorders and indecencies were horrible. Numbers were praying and shouting at the top of their voices, "Glory, glory, He is coming, He is here, I feel it, He is saving, Glory Glory, He has pardoned my sins, I am saved" The preachers then would shout out, "Another soul saved, let us praise God". This went on for several hours until the leaders were completely exhausted and they had lost their voices and then the meeting was dismissed. The meetings went on for several weeks and hundreds were said to have been saved but, of these, some were said to have been saved several times over and many fell away.

By 1830, the Primitive Methodist Camp Meetings were strictly organized, however, and their Conference that year stipulated that preaching services were to last no more than forty-five minutes and prayer services thirty minutes. There were to be two speakers in a preaching service, who were each to speak for twenty minutes only, unless sinners were actually falling down under their preaching. All repetition, cant, and "chaffy" or "trashy" expressions such as, "my time's short" or, "doing justice to my subject", were to be avoided! The conductor (chairman) was to press the point of an umbrella or something else against the speaker's foot five minutes before his time had expired! The speaker was then to urge the need of a present faith and salvation, leaving the strongest possible impression on the people and, if a second signal had to be given, he was to stop immediately. The following year, the time limit after a warning to stop was one minute, with a fine of one shilling for exceeding it!

It is understandable that many ministers and churches reacted as they did to such extreme forms of revivalism, especially as they produced schism, rather than unity and prejudiced many against a spontaneous revival of the Holy Spirit. In some cases, however, it seems that denominational leaders, overreacted. It is sad that Wesleyan Methodism, should show a similar objection and spirit to unofficial preaching within their circuits, however successful, that Anglican leaders had shown to the unauthorized preaching of the early Methodists. H.B. Workman, in his book, *Methodism,* stated that:

> If Methodist officials had been wise, they might perhaps have controlled these extremists by giving them fair latitude as mission bands auxiliary to the regular societies, or as irregular cavalry in the host of the Lord. As it was, they acted towards them with the lack of wisdom with which the Anglican bishops had acted towards their fathers. Wesleyan Methodism, in fact, at this time was setting its house in order; it was cautiously constituting its organization and complete independence. The thing dreaded was irregularity. [90]

Even the Primitive Methodists, who had earlier been most involved in revivalism, later repudiated any unauthorized form of it. In June 1862, their Conference passed a resolution urging all its pastors, "to avoid the employing of revivalists so-

---

[90]   Workman, H.B. *Methodism*, pp. 95

called". Their policy was to use only accredited denominational pastors and evangelists in revival! The next month, the Wesleyan Methodist Conference followed suit and directed its superintendents not to sanction the use of their chapels for continuous services by outsiders. Revival campaigns were to be held only by their ministers, who were subject to regular discipline, so as to, "prevent irregularities which tend to impair the true and lasting prosperity of the church".

Yours as ever
D L Moody

The life of D L Moody", Morgan & Scott, n. d. c.1900.

CHAPTER ELEVEN
THE "REVIVAL" CAMPAIGNS OF FINNEY AND MOODY IN BRITAIN

The nineteenth century was characterized by an unparalleled degree of evangelistic activity. Never before or since have so many itinerant evangelists been involved in such an on-going crusade to win the masses for Christ, in cities and towns and villages throughout the United Kingdom. This extraordinary effort took place mainly in the second half of the century, largely as a result of the spiritual impetus of the 1859 revival and of the widespread premillennial view of the imminent return of Christ and the urgency to fulfil the Great Commission (Matthew 28:19, 20). Many of these evangelists were household names and were greatly used by God in evangelizing people of their own social class. Men such as Henry Grattan Guinness, Brownlow North and Reginald Radcliffe were particularly effective among the middle and upper classes, while men like Richard Weaver, Duncan Matheson and Henry Moorhouse especially appealed to the working classes. Of all the many itinerant evangelists of that time, however, the two which had the most impact were Charles Finney and D.L. Moody.

Finney's Early Life.

Finney, called "The Father of Modern Revivalism", was born on August 29th 1792, the youngest of nine children, and spent his earliest years on his father's farm in Warren, Connecticut. When he was two years old the family moved to the little town of Adams on the shores of Lake Ontario. He didn't have a religious upbringing and knew nothing of the Gospel until he was twenty years old. Neither his parents nor many of his neighbours were religious and, although the community had a school, which Finney attended, he had little access to religious books and he seldom heard a sermon. Also, the few sermons he heard were from local uneducated preachers, whose mistakes and absurd comments caused their hearers considerable amusement rather than conviction. Finney began work as a teacher and then, when he was twenty-six, he joined a law firm in Adams and qualified as a lawyer. Also, although he had no religious convictions, he attended the local Presbyterian Church, where he apparently led the choir. The church members were concerned about his spiritual state and asked if he wanted them to pray for him and he told them he didn't! Having a logical mind he had been analysing their prayers and couldn't see that they were being answered. He told them:

> No, I suppose I need to be prayed for, for I am conscious that I am a sinner; but I do not see that it will do any good for you to pray for me, for you have been praying for a revival of religion ever since I have been in Adams, and yet you do not have it. You have been praying for the Holy Spirit to descend upon yourselves, and yet are still complaining of your leanness…You have prayed enough since I have attended these meetings to have prayed the devil out of

Adam, if there is any virtue in your prayers. But here you are praying on, and complaining still.[91]

Finney's Conversion and the Baptism of the Holy Spirit.

That autumn, in 1821, however, aged twenty-nine, he came under a great conviction of sin and was powerfully converted on the 10th of October while praying alone in the woods outside the town. He had begun to read the Bible, being interested as a lawyer in the Mosaic legal code and became convinced of its authority and the truth of the Bible. In his office that evening he had a vision of Jesus and was powerfully baptized with the Holy Spirit. He said he had not expected it and had no thought that there was such a thing for him and it was at a time entirely unexpected by him. The next day he again had an experience of the filling of the Spirit, and he witnessed to many friends and neighbours and said that he could not remember one of them who were not afterwards converted. He said:

> I received a mighty baptism of the Holy Spirit without any memory of ever hearing the thing mentioned by any person in the world. The Holy Spirit descended upon me in a manner that seemed to go through me, body and soul. I could feel the impression, like a wave of electricity, going through and through me. Indeed, it seemed to come in waves of liquid love, for I could not express it in any other way. It seemed like the very breath of God. I can remember distinctly that it seemed to fan me, like immense wings. No words can express the wonderful love that was spread abroad in my heart. I wept aloud with joy and love...These waves came over me, and over me, and over me, one after the

---

[91] Finney, The Memoirs of Charles Finney, p.23

other, until I remember crying out, 'I shall die if these waves continue to pass over me'. I said, 'Lord, I cannot bear any more', yet I had no fear of death.[92]

He was then so full of the love of God and the desire to witness to everyone in his village and in the surrounding countryside that, for more than a week, he didn't feel inclined to eat or sleep. He said he was then endued with such power from on high that every day a few words dropped here and there to individuals were the means of their immediate conversion and that his words seemed to fasten like barbed arrows in the souls of men, cutting like a sword and breaking hearts like a hammer. Revival then broke out in his village and almost everyone he spoke to was converted. Like all those used by God he spent hours in prayer, whether alone or with others, often having a great burden for some individual until he had the assurance that person would be saved. However, he said that sometimes, if he lost the spirit of grace and supplication, he found himself empty of spiritual power and he would be unable to preach effectively or win souls by personal conversation. He would then set a day apart for private fasting and prayer, afraid that the power of the Holy Spirit had departed from him but, after humbling himself and crying to God for help, the power of the Spirit would return with all its freshness.

It soon became clear to him that God was calling him to devote himself to preaching the Gospel and he began his public ministry in neglected backwoods, going from place to place as he was led by the Holy Spirit. He said he was unwilling to do anything else. He no longer had any desire to practice law and it had no attraction for him at all, nor did he have any disposition to make money or to desire any worldly pleasure or amusements. His whole mind was taken up with Jesus and his

---

[92] Duewel, Wesley, L., *Ablaze for God*, p. 302

salvation and nothing could compare with holding forth Christ to a dying world. He also helped the Rev. George Gale, the Presbyterian minister, in the work of his church in Adams, and he was accepted as a candidate for the Presbyterian ministry and ordained in 1824. Speaking of the effect of his preaching at this time, Finney said that the Spirit came upon him with such power that it was like a cannon being fired at the people. It seems people came under great conviction and were converted wherever he preached, but he also encountered opposition from unconverted people and from Christians, including older Calvinistic ministers of the Presbyterian Church. They disliked his methods, especially as once he was licensed and ordained as a Presbyterian minister, he took every opportunity to oppose the traditional, Calvinistic beliefs of Presbyterianism. Finney, however, charged those who were critical of his methods as being enemies of revival.

In October 1824 he conducted a series of meetings at Evans Mills in Oneida County, New York State, which went on until the spring of 1825. For several weeks he preached without results and he then told his audience that he wouldn't preach to them again unless someone received Christ as Saviour. Still no one responded so Finney told his audience, "You have rejected Christ and the Gospel. You may remember as long as you live that you have publicly committed yourselves against the Saviour". He assumed they had decided not to accept Christ and didn't ask them to change their decision. However, during the night scores under conviction tried to contact him but at first he couldn't be found. Such a concern then arose among the people that almost every one of them was converted, including atheists.

This was the beginning of his wider public ministry and, from this time, an unusual power attended it. In October 1825 he again met Gale, who had moved to Western in Oneida

County. He urged Finney to stay with him and to take part in what became known as the "Western revivals". Gale later wrote of the majority of those converted under Finney's ministry at that time:

> They were not women and children but strong men, educated men...Lawyers and judges, men all professions and conditions of life...The great secret of his success was that he was a powerful reasoner. Though he was a bold and fearless preacher of the Gospel he was a man of much prayer and singleness of purpose. It was to win souls to Christ that he laboured. His own reputation or interest came in for no share of his aims, any further than the cause of Christ was to be effected. Like Barnabas he was full of the Holy Spirit, as well as a good man, and much people were added to the Lord. [93]

In the summer of 1826 Finney had a further experience of the power and presence of God. He was invited to preach at Auburn, New York, but some of the professors in the Seminary there were opposed to his preaching, because he had not been theologically trained. However, God gave him a vision, showing him that though he would face opposition there it would not prevail against him. In the vision Christ drew so near to him that, as he prayed, his whole body trembled from head to foot. He said that instead of feeling like fleeing, he seemed to be drawn nearer and nearer to God, nearer to a Presence that filled him with such unutterable awe and wonder.

One of his early missions was held in the town of Antwerp which, unknown to Finney, was nicknamed "Sodom", because the place was so wicked and that there was there a godly man of prayer who was derisively called "Lot". Finney happened to

---

[93] Murray, Iain, H., *Pentecost Today*, p. 36

preach on Genesis 19:14, "Up, get you out of this city, for the Lord will destroy the city". The congregation thought Finney had deliberately chosen that text and was being facetiously offensive but, as Finney began to apply the message their anger and resentment turned to conviction and there were many conversions.

In 1829 Finney preached for some months in Philadelphia among lumbermen who brought logs down the Delaware River to sell. Many were converted and went back up river with a concern for other lumbermen and began praying for them. There were many instances of two or three lumbermen living alone in little shanties, who didn't attend any of Finney's meetings and who were ignorant of spiritual things, who were suddenly convicted and who then asked the converted lumbermen what they should do. It was said that five thousand of them were converted in this way.

Finney always placed great emphasis on the need of ministers to experience the Baptism of the Holy Spirit if they were to be effective. He said:

> I would repeat with great emphasis, that the difference in the efficiency of ministers does not consist so much in difference of intellectual attainments as in the measure of the Holy Spirit they enjoy…Until he knows what it is to "be filled with the Spirit", to be endued with power from on high, he is by no means qualified to be a leader in the Church of God. A thousand times as much stress ought to be laid upon this part of a thorough preparation for the ministry than has been.[94]

In 1830-31 Finney conducted a campaign in Rochester and it was said that one tenth of the city's ten thousand population

---

[94] Duewel, Wesley, L., *Ablaze for God*, p. 273

was converted, including a large number of the leading men of the city. The whole character of the city was changed and twelve hundred people became members of the churches there. A spiritual Awakening then swept throughout the country and, in 1831, an estimated one hundred thousand people joined the churches. Finney became a national figure and was invited to conduct campaigns in all the larger cities of the United States. Twice he preached extensively in Britain, from 1849-1851 and then from 1858-1859.

In 1834 he left the Presbyterian Church, having moved in his theology away from Calvinism and become a Congregationalist. Also, the church in New York, of which he was pastor at that time, adopted Congregational views. The next year he became the Professor of Theology at the newly formed Liberal Arts College at Oberlin, Ohio and, for a while, he combined this post with his pastorate but, from 1838, his time was divided between his college work and itinerant ministry. Then, from 1851 to 1866, he took on the extra role of president of the College and, during this period, twenty thousand students are said to have come under his influence. He retired from the College in 1872 but continued to teach in the seminary and kept up his involvements with the students until a few days before his death.

Finney's Marriages.

Finney was married three times and was twice a widower. In 1824 he married Lydia Root Andrews (1824-1847), while he was living in Jefferson County. They had six children. In November 1848, a year after Lydia's death, he married Elizabeth Ford Atkinson (1799-1863) in Ohio. Then in 1865 he married Rebecca Allen Rayl (1824-1907), also in Ohio. Each of his wives accompanied him on his revival tours and joined him in his evangelistic efforts.

The First Visit to Britain of Charles Finney, 1849-1850.

His first visit to Britain was in early November 1849, in response to invitations to hold revivalist meetings in the Congregational church in Houghton, Huntingdonshire, and the surrounding district.

He was accompanied by his second wife, Elizabeth. According to Finney the church had recently had some blessing and conversions under a new minister, the Rev. James Harcourt but, he said, the minister did not know how to promote a revival and couldn't reach the social middle classes. Harcourt had read Finney's revival lectures, however, and wanted Finney to preach for him. According to Finney a revival began immediately after he began to preach there, on November 11th 1849, and soon spread throughout the area, people coming from the surrounding villages to hear the Gospel. Potto Brown, the wealthy patron of the church and Finney's host, opened his home to all his friends that they might meet and hear Finney and, according to Finney, they were all saved. Finney preached in Houghton and nearby St. Ives for about three weeks. The church, seating four hundred, proved to be too small and a tent holding one thousand was erected. After the public meetings inquirers' meetings were held, which were so largely attended that Finney had to ask for the help of other ministers. It was said that of the seven hundred inhabitants of the two villages, probably one hundred were converted and fifty united with the local churches, although others, "minutely acquainted with the work", said that the claims were exaggerated and the long-term results were doubtful. The *British Quarterly Review,* in fact, said one had to take some of Finney's statements with a grain of salt!

In mid-December, Finney went from Houghton to Birmingham at the invitation of a Rev. Peter Roe, a Strict Baptist minister, preaching there twice on Sundays and three or four times during the week. Here he met the Rev. John Angell James, the minister of Carr's Lane Chapel, a famous Congregational minister of the time, who wrote an introduction to Finney's *Lectures on Revival* when they were first published in England in 1839. James retracted his recommendation four years later, however, concerned with what he called the "self-conversionism" in Finney's meetings. Finney remained in Birmingham for three months and, he said, there was a powerful revival in Roe's church such as they had never seen and, "it swept through the congregation with great power and a large number of the impenitent in the congregation were turned to Christ". The church then examined a "large number" of converts for admission by baptism, and thirty-six were admitted and a further twenty-two in the following two months, all the minister's time being taken daily in dealing with the inquirers.

Finney preached by invitation in numbers of other churches in the city for the next four or five weeks, including Carr's Lane. Church. The congregations everywhere were said to be crowded and the largest vestries were packed with inquirers whenever Finney made a call for them to go to them for instruction. In the meantime, John Angell James was receiving letters from America warning him against the influence of Finney's work, but Finney finally found a supporter in a Dr. George Redford, a leading Congregationalist of Worcester. Finney described him as, "a theologian second to none in these realms". He read and generally approved of Finney's *Systematic Theology*, and subsequently wrote the introduction to the English edition.

Redford, however, was already in sympathy with Finney's methods and had pioneered the use of "protracted meetings" in England as early as 1837. Finney recorded that there were many interesting conversions in Birmingham, but that ministers there were, "not prepared to commit themselves heartily to the use of the necessary means to spread the revival over the city". Apparently the ministers admired his zeal and wished him well, but had doubts about the correctness of some of his views. John Angell James said that Finney excited considerable attention but did not succeed to the extent of his expectations as many ministers stood aloof from him. James himself couldn't bring himself to do that, however, since Finney preached for him five or six times and with great power.

Finney's Views on Revival.

Finney spoke of revival simply as multiplied conversions and believed it was possible to promote, "a widespread and thorough revival throughout Protestant Europe", and that Christians were to be blamed if there was no revival because God had placed the Holy Spirit at their disposal. He told people on one occasion that they did not have a revival because they didn't want one, were not praying for one or making an effort to get one. Also, he maintained that were it not for the evil reports about him from America, claiming that his "revivals" there had turned out disastrously for the churches, and causing English ministers to be hesitant about supporting him, a far reaching and powerful revival would have swept over not only Birmingham but also all over Britain. This was against the older view of revival, that even the most eminent ministers are simply God's instruments and that however excellent the preaching, it is the Holy Spirit alone who can revive or, as someone crudely put it, revival is prayed down not worked up!

Finney's own well-known analogy from the laws of nature was that:

> Revival is naturally a result of the use of the appropriate means as a harvest crop is of the use of its appropriate means, and if the right means continue to be employed, revival would never cease.[95]

From Birmingham Finney went to Worcester and, from March to May 1850, preached for Dr. Redford and for a Baptist congregation there. Finney said that a powerful work was done there and that there were many interesting conversions in the city. Mrs. Finney's letters also described the effect the preaching had on all classes and on many from surrounding areas. There were so many in the inquiry meetings that the church had to be used and was filled. Redford remarked he had never seen anything like it nor expected to do so. The work didn't then stop when Finney left, but continued for months under the ministry of Redford. While Finney was in Worcester some wealthy men offered to provide him with a portable Mission Hall, one hundred and fifty feet square, to hold five or six thousand people for his use in England, provided he would preach in it from place to place for six months. He declined, after ministers persuaded him he ought rather to preach in churches, but he later regretted this decision. He came to believe he could have done much more good if he had had the independence of having his own mission hall, as he found the churches he visited generally so small and poorly ventilated.

From Worcester, Finney went straight to London and began preaching at Whitefield's Tabernacle, Moorfields, in Finsbury, whose pastor was Dr. John Campbell. Finney said that, although Whitefield's name was honoured, Whitefield's

---

[95] Murray, Iain, H., *Pentecost Today*, p. 8

spirit was not very apparent there! The church building, the largest of the time, held upwards of three thousand people and Finney preached there to large congregations, from May 12th 1850, to April 2nd 1851, with one thousand five hundred to two thousand people allegedly responding to an invitation to receive Christ and, on his second visit to Britain, he was told that almost all the converts were faithfully following Christ. Like Spurgeon four years later, Finney soon attracted the attention of London and of the nation partly because, like Spurgeon, he published his sermons. One observer reported that:

> His preaching is marked by strong peculiarities. It is highly argumentative and keenly logical, yet being composed of good, strong Saxon, is intelligible to the common people. Boldness, verging on severity, is one of its characteristics. Unpalatable truths are urged with a fearless courage...masks, pretexts, subterfuges of all sorts are exposed; and the selfish, the worldly, the cowardly, the inconsistent, are driven from their retreats. Then comes the Gospel, with its full and free antidote to despair, its gracious invitations to the penitent, its pardon and peace to the believing. [96]

From the beginning Finney worked, "in earnest for a revival and to convict people of sin as deeply and universally as possible". He believed in addressing sinners directly, not in the third person, and commented that one would not get the idea from sermons heard in America or Britain that the ministers expected or intended to be used in converting anyone "on the spot". He preached a great deal on the need of confession and restitution and said he believed thousands of pounds had been repaid as a result. He also had cards printed and distributed

---

[96] Orr, J. Edwin, *The Second Evangelical Awakening in Britain*, p. 159

around the district with titles of his sermons such as, "Life and Death", "Heaven and Hell" etc. Crowds came to hear and every week he saw the Word of God taking great effect. After three weeks, Finney asked Campbell for the use of a large room for an inquiry meeting. Campbell hesitated but suggested a room holding about two dozen, not believing half the number would respond. When Finney said he wanted a room holding hundreds Campbell laughed, but finally agreed for the use of a schoolroom, which was a little distance from the Tabernacle and which could accommodate over a thousand. To Campbell's amazement this was then regularly filled with inquirers after Finney's instructions that God required them to repent and submit themselves to Him there and then, and to abandon the idea of waiting God's time, as hyper-Calvinists taught. When he asked the people to kneel down and commit themselves entirely and forever to Christ, some cried out in distress of mind and there was great sobbing, but Finney told them to be as quiet as possible, in order to hear the prayer he was about to offer for them, before he dismissed the meeting.

Meetings of this kind went on for the time he was engaged at the Tabernacle. He said that the inquirers became so many that they could not be accommodated in the schoolroom or come to the "anxious seat", as the aisles were so narrow and packed, so he had to ask the convicted to stand in their places while he prayed for them. Hundreds would rise and as many as two thousand at one time were said to have done so. The interest he created was so great, with thousands converted of all classes of society. Finney said that if the Tabernacle had seated forty thousand, he had no doubt that it would have been filled! Campbell, however, reported simply that "not far above a hundred" had offered to join his church as a result of Finney's mission, although Finney commented that comparatively few converts joined due to Campbell's unpopularity! In reporting

Finney's death in 1875, *The Christian World* stated that, after Finney returned to America in early April 1851, Campbell regretted that he had welcomed him to the Tabernacle or praised and defended him in his paper, *The Banner*, because the church had been greatly injured by the hastily made converts of the revivalist preacher.

Finney's Second Visit to Britain, 1859-1860.

On New Year's Day 1859, Finney returned to Britain, going to Houghton and ministering there and in nearby St. Ives for several weeks where, he said, "we saw precious revivals". The old minister at St. Ives was opposed to Finney and left the district while Finney was there! Finney then went to Borough Road Chapel, London, allegedly transforming the church, which had been torn by feuds and demoralized. From April 21st to May 13th Finney was in Houghton again, and then went to Huntingdon until June 20th, where he preached for about five weeks in the Baptist church. Again Finney speaks of a revival taking place which, "spread extensively among the unconverted and greatly changed the religious aspect of that town". The United Free Churches in London, (formed in 1857 by the Wesleyan Methodist Association and Wesleyan Reformers), also invited Finney to minister among them. He began on June 26th and continued until August 7th 1859, preaching in their largest churches, "having a glorious work of grace". From London he went to Edinburgh on August 10th and preached there from August 21st to November 9th, mostly in the Rev. John Kirk's Evangelical Union Church. He had "a very interesting revival and many souls were converted". The church members were greatly blessed and the minister was continually busy dealing with six hundred inquirers. There was much opposition to Finney among other ministers in the city, however, and Finney was not invited to preach for them. Finney thought there was little hope of seeing a widespread revival in Edinburgh because of their prejudice and believed that thousands would have been saved but for that prejudice. Also, in the light of denominational rivalry that he often found in Britain, he came to the conclusion that the best way to promote a revival here was to hold independent meetings in large halls, not attached to churches, to which people of all denominations might come, a policy followed by twentieth century evangelists.

On December 14th he went with Mrs. Finney to Bolton, holding meetings in various churches in the town. Bolton was a Methodist centre and the Methodists co-operated fully in the revival. During the first Universal Week of Prayer in the second week of January, when Christians throughout the world joined in prayer for revival, the Temperance Hall, the largest hall in the town was crowded with those who attended his meetings. Under his direction the whole town was canvassed, attracting large numbers to the meetings. He encouraged Christians to visit in pairs and to witness and pray in every house in the town, and a large number of posters, tracts and various invitations were distributed. Finney said that the meetings had greater and greater power and that all classes became interested. Also, great numbers came forward, in response to his appeal for them to receive Christ, pushing as best as they could through the dense masses that filled every nook and corner.

The Bolton Evangelical Revival Committee was formed and the denominations united in the work. Very many inquirers went forward and knelt for prayer, but Finney eventually had to restrain some of the Methodist helpers who were adopting methods used in their Camp Meetings. Finney felt they were hindering the decisions of the inquirers when they prayed for them, by excitedly pounding the benches, praying very loudly and sometimes more than one at a time! Soon large numbers of people began attending from Manchester and Finney was invited there but he remained in Bolton until the beginning of April. Finney spoke of the revival becoming so powerful that the whole town was stirred, affecting all classes and extending to the Cotton mills. One owner stopped the machines in his mill, in order for the workers to attend a prayer meeting addressed by Finney and himself, and numbers of workers were converted. Here, too, Finney preached with great effect on confession and restitution, which made a profound impression on people and varying amounts, from a few shillings to many hundreds of pounds, which had been misappropriated, were restored to their rightful owners. Finney maintained that the interest was such that ten thousand would have attended each night if a large enough hall had been available. As it was, the Temperance hall was densely packed every night, long before the commencement of the service, and on Sundays hundreds were turned away. At the end of Finney's stay, a local newspaper stated that there had been more than two thousand enquirers and not less than one thousand of them had been converted. Also, of this number, nearly three quarters had previously made a profession of faith but had never really been truly saved. It added that probably thousands had been instructed in the Christian Faith and their ignorance of it removed, and that no doubt they would in the future lead a better life, if not a spiritually renewed life.

Another report stated:

The Rev. C.G. Finney, by whom these services are conducted… is close on seventy years of age. His style of address is singularly direct. There is a total absence of display, and a complete forgetfulness on most occasions at least of the graces of elocution. There is the most rigid exactness of statement, the severest simplicity, the closest reasoning and, as the discourse proceeds step-by-step, the judgement of the hearer is forced along with it until the end.[97]

On April 22nd, Finney began a mission in Manchester among the Congregationalists and Methodists and, in early May, he started to preach in the huge Free Trade Hall and then at Salford and Pendleton. Unlike Bolton, however, there was a lack of unity among the ministers and they did not, generally, attend his meetings. Some who did regarded him as a disappointment leaving his meetings, "with a worse opinion of revivalists than ever". Nevertheless, there were more than a hundred inquirers each night in Manchester and Finney maintained that large numbers were converted and that the revival continued to increase and spread up to the time he finally left for America in early August 1860. He then continued his revival services throughout the States for the next fifteen years until his death. He died of a heart attack on August 16th 1875, two weeks before his eighty third birthday.

Despite Finney's phenomenal success as a preacher, his greater influence probably resulted from his written work on revival. In 1834, the editor of *The Evangelist* asked him to write a series of articles on revival. After praying about it Finney promised to give a series of lectures on the subject once a week. A reporter of the paper was to attend the lectures and write them up in the required series of articles. They were then published as, *Finney's Lectures on Revival*. The book became a

[97]   Orr, J. Edwin, *The Second Evangelical Awakening in Britain*, p. 158

phenomenal best-seller, with more than two hundred thousand copies in circulation at a time and it was reprinted many times in England, France and Germany. Many Christian leaders claimed to have been greatly influenced by the book and it was used by God to encourage prayer for revival in many parts of the world including, some believe, the 1858-1959 revivals in America and the British Isles. Probably this book, and *The Memoirs of Charles G. Finney* , written between 1866 and 1868 and published a year after his death in 1876, were used by God more than anything else in calling people to pray for revival.

Repeatedly in the Memoirs there are references to the "New Measures" Finney used in his meetings to bring people to Christ, and which were the subject of much criticism by conservative church leaders as unwarranted innovations. In these scattered references throughout the Memoirs he stated:

> I called upon any who would give their hearts to God, to come forward and take a front seat (the so-called "anxious seat"). We insisted on immediate submission.

> I called upon them to kneel down and then and there commit themselves forever to the Lord.

> I called on those only to kneel down who were willing to do what God required of them, and what I presented to them.

> I called for those whose minds are made up to come forward, publicly renounce their sins, and give themselves to Christ.[98]

---

[98] Murray, Iain, H., *Pentecost Today*, p. 40

Moody's Early Life.

The importance of Moody is seen in that, it has been said that Finney was the greatest evangelist in the nineteenth century, with the exception of Moody, and that as Finney dominated the middle third of the nineteenth century, Moody dominated the final third.

Moody was born in Northfield, Massachusetts on February 5th 1837, the sixth child of Edwin Moody and Betsy Holton. He came from Puritan stock, his paternal and maternal ancestors landing in America in the early 1630s. When he was four years old, his father died suddenly, aged forty-one, and his mother was left with practically no means of support for herself and her nine children, including twins born after the father's death. The house was mortgaged and, though that was secured under dower rights, creditors took everything else they could, even the firewood in the shed! Moody, therefore, grew up in extreme poverty and, as a young boy, earned a few cents driving cows for a farmer or working for a neighbour in exchange for his board. His mother, however, insisted on a religious upbringing for her children, including regular church attendance and they were christened in the local Unitarian church. Also, they not only attended Sunday school themselves but they were encouraged to recruit other children so, in a sense, Moody's well-known Sunday school mission work began earlier than is commonly supposed!

Moody was ambitious to get on in the world and one day, when he was seventeen, and cutting and hauling logs on the mountainside with his brother he said, "I'm tired of this! I'm not going to stay around here any longer. I'm going to the city". He then moved to Boston to work for an uncle in his shoe shop. As part of the employment agreement he began to attend the Mount Vernon Congregational Church, as well as a young men's Bible class conducted by a Mr. Edward Kimball. Kimball, concerned about Moody, visited him in the shoe shop and appealed to him to receive Christ. He thought what he said was fairly feeble but Moody was ready to respond and, from that moment, his whole life was changed and his church attendance was no longer regarded as a duty. The next morning he thought the sun shone brighter than before and that the birds were all singing for him! He said that it seemed that he was in love with the whole creation and that he didn't have a bitter feeling against any man.

In May 1855 he applied for membership in the Mount Vernon Church and the membership record stated:

> Has been baptized. First awakened on May 16th. Became anxious about himself. Saw himself as a sinner, and sin now seems hateful and holiness desirable. Thinks he has repented; has purposed to give up sin and feels dependent upon Christ for forgiveness. Loves the Scriptures. Prays. Desires to be useful. Religiously educated. Been in the city for a year. From Northfield, this State. Is not ashamed to be known as a Christian. Eighteen years old. [99]

At this time, however, Moody was fairly ignorant of the Bible and the doctrines of the Christian Faith. Mr Kimball stated that he could truly say that he had seen few persons whose minds were spiritually darker than Moody's when he first came into his Sunday school class! Then, when Moody was examined for church membership and asked, "What has Christ done for you and for us all", he replied, "I think he has done a great deal for us all, but I don't know of anything he has done in particular". As a result the committee examining him deferred recommending him for membership, and some of them were

---

[99] Moody, W.R., *The Life of Dwight L. Moody*, pp. 41, 42

appointed to explain the Christian Faith more fully to him. In March the following year he applied again for membership and, in the light of his progress in the meantime, he was accepted.

After two years working in the shoe shop, however, he felt there were greater opportunities for him elsewhere and, in September 1856, he decided to go to Chicago, where he obtained a job in another shoe shop, with the ambition to earn a fortune of $100,000. The next year, however, the great American revival of 1857-1858 reached Chicago and made a big impact on Moody as a zealous young Christian. The churches of every denomination were packed to overflowing and Moody enjoyed the opportunity and blessing the revival brought. In January 1857 he wrote to his mother, "There is a great revival of religion here. I go to meetings every night. Oh how I do enjoy it! It seems as if God were here Himself". The crowded churches and the rapidly growing city provided plenty of opportunities for evangelism and his first attempt at Christian work there was renting and filling rows of church seats with young men, believing he had a talent for recruiting young people for Sunday school. He therefore rented a pew in the church he attended and brought in young people from street corners, boarding houses and even saloons. Before long he rented four pews, which he filled every Sunday. In addition to recruiting young people to attend church, he applied to teach a class in a little mission Sunday school. There were more teachers available than children and he was told he had to provide his own class, which he did, arriving the next Sunday with sixteen little "hoodlums", and he also gathered new scholars for others to teach. He attracted so many children that, in the autumn of 1858, he started his own Sunday school with five or six hundred scholars in another part of the city, which increased to fifteen hundred and became the largest Sunday school in Chicago. This work developed later into the

Chicago Avenue Church, which he pastored for a while and where he was a member during the later years of his life.

At this time Moody began to think of his need to be full-time in Christian service. He was successful as a salesman in the shoe shop and had been given the more responsible job of a commercial traveller. However, the Sunday school work was demanding more time and effort than he could give and still continue as a commercial traveller. In addition, he had also begun Gospel services during the week in a room formerly used as a saloon, where he was gaining experience as a preacher that was useful to him in later years, though his first efforts were not auspicious. When he attempted to speak in a church prayer meeting, one deacon told him he would serve God best by keeping still! Another critic suggested he should keep to filling church pews and make no attempt to speak in public, as he made too many mistakes in grammar. In his typically blunt way he replied, "You've got grammar enough; what are you doing with it for the Master"!

Moody was very ambitious and, as mentioned, he determined he would "make" $100,000 and then retire. By the time he was twenty-three he had already saved $7,000 and, because he was such an excellent salesman, he earned over $5,000 in one year in commissions, in addition to his salary. The following year, however, he decided to give up business and enter full-time Christian service, supporting himself on his savings for as long as possible and depending on God for the future.

The same year Moody's ministry was transformed again when he received a mighty filling of the Holy Spirit. He said later;

> I was crying all the time that God would fill me with His Spirit. Well, one day, in the city of New York; oh, what a

day, I cannot describe it and I seldom refer to it; it is almost too sacred an experience to name. Paul had an experience of which he never spoke for fourteen years. I can only say that God revealed himself to me, and I had such an experience of His love that I had to ask Him to stay His hand. I went to preaching again. The sermons were not different: I did not present any new truths; and yet hundreds were converted. I would not now be placed back where I was before that blessed experience if you should give me all the world. [100]

He later said that he didn't know of a sermon that he had preached since that experience when God had not saved some soul. The sermons he was preaching were the very same he had preached previously, word for word. Then he had preached and preached, but it was as one beating the air. It was not new sermons that made the difference but the power of God, not a new Gospel but the old Gospel with the Holy Ghost power.

The Beginning of Moody's Full-Time Christian Service.

In 1861, when he was only twenty-four, he believed he had saved enough money to begin full-time Christian service without the need of a salary. He turned his back on an income of $5,000 a year and, in the first year of his full-time service, he received only three hundred dollars from friends who supported his work with children. It was at this time, when he had renounced worldly ambitions that, against the advice of his friends, he was engaged to a seventeen year old girl, Emma C. Revell, whom he married in 1862. It was a happy marriage which was to last until his death in 1899.

Moody joined the newly formed Young Men's Christian Association in Boston after he left home to go there in 1854,

---

[100] Murray, Iain H., *Pentecost Today*, p. 98

commenting to his brother, "I shall have a place to go to when I want to go away anywhere, and I can have all the books I want to read free and only have to pay one dollar a year"! He also once said, "I believe in the YMCA with all my heart. Under God it has done more in developing me for Christian work than any other agency". Then, in 1861, after giving up business he devoted much of his time to Association work, and made a wider reputation for himself as an organizer and fund raiser for the Y.M.C.A. in Chicago. That year, at the beginning of the Civil War, he began to hold services for the Union soldiers, as well visiting the battlefields and ministering to the wounded and dying. Throughout the war he continued to try to win the soldiers for Christ by Gospel services, the gift of Bibles, books and tracts. Then, when numbers of soldiers were converted, he formed branches of the YMCA in the camps. The war conditions under which the work was conducted made it necessary to urge his hearers to immediately accept salvation, and this was a conspicuous feature of his work afterwards.

In 1865 Moody became president of the Y.M.C.A. in Chicago and when the war ended that year, he returned to his Sunday school work in Chicago and held conventions for Sunday school workers, which were attended by thousands and where his evangelistic methods were explained. News of these conventions spread through America and then national and international Sunday school conventions were held on similar lines. It was at a convention in Indianapolis that Moody met Sankey. There was a difficulty in starting the singing and someone persuaded Sankey to sing a hymn. He sang, "There is a fountain filled with blood…" and all the congregation joined in. Moody approached him at the end of the service and said he was the man he had been looking for and he wanted him to come to Chicago and help him in his work. Then, after taking part in several meetings with Moody, Sankey was sufficiently

C. G. Finny.

Ira D. Sankey and Fanny Crosby

impressed to give up his business and become Moody's full-time accompanist in his campaigns.

Moody's First Visit to Britain in 1867.

In 1867 Moody decided to go to Britain as a representative of the Y.M.C.A. and to learn English methods of evangelism. He met many of the most well-known British evangelical leaders and made a deep impression on all who heard him. He particularly wanted to meet George Muller who, by faith, cared for one thousand one hundred children, later two thousand, in his Children's Homes in Bristol, and he also met the famous London Baptist preacher, C.H. Spurgeon, known as "the Prince of preachers". He soon went to the YMCA in Aldersgate Street in London and established a noon prayer meeting, where he told of his work among the rough and lawless children of Chicago. This was attended by two to three hundred men and it was soon followed by many such meetings throughout the city and the country. It was at this time that Moody heard the words, "The world has yet to see what God will do with, and for, and through, and in, and by the man who is fully and wholly consecrated to him". Moody thought, "he said 'a man'; he did not say a great man, nor a learned man, nor a rich man, nor an eloquent man, nor a smart man, but simply a man. I am a man and I will try my utmost to be that man who is fully and wholly consecrated to God". Moody then went to Edinburgh where he spent two months and spoke of the new methods of evangelism in America, especially in Chicago, which moved everyone in his meetings. In later years, however, Moody referred to his earlier efforts as "zeal without knowledge", but added that was better than knowledge without zeal! Before he visited Britain again, however, there came an important turning point when his ministry was transformed, from an emphasis on the judgement of God to one on the love of God, through the influence of Henry Moorhouse, an English evangelist, known as "The Boy Preacher".

Moorhouse was converted in the 1861 revival in England and began a remarkable career as an evangelist with a world-wide reputation. He wrote to Moody saying he would like to come to Chicago and preach for him but, not knowing him, Moody didn't respond. However, Moorhouse turned up in Chicago and, while he was away, Moody reluctantly gave him permission to preach. When he returned home people enthusiastically told Moody of how Moorhouse had preached from John 3:16, stressing the love of God throughout the Scriptures and that he told the worst of sinners that God loves them. Used to preaching on the judgement of God Moody said Moorhouse was wrong, but was persuaded to hear him. Moody had never heard anything like it. Moorhouse then preached night after night on John 3:16, every sermon being more impressive than the one before, when he powerfully quoted examples from every part of the Bible to demonstrate the love of God. Moody was completely captivated and his views were radically changed. He said:

> I never knew up to that time that God loved us so much. This heart of mine thawed out; I could not keep back the tears. It was like news from a far country: I just drank it in. So did the crowded congregation...He just beat that truth into my heart, and I have never doubted it since. I used to preach that God was behind the sinner with a double-edged sword ready to hew him down. I have done with that. I preach now that God is behind him with love, and he is running away from the God of love. [101]

---

[101] Moody, W.R., *The Life of Dwight L. Moody*, p. 127

It is said that it became common in the late nineteenth century to, "put the soft pedal on hell". Instead, reference was made to exclusion from the presence of God, which was not God's will, but the choice of the individual. Certainly Moody from this time spoke more of heaven than of hell.

Moody's Second Brief Visit to Britain in 1872.

In June 1872 Moody returned to Britain, being free from his work in Chicago, with the intention of learning more of the Bible from English Bible expositors. He wanted a rest and was determined not to work if he could help it but, at the close of a prayer meeting, a Rev. Lessey, pastor in a church in North London, asked him to preach the following Sunday. That day the people didn't show much interest in the morning service but, in the evening, while he was preaching, the very atmosphere was charged with a sense of the Spirit of God. When he finished he asked all who would like to become Christians to rise so he could pray for them. People rose all over the church until it seemed the whole congregation was getting up. Moody had never seen such results before and thought the people didn't understand him, so he asked all who wanted to become Christians to step into the inquiry room. Again all the people responded crowding into the room. When he once more asked those who really wanted to become Christians to rise they all stood up. Moody at this time was inexperienced, and didn't know what to do, so he told all who were really in earnest to meet the pastor there the next night. The next day he went over to Dublin but, the following day, he had a message from the pastor urging him to return as there were more inquirers on Monday than on Sunday! He went back and held meetings in that church for ten days and four hundred were converted and joined the church. Both Moody and the minister were puzzled by the size of the results until they learned of the prayers of two ladies in the church. In his biography of his father Moody's son recorded:

> There were two sisters belonging to that church. One was strong, the other was bedridden. One day as the sick woman was bemoaning her condition, the thought came to her that she could at least pray, and she began to pray God would revive her church. Day and night her prayer went up to God. One day she read in a paper an account of some meetings Mr. Moody had held in America and, though she did not know him, she began to pray that God would send him to her church. On the Sunday Mr. Moody preached, her sister went home and said: "Who do you think preached this morning?" She suggested the name of several with whom her pastor was in the habit of exchanging. Finally her sister told her, "It was Mr. Moody, from America". "I know what that means", cried the sick woman; "God has heard my prayers!" Mr. Moody believed that it was this revival that carried him back to Britain the next year.[102]

The First Extended Mission of Moody and Sankey in Britain, 1873-1875

After a second brief visit to Britain in 1872, Moody was invited to return in June 1873 and hold meetings in Newcastle-on Tyne with a promise the travelling expenses of his party would be met but no funds came. When he landed in Liverpool he learned that the three men who had invited him had died! He was then invited to York by the secretary of the York Y.M.C.A., where mission meetings were arranged, and he

---

[102] Moody, W.R., *The Life of Dwight L. Moody*, pp. 139, 140

was accompanied by Ira Sankey as a soloist and accompanist. Moody was very different from previous American evangelists and he was accepted on both sides of the Atlantic to a greater degree than anyone before or since. Moody's English, as an uneducated man, was imperfect, and he was not an orator or theologian, but these characteristics were considered of little consequence in the light of his transparent sincerity, integrity and love and zeal for Christ and the souls of men, as well as his complete faithfulness to Scripture and the essential truths of the Gospel. His teaching was in simple everyday language, with plenty of homely illustrations and the extraordinary and consistent success of his ministry to the saved and unsaved alike demonstrated the blessing of God upon him. Unlike some evangelists, Moody was never negative. He avoided criticizing other ministers and denominations and did not take sides on controversial issues. His one concern was for the salvation of souls and he welcomed all who would assist him in that task.

Initially, the situation of the first mission in York was not encouraging. Few people had heard of Moody and the Y.M.C.A. secretary said the city was so cold and dead it would take a month to prepare for the mission. Moody, however, began at once, and gradually the churches co-operated in the mission and he held services in several of them. Only eight people turned up for the first meeting in York, but there were conversions from the start and, at the end of five weeks, they finally totalled seven hundred. Several chapels and halls were opened for Moody's services, and prayer meetings were held every day at noon in the Y.M.C.A. In the evening services, aisles, vestries, lobbies and even the pulpit stairs were crowded an hour before the service commenced. The Holy Spirit worked mightily and people from all walks of life sought the Lord earnestly. Also, Christians from all denominations helped by speaking and praying with the enquirers. The Rev. F.B. Meyer, who assisted in the mission, said the first ten days of meetings were only moderately successful, but Moody accepted his invitation to come to the chapel where he ministered and there they had a fortnight of most blessed and memorable meetings. He later wrote:

> I have known Mr. Moody since a memorable Monday morning in 1873. I can see him now, standing up to lead the first noon prayer meeting in a small, ill-lit room in Coney Street, York, little realizing that it was the seed-germ of a mighty harvest... the birth of new conceptions of ministry, new methods of work, new inspirations and hopes. What an inspiration when this great and noble soul first broke into my life. I was a young pastor and bound rather rigidly by the chains of conventionalism. The first characteristic of Mr. Moody's that struck me was that he was so absolutely unconventional and natural. That a piece of work had generally been done after a certain method would probably be the reason why he would set about it in some fresh and unexpected way. That the new method startled people was the greater reason for continuing with it, if only it drew them to the Gospel. But there was never the slightest approach to irreverence, fanaticism or extravagance; everything was in perfect accord, with a rare common sense, a directness of method, a simplicity and transparency of aim, which were as attractive as they were fruitful in result...We had our all-day meeting, the first of its kind in England...Ah, blessed days! That will live as long as memory endures- days of heaven, of wonder...[103]

Moody's intention was to hold missions in the large cities of Britain and, from the start, in each place he visited, he introduced the practice of the midday prayer meeting, which

---

[103] Ibid., The Life of Moody, 144, 145

had been so successful in the 1858 American revival. Sankey's singing was a valuable asset, but behind both his impressive rendering of Gospel songs and Moody's arresting preaching, was the manifest power of God.

The evangelists then went to Sunderland and Newcastle, where they had increasing numbers, requiring the use of the largest halls in the north of England and many, especially men, were converted. It was not thought likely that any impression would be made on Newcastle, as it had a reputation for being irreligious, but crowds attended the daily prayer meetings and services and many were converted. Moody was determined to stay there until he had overcome the prejudice there was against his methods and motives, which he did. The evangelist Henry Moorhouse, who helped in the work at Newcastle spoke of the four things that summed up Moody's methods:

1. He believes firmly that the Gospel saves sinners when they believe, and he rests on the simple story of a crucified and risen Saviour.

2. He expects, when he goes to preach, that souls will be saved, and the result is that God honours his faith.

3. He preaches as if there never was to be another meeting and as if sinners might never hear the Gospel sound again; these appeals to decide now are most impressive.

4. He gets Christians to work in the after-meetings. He urges them to ask those who are sitting near them if they are saved. Everything about their work is very simple, and I would advise the workers in the Lord's vineyard to see

and hear our beloved brothers and, if possible, learn some
blessed lessons from them in soul-winning. [104]

The evangelists were then invited to Scotland and, for six
weeks beforehand, daily united prayer meetings were held in
Edinburgh for God's blessing on their ministry and no building
proved large enough for the crowds who wanted to attend.
Moody, unlike Finney before him, soon won the wholehearted
support of the great majority of ministers and churches. Some,
at first, were unsure of Moody's theology and were against
instrumental music in public worship but, as the weeks went
by, these prejudices were overcome. The first service was in the
Music Hall, the largest in the city, and not only was the hall
densely packed in every cranny, but the lobbies, stairs, and
entrance were all crowded, and several thousand people went
away unable to get admission. Similar crowds went to the large
Barclay Free Church and the attendance at each meeting was
said to have exceeded two thousand.

The whole city was stirred and three thousand converts
were registered, including people of all classes, religious and
irreligious, respectable and immoral.

The Edinburgh Review reported:

> The part of the service toward which all the rest tends, and
> in which the power culminates, is the address of Mr. Moody
> in which, in simple figures and telling language, he holds up
> before men the truth as it is in Jesus, and makes the most
> earnest and powerful appeals to heart and conscience. He
> is free from all pretence and parade; he speaks as one who
> thoroughly believes what he says, and who is downright
> earnest in delivering his message. His descriptions are

---

[104] Ibid., p. 152

characterized by a remarkable vividness and graphic power. He has a great wealth of illustration, and his illustrations are always apposite, bringing into the clearest light the point he intends to illustrate, and fixing it forever in the memory. There is very little excitement; there is no extravagance; but the effect of the services is seen in the manifest impression produced on the audience generally, in the anxious inquirers who remain for spiritual conversation and prayer after every meeting, and also in the hundreds of persons in all grades of the social scale scattered through Edinburgh and the neighbourhood, who are more or less awakened to realize the importance of eternal things, and are burdened with a sense of sin and a longing to obtain salvation. Not a few also profess to have been brought out of darkness into marvellous light, and to be going on their way rejoicing. [105]

After Edinburgh and special meetings in other Scottish towns, a hundred ministers and laymen of all the evangelical churches of Glasgow prepared for the visit of Moody and Sankey there in February 1874, and a great impact was made on the city. A 9 a.m. service was held for Sunday school teachers in the City Hall and was said to have been attended by about three thousand. At 6 p.m., the evening evangelistic service was held in the same place, which was crowded an hour before the meeting began, with a great multitude outside being sent to the three nearest churches which were soon filled. Dr. Andrew Bonar commented on the meetings soon after they started and stated:

There have been not a few awakened of late, and the interest is deepening. The ministers of all denominations take part most cordially. Men are coming from great distances to ask

---

[105] Moody, W.R., *The Life of Dwight L. Moody*, pp. 164, 165

the way of life, awakened to this concern by no human means, but evidently by the Holy Spirit, who is breathing over the land. It is such a time as we have never had in Scotland before...[106]

Moody's visit to Glasgow was attended with equal or even greater results. Meetings were held in the Crystal Palace Botanical Gardens which were crowded with five thousand people night after night, mostly men and many had to be turned away. The final Glasgow meeting was also held in the Botanical Gardens. Six or seven thousand were said to have been crushed together there and the crowd outside was so great, being estimated at twenty to thirty thousand, that Moody himself could not get inside. He stood on the coachman's box of the carriage in which he had arrived and asked members of the choir to sing. They had to find a place for themselves on the roof of a shed nearby and, after they had sung, Moody preached for an hour on "Immediate Salvation", and his voice was so distinct that the great crowd was able to hear him. Someone who was present said, "we thought of the days of Whitefield, of such a scene as that mentioned in his life when, in 1753 at Glasgow, twenty thousand souls hung on his lips as he bade them farewell". It was said that when the call for those who were unsaved and anxious to stand, two thousand people responded. From Glasgow occasional meetings were arranged in nearby towns and the ministers of Glasgow and other places conducted the regular meetings in the city during Moody's absences.

Many organizations for evangelism and social relief were started as a result of the Glasgow campaign. The work began among the middle class, but Moody inspired Christians to attempt missions to the criminal classes and the destitute. Lodging houses and the haunts of vagrants were visited.

---

[106] Ibid., p. 178

Temperance work was organized and many drunkards were reformed. Poor children were fed and clothed. Up to two hundred inquirers responded after every meeting, when groups of anxious men and women gathered together, many weeping, while Christian workers spoke to them of Christ. On Mondays there was a meeting for converts and, at the last meeting, three thousand five hundred were present. When the evangelists visited other nearby towns, those who had been blessed in the Glasgow mission prepared the way for them. Fifty thousand are said to have listened to Moody's farewell address in the open air. The work continued after the evangelists left and further services were held to reach the un-churched.

From Glasgow, in the spring of 1874, Moody went to Dundee. After three weeks there hundreds of irreligious people accepted the Gospel, including four hundred young people, and many church members were awakened to new spiritual life and activity. Vast crowds attended the services, thousands were converted, including hundreds of young men, religious and irreligious. Then, in September 1874, Moody and Sankey held a mission in Belfast. He started with a service at 8 a.m., exclusively for Christian workers, and long before the meeting began the chapel was crowded. The evening services were held in the largest church in the city, capable of holding two thousand people, but again the streets were crowded with people being unable to get in. Even the daily noon prayer meetings were overcrowded and had to be moved to a much larger building. As elsewhere, the midday prayer meeting proved to be a blessing to the work and the workers. Soon after these meetings began Moody published a letter, calling on Christians throughout Britain to hold daily prayer meetings. He stated:

> During the revival of God's work in America in 1857 and 1858, in nothing was the power of God's Spirit more

manifest than in the gatherings that came together at twelve o' clock for prayer and praise…if such meetings were started in the different towns of the kingdom, similar to those in Edinburgh and Glasgow, they might be the means of a very great blessing. Could no such meetings be started? The noon prayer meetings at Newcastle, Edinburgh and Glasgow are still kept, and if God blessed these places, as we believe, in answer to prayer, is He not able and willing to bless others? …Again I urge, will not God's children all over the United Kingdom meet at the noon hour and unite their prayers with those of other Christians in different towns for a mighty blessing. He says, "Call unto Me, and I will answer thee and show thee great and mighty things" [107]

Further services were held in Londonderry, attended by all ages and classes of society from the city and the surrounding districts. Trains brought increasing numbers to the meetings, while hundreds walked or drove many miles to them. All the meetings were marked by an intense earnestness and solemnity. The inquiry meetings were also very well attended, with many remaining for counselling and prayer with Moody and other Christian workers. In Dublin, the preaching services were preceded by a united prayer meeting which was attended by so many members of all the evangelical denominations in the city that they had to meet in the Exhibition Palace, the largest building that was available for Moody's use. Even that, where the Industrial Exhibition had just been held, was not large enough for the crowds who turned up for admission, including many Roman Catholics. Moody avoided any insult to the Roman Catholic Faith and again, there were several thousand professed conversions. Thirty thousand free copies of *The Revival* paper, reporting the success of the Dublin mission,

---

[107] Ibid., pp. 188, 189

were then distributed throughout Britain to encourage support for the work. One report in the paper stated:

> The inhabitants of Dublin are becoming alive to the fact that we are now in the enjoyment of a great time of refreshing, and that our gracious God is working powerfully among us by the instrumentality of these, His honoured servants. Such a sight has never been witnessed here as may now be seen every day – thousands flocking to the prayer meeting and the Bible reading and, most of all, to the evening services in the great Exhibition Palace…The leading Roman Catholic paper in the city gave full information respecting the work, and was extremely friendly toward it. In The Nation an article appeared, entitled "Fair Play", in which the editor informed his constituents that, "the deadly danger of the age comes upon us from the direction of Huxley and Darwin and Tyndall, rather than from Moody and Sankey. Irish Catholics desire to see Protestants deeply imbued with religious feeling rather than tinged with rationalism and infidelity; and so long as the religious services of our Protestant neighbours are honestly directed to quickening religious thought in their own body, without offering aggressive or intentional insult to us, it is our duty to pay the homage of our respect to their conscientious convictions; in a word, to do as we would be done by". [108]

From the end of 1874 other successful missions followed, with packed services in Manchester, Sheffield, Birmingham and Liverpool. In Manchester, in the Free Trade Hall, the daily midday prayer meeting alone was attended by two to three thousand people. In Liverpool, in February 1875, hundreds crowded the inquiry rooms; rich and respectable people,

---

[108] Ibid., pp. 192, 193

drunkards, prostitutes and the "ragged" people from the slums. Even greater crowds gathered in Birmingham, where Moody held a two weeks' series of meetings. Twelve to fifteen thousand people of all classes assembled daily in the Bingley Hall and all the churches in the city were said to have been affected. Dr. R.W. Dale, minister of Carr's Lane Chapel in the city, was initially critical of the meetings but he soon became impressed. He commented:

> Of Mr. Moody's power, I find it difficult to speak. It is so real and yet so unlike the power of ordinary preachers that I hardly know how to analyse it. Any man who can interest and impress an audience of from three to six thousand for half an hour in the morning and for three quarters of an hour in the afternoon, and a third audience of thirteen to fifteen thousand for three quarters of an hour in the evening, must have power of some kind. [109]

The climax of the visit, however, was the London campaign, which lasted for twenty weeks, from March until July 1874. Several of the very largest buildings across the city were hired for the Campaign, including the Agricultural Hall, Islington, which seated thirteen thousand seven hundred, and had standing room for four to five thousand more. There, for a month before the campaign began, a thousand people met to pray for God's blessing on the meetings. There too, Moody preached to crowds of twenty thousand or more every night. He also preached to the upper classes in the Opera House, Haymarket, as well as to the poorest, in the Bow Road Hall in the East End, which was specially erected, with seating for over nine thousand. It was in a poverty stricken area, which Moody thought came nearer to hell than any other place on earth!

---

[109] Ibid., p. 196

There, every night also, all seats were filled and standing room occupied and police had to turn away late comers. Moody had to appeal to Christians to stop attending the London meetings and occupying seats but rather to go out and bring in the unconverted. He also said, "You've had enough pulpit preaching, what we want now is personal witness, individuals going to people and pressing on them the claims of Christ".

The midday prayer meetings were held in Exeter Hall and one thousand eight hundred attended them daily. Often, as prayers were offered for unsaved relatives and, as one after another stood in obvious distress to indicate their request for prayer, an overpowering sense of the presence and love of God pervaded the meeting. In total, an estimated two and a half million people attended the London meetings, although it was reported that many were unable to hear the message! The beneficial results consisted not only in the numbers converted. Denominational differences were put aside to a remarkable extent and there was a greater unity and co-operation between the churches. Bible reading was increased; churches were revived; prayer meetings were commenced in churches and homes; Christians became more aware of their spiritual and social responsibilities and aggressive Christian and social work was begun everywhere.

Sankey's innovative solos came in for criticism at first but, when many were known to have been converted through them, opposition to them died away. Moody achieved a popularity and success no other evangelist had done and many public figures attended his meetings including William Gladstone, who was Prime Minister several times, though the Queen and the Archbishop of Canterbury did not do so. The Queen is said to have replied to an invitation from the Dowager Countess of Gainsborough that it would never do for her to go to a public place to hear the evangelists, though she was sure they were very good and sincere people. She also thought that a sensational style of service was not the religion that could last and was not wholesome for the mind or heart, though there might be instances where it does do good!

Some claimed that the work of God on this mission was one which had not been seen since the days of Whitefield and Wesley and that it was wider in its results than the work of those men, and that as the Methodist revival stopped the progress of deism so the work of these plain American laymen turned the tide of materialism and atheism. Neither in America or in Britain did people have any idea this visit would have produced the remarkable spiritual interest and results that it did, and it was only the grace and power of God that was behind these men that can explain.it. On returning to America Moody and Sankey continued to evangelize, holding missions throughout the Eastern states until they returned to Britain in 1881.

The Second Extended Mission of Moody and Sankey in Britain, 1881-1884

Moody returned to the United States in August 1875, and did not revisit Britain until the autumn of 1881, and again there was the same general interest and support for his mission. Wherever he preached, the churches were filled to overflowing, with hundreds turned away. He began in Newcastle-on-Tyne and then went to Edinburgh for six weeks and Glasgow and district for five months, where he was again assisted by Professor Henry Drummond, finishing there in June 1882. One new feature was the conducting of meetings for children on Saturday mornings, with "illustrated sermons", when he used various objects to simply explain the Gospel. Again in these and other meetings many were converted, especially working-class men. He also made short visits to other towns and cities, holding Conventions and organizing evangelistic efforts.

Moody then visited cities in the South of England, Oxford and Cambridge, the Midlands and again in the North. He went to Cambridge in November 1882 with some trepidation, as he had had no higher education and the prospect of speaking to university students was daunting. The meetings were held in the Corn Exchange. Seventeen hundred students attended the first meeting and constantly interrupted the proceedings with banter and barracking. Many left the service before the end, but four hundred remained for a brief prayer meeting, including some of the worst trouble makers. During the following days of the week's mission the atmosphere changed and more and more students responded to the Gospel appeal including Gerald Lander, who was a ring leader of the disturbances, and who later became a missionary bishop in China. C.T. Studd, captain of the England cricket XI, already a Christian, took several of the team to the meetings, some of whom, including Studd, also later went as missionaries to China. Throughout the week there were conversions which proved to be genuine and lasting and, in the final meeting, one thousand five hundred attended. On the final night eighteen hundred men assembled in the Corn Exchange and a hundred and sixty-two gave their names as wanting to receive a Gospel booklet. Some went to Moody afterwards and apologized for the bad behaviour on the first night. From Cambridge Moody went to Oxford and, at first, there were similar disruptions in the packed meetings as in Cambridge, but Moody soon overcame the opposition and before the week's mission was over scores of students had responded to the call to receive Christ. Some of them helped him in the mission that followed in London and numbers of them later devoted their lives to overseas missionary work.

Moody spent the rest of the year in the south of England. In 1883 he revisited Ireland and Northern and Midland towns in England, ending his visit as previously, with a mission in London, which began in November 1883 and lasted eight months. Here it was said that no movement in living memory had so bound together the clergymen and Christian workers of the various denominations. Even greater preparations were made for this London mission than for the previous one, by a committee consisting of many of the leading Christian men in the capital. In the 1875 mission, meetings were held in a few large buildings. In 1883 the aim was to reach the multitudes who could not or would not go to the central halls. Two large temporary halls were erected, therefore, each with seating for five thousand, and three-week missions were held in them alternatively on eleven sites in succession, from Hampstead in the north to Croydon in the south and from Stepney in the east to Kensington in the west. Moody spoke in these crowded halls at least twice a day and sometimes four or five times. Entrance to many of the meetings was by ticket only and, during the mission, four million were issued. All classes attended, from peers to the very poorest, and the climax of the mission, in June 1884, was a memorable Holy Communion service, in which thousands participated. At the opening meeting, Moody replied to criticisms that the professions of the converts didn't last. He said:

> I have come to London with high hopes and great expectations. I have one hundred times more faith than I had when I came here eight years ago. Some people have said that the former work in London hasn't lasted. I want to say that since then I have been preaching all through America; from Maine to the Pacific slope; and that wherever I have

gone, I have found fruit of that London work; it is scattered all over the earth. [110]

Moody's Final Visit to Britain, in 1891-1892

This visit was on a much smaller scale, consisting of a six-day mission at the London Polytechnic and then visits to Manchester and Scotland, where he stayed for four months, speaking in ninety different towns and cities. As a young man, The Rev. Poole-Connor, Founder of the Fellowship of Independent Evangelical Churches, attended a service conducted by Moody in the Metropolitan Tabernacle in 1892. In his book, *Evangelical Unity* he writes:

> The present writer and two friends were just able to squeeze in about an hour before the meeting was advertised to begin and, as the building was now filled to capacity, the doors were shut and the service commenced. There was a very large choir, and Mr. Stebbins was the soloist. He sang, "It may be at morn, when the day is a-waking…" Mr. Moody's text was Luke xxiii, 51, and his subject was the moral courage to confess Christ. 'I guess there are as many cowards to the square foot in England as in Amurrica', he said. He was, as we recall, stout, very thick-set, bearded, his head rather humping down on his shoulders. His general appearance was that of a keen, rather prosperous business man, very intent on the job before him. He did not seem in the least ministerial, the somewhat Gladstonian collar that he wore heightening the "lay" effect of his dress and the absence of all rant or undue pietism contributed to the business-like directness of his manner. His speech was alert, racy,

---

[110] Ibid., p. 269

and straight to the point, and enlivened with interesting anecdotes. We do not recall noticing any grammatical errors, such as are sometimes related to him. There seemed no great power in his words while he was speaking, but the effect at the close of his address was electrical. When he asked for those of his hearers, particularly men, that were prepared to confess Christ for the first time to stand up and say, "I will Sir," a wave of intense emotion swept the great audience, and from every quarter men arose to respond, "I will Sir". "I will Sir". "I will Sir". Nearly everyone around us was in tears, and murmured prayers could be heard all over the building. We learned that some three hundred professed conversion that night. [111]

Moody spent more time evangelizing in Britain than in any other country outside the United States, working here for at least five or six years in all on his five visits, from 1867-1892. Such were the number of invitations he received from all over Britain in the various visits that he probably could have spent his whole public ministry in Britain. However, despite preaching in so many places in England, Scotland, Wales and Ireland he had to decline most invitations because he naturally felt his main mission was to evangelize his own country. Therefore, for thirty years or so, apart from his ministry in Britain, he held evangelistic campaigns throughout America, from the New England cities of Boston, New York and Philadelphia to the West Coast cities of Vancouver, San Francisco and San Diego, resulting in multitudes being converted and added to the churches. It has been claimed that no other evangelist, under God, has turned so many to righteousness. (Daniel 12:3)

---

[111] Poole-Connor, E. J., *Evangelical Unity*, pp. 98, 99

Elizabeth and Charles Finney

Phoebe and Walter Palmer

William Booth

CHAPTER TWELVE
IS IT POSSIBLE TO PROMOTE A REVIVAL?

The question as to whether we can promote revival has been debated for at least the last two hundred years. The answer depends, of course, on what we mean by revival and various definitions have been given, although these fall into two main categories. Until the end of the eighteenth century, the common view was that revival was a sovereign act of God, in which He, and not man, took the initiative and for which the Church could only prepare by obeying Scriptural commands regarding it and praying for it. It was not thought of in terms of activity, organization, meetings or personalities. It was believed to be more than believers being filled with the Holy Spirit or what people may now call "renewal" or "restoration"; more than an ingathering of souls or a successful evangelistic mission and certainly more than religious excitement or excessive emotionalism. It was, rather, a powerful outpouring of the Spirit and a manifestation of God, which of necessity made an impact on the community.

Revivalism-The Introduction of Appeals for a Public Response to Gospel Preaching.

Both Wesley and Whitefield held the old view of revival being a sovereign visitation from God. Accordingly, during the Eighteenth Century Revival, they did not publish the number of their converts and, since they did not ask for a public confession of faith after they had preached, they could only assess results by the number who joined the Methodist societies. Whitefield stated, "There are so many stony-ground hearers that I have determined to suspend my judgement till I know the tree by its fruits". Before the end of the eighteenth century, however, the custom arose in America to count responses to Gospel preaching. At first, American Methodists counted the number who fell down during preaching services, believing the physical prostration indicated a spiritual response had taken place. Then, in the 1790s, the "falling exercise" was replaced by, "the invitation to the altar", when "mourners" were invited to the front and exhorted. Also, in Britain, from the late 1790s, William Bramwell (1759-1818), a Methodist itinerant and a pioneer of the appeal system, was making "altar calls", after preaching for those in spiritual distress to stand up and be prayed for.

Then, at the turn of the century, when the American Methodists began to organize their Camp Meetings, the practice was for an area to be roped off as an "altar" and "mourners" were directed to it. The reason for this was that, by individuals identifying themselves publicly, it was possible to pray with them and give them instruction. No one at first thought of it as a means of conversion but, before long, responding to the altar call came to be regarded as being converted and, under pressurized threats of certain hell if an immediate public decision was not made, it was common for hundreds to respond in these meetings. An example of this is the method used by one of Finney's early companions, Jedediah Burchard:

> After repeated prayers and appeals, by which he almost compelled multitudes to repair to the anxious seats, he asked again and again if they loved God. They were silent. "Will

you not say that you love God? Only say that you love or wish to love God". Some confessed; and their names were written down in a memorandum book, to be reported as so many converts. It was enough to give an affirmative to the question: but many were not readily, and without continual importunity and management induced to the admission. He would continue: "Do you not love God? Will you not say you love God?" Then taking out his watch he would say: "There now, I give you a quarter of an hour. If not brought in fifteen minutes to love God there will be no hope for you, you will be lost, you will be damned". Then was a pause and no response. "Ten minutes have elapsed, five minutes only left for salvation! If you do not love God in five minutes you are lost forever!" The terrified candidates confess; the record is made and a hundred converts are reported. [112]

The new practice of going forward at the end of a challenging Gospel message spread and some people responded in this way, even when evangelists who did not believe in this innovation did not make an appeal! In Britain, in 1806, the American evangelist Lorenzo Dow developed what William Bramwell had begun by introducing the appeal system of the American Camp Meetings, particularly among the Primitive Methodists. Until about the mid-1830s, however, such appeals for an immediate public response were widely regarded with suspicion as an unwelcome innovation but, from that time, many believed they were a necessary part of revivalism.

Finney believed that the "anxious seat", or its equivalent, was vital to evangelism because it produced quick conversions, as he thought conversions should be. "People", he said, "should be brought to a point of immediate submission to God by the appeal. If they do not submit the Holy Spirit forsakes

---

[112] Cox, F.A., and Hoby, J., *Baptists in America*, pp. 180, 181

them and their state is well-nigh hopeless". Moreover, since it was thought that conversion was the sinner's decision and it was the preacher's responsibility to secure that decision, any measure to secure it had to be good. He said that for men to be converted "it is necessary to raise an excitement among them". It was claimed that the use of the "anxious seat" always saw a multiplication of converts, therefore God must be blessing such means and the numbers produced were seen as a justification of the means. Finney also adopted this method wholeheartedly, because he believed Man's only problem was in his will and that it was man's will, not his nature, that controlled his actions. He also adopted the Pelagian position, which denies the reality of man's fallen nature, and insisted that sinners have the power to turn to God. The new birth, he said, was simply the beginning of obedience to God and when an individual chooses to obey God, he is a Christian. He maintained that the sinner has all the faculties and natural abilities requisite to render perfect obedience to God, and that all he needs is to be induced to use those powers and attributes as he ought.

Objections to the Practice of Calling for a Public Response to the Gospel Message.

Those against these "altar calls", however, made the following objections:

1. The call confused an outward with an inward change.
2. It trivialized the Christian experience. Also, those who go forward and experience no saving change are liable to become worse than before, being convinced there was no reality in their so-called Christian experience.

3. The many who go forward and who subsequently lapse into the world bring dishonour to God and discredit to the Gospel.

4. Those making the altar call guarantee salvation to those who go forward. They are told they can be sure of salvation, since Christ said, "Whoever comes to me I will never drive away". The old doctrine of the witness of the Spirit is neglected, as preachers want instant results and to do away with any doubts.

5. The implication is that those who do not go forward, there and then, in response to the preacher's appeal, are deliberately rejecting Christ and will go to hell.

The Propagation of the New Theory of Revival.

The new view of revival, which was called revivalism by its opponents, was most strongly expressed by Calvin Colton, an American Presbyterian minister, who wrote his *History and Character of American Revivals of Religion* for British readers, which was published in London in 1832. In his book he distinguished what was, in his clearly exaggerated opinion, the difference between the old and new revivals, stating that in the old nobody expected, nobody prayed, nobody apparently tried for such a work, and that it was only within the past few years that the promotion of revivals by human instrumentality had, to any extent, been made the subject of study and systematic efforts. He said:

> The old (type of revival), which came mysteriously and unexpectedly directly from the presence of the Lord with overwhelming effect, were, till a few years past...the more ordinary character of revivals in America. Churches and Christians waited for them, as men are wont to wait for

showers of rain. The new were the same in character and nature, but they had only begun to occur in recent years because previously men had not learned how, as instruments, to originate and promote them. [113]

His aim was to convince the British public of the need to forsake the old notions of revival and to adopt the "new measures", such as were being used by Charles Finney and other American evangelists. He dismissed the old view that men ought to wait for God's time as, "an expression of sloth". Now, he said, there were scores of ministers and thousands of influential Christians in America, who *believe* in revival, and believe too that man may be the successful instrument in originating them and they see it as a fact, because their own experience has proved it. "Let loose from the chains of predestination", he said, the scheme has been set on foot in America of converting the world at once". It was natural to him that the date of a revival should be fixed in advance and posters printed and a hall booked ahead of time. One might also take it for granted, he claimed, that provided enough prayer was offered, God was bound to co-operate. In fact, if God did not, this meant that there was a lack of faith among Christians. These ideas appeared in a Wesleyan society in Derby in 1831, and led to a split of people who formed themselves into a sect called the Arminian Methodists. They said it was wrong to pray for faith, for all have it and can exercise it if they will. These "Derby faith" people were expelled by the Wesleyan Conference in 1832.

Colton, however, changed his mind and published his changed views in 1836, writing of "the evil effects of special efforts, protracted meetings, novelties, rash experiments and over-heated excitements", etc. The influences he previously attributed to the Spirit of God he came to believe were

---

[113] Murray, Iain, H., *Revival and Revivalism*, p. 375

explainable on a purely natural level. His point underlined the fact that secular writers can point to such manipulative methods, which are used by groups and organizations which are not religious at all and, when associated with revival, the supernatural element in true revival is discredited.

Finney's Revivalism.

Finney, unlike Colton, never changed his mind about the new views of revival. He became, in fact, the chief representative of them, in spite of the fact that Christians prayed in faith and godly ministers preached in faith for years without seeing results and then, suddenly, without apparent reason, a spiritual Awakening occurred, Finney maintained that Christians were to be blamed if, at any time, there was no revival, for God had placed His Spirit at their disposal. If they did not have a revival it was because they did not want one. He stated:

> For a long time it was supposed by the Church that a revival was a miracle, an interposition of Divine power, with which Christians had nothing to do, and which they had no more agency in producing than they had in producing thunder, or a storm of hail, or an earthquake. It is only within a few years that ministers generally have supposed revivals were to be promoted, by the use of means designed and adopted specially to that object. It has been supposed that revivals came just as showers do, sometimes in one town, and sometimes in another, and the ministers and Churches could do nothing more to produce them than they could to make showers of rain come on their own town, when they were falling on a neighbouring town... [114]

---

[114] Ibid., p. 247

He also maintained that if the whole Church had gone to work for revival years beforehand there might not have been an impenitent sinner in the land, and that if the Church did all her duty, she would soon complete the triumph of religion in the world and the millennium might come in three years.

A revival, then, was purely the result of the right use of the appropriate means or the powers of nature, as the production of a natural harvest was. It was just that and nothing else. He believed that if the facts were known it would be found that, when the appointed means had been rightly used, revivals had been obtained more regularly than harvests! He further argued that if the belief that revival was in the sovereign will of God was applied to farming we would starve, and said that the idea had been the devil's best device for destroying souls.

Finney propagated this theory of revival by means of his *Lectures on Revival*, published in 1835, which made a profound impression on both sides of the Atlantic in the next few decades. One lecture was entitled, "How to Promote a Revival" and in it he stressed the need of self-examination and of listing, one by one, all known sins, then repenting of them one by one. In another lecture, entitled "Strategies to Promote Revival", he defended the use of the "new measures" which were being widely criticized. His argument against his critics was that no specific forms or measures were laid down by Christ or the apostles about how Christians were to evangelize. Also, he pointed out how many changes had taken place over the years in church life and he listed a number of church leaders who were innovators, including the Reformers and the leaders of the eighteenth century revival, Edwards, Whitefield and Wesley.

The Controversial "New Measures".

Finney defended three "new measures" in particular: the protracted or extended meetings, since successive meetings lasting several days or weeks were not common at that time; the altar call, or the invitation for people to make a public commitment by standing up or going forward and the "anxious seat". The use of the last named reached England in 1807 and those responding to the appeal went to it for further instruction or exhortation. Later, the inquiry room replaced the anxious seat. Finney claimed that if speakers adopted his convictions and methods, the revival that would "never cease" would come. Many ministers did adopt his methods but they did not see revival, nor did they continue when they occurred. Moreover, the idea that revivals could be produced if only the right means were used led to dissatisfaction with, and criticism of, ministers. People who had been spiritually blessed by their ministers for many years now wrote anonymous letters to them, asking them to create and continue a revival or, if not, to resign and not stand in the way of souls. We may define revivalism, therefore, as evangelism plus certain manipulative measures to obtain immediate results. When a significant number responded in revivalist meetings, the revivalist was likely to describe the response as revival, rather than simply the result of an evangelistic effort.

Opposition to the New Measures.

The principal opponent of the new measures adopted by Finney and others was the Rev. Asahel Nettleton (1783-1843), an American Congregationalist, who had been greatly used by God in revivals. In 1828, lengthy letters of his and of the Rev. Dr. Lyman Beecher, were published under the title, *New*

Measures in Conducting Revivals of Religion and, in the letters, the methods of the new revivalism and of Finney in particular were analysed. Nettleton complained that the broadcasting of results was grieving the Holy Spirit; that the names of God were being used irreverently and that division was being caused by ministers and colleges not favourable to the new measures being denounced as enemies of revival. Also, young ministers were excluding themselves from pulpits by their criticism of older pastors. Some churches, Nettleton said, had had a revival of anger, malice and evil-speaking, without the knowledge of a single conversion, in attempting to introduce the new measures. He maintained that Finney's supporters, in fact, were more anxious to convert people to the new ideas than to convert sinners to Christ. Yet some, so persuaded, had advised others not to introduce this spirit into their churches. Those who were the most superficial were the ones who first agreed with the new measures and those who had experienced true revival were the last to have fellowship with those who adopted them.

Nettleton went on to criticize the practice of congregational praying in a negative way for named or identifiable unconverted people in their presence in public, presumably to shame them and lead them to repentance. It had caused general indignation and was to be discouraged as showing a Pharisaic spirit. Christians were also objecting to young boys publicly describing senior ministers in prayer as old hypocrites or apostates who were "leading souls to hell". Some young men had gone to a church saying they knew how to promote a revival and had accused the minister of being "an Achan in the camp", and that his character was as black as hell, thinking this was the way to wake up or "shake off" the minister. Some maintained that if the unconverted in a congregation were pleased with their minister he must be a sleepy one and must be "shaken off". Individuals then simply had to ask if a congregation was pleased with its minister and, if it was, it was its duty to drive him away! Finney maintained that a revival would always attract opposition and that, if it did not, it could not be revival. The ministry of Christ and the apostles was quoted as always attracting opposition and a parallel was drawn between the Pharisees and opponents of the new measures.

Nettleton also objected to the error of thinking and teaching that the only danger in religion is "coldness, deadness and opposition", while saying nothing about an enthusiastic hypocrite or self-deceived person. He quoted Jonathan Edwards as saying that the greatest danger to revivals is not opposition but counterfeit experiences, the devil establishing many in a strong confidence that they were holy, when in God's sight they were the vilest of hypocrites. There needed to be discrimination between true and false zeal and true and false conversion. Preachers had to preach and exhibit the fruit of the Spirit, for it was a mark of pride when people criticized others in the most harsh language, saying they were "cold" or "dead" and "from the devil" or "from hell", for humble Christians have enough to do dealing with their own hearts.

Later Criticism of Revivalism.

A generation after Nettleton, Samuel Prime, who was one of the first to record the events of the 1858 American Revival in *The Power of Prayer*, published in 1859, wrote of the work of God in the daily prayer meetings, which led to that revival. He stated that in the revival there were no revivalists or revival machinery and that the "anxious seat" was unknown. The nationwide united prayer meetings had not been appointed to create religious feeling, he said, but rather to give expression to and increase the feeling already existing. The revival was nowhere attended by any special measures intended and adapted to produce excitement on the subject of religion. Also, Gardiner Spring writing in his *Personal Reminiscences* in 1866, in reference to the revivalist meetings of the time stated:

> With the obvious signs of the times in view, who does not see that this artful foe (the devil) would enjoy his malignant triumph if he could prejudice the minds of good men against all revivals of religion? This he does, not so much by opposing them, as by counterfeiting the genuine coin and by getting up revivals that are spurious and to his liking. Revivals are always spurious when they are got up by man's device, and not brought down by the spirit of God. [115]

Similarly, C. H. Spurgeon once said that Christians should never speak of *getting up* a revival for where could they get it up from, except the place which is better to have no connection with, and that it is to be *brought down* if it is worth having.

Duncan Campbell also expressed this view in his description of the Lewis Revival: he stated:

> I would like first to state what I mean by revival, as witnessed in the Hebrides. I do not mean a time of religious entertainment, with crowds gathering to enjoy an evening of bright gospel singing; I do not mean sensational or spectacular advertising; in a God-sent revival you do not need to spend money on advertising. I do not mean high-pressure methods to get men to an inquiry room; in revival every service is an inquiry room and the road and hillside become sacred spots to many. Revival is a going of God among His people and an awareness of God laying hold of the community. Here we see the difference between a successful campaign and revival; in

---

[115] Murray, Ian, H., *Revival and Revivalism*, p. xv

the former we may see many brought to a saving knowledge of the truth and the church or mission experience a time of quickening but, so far as the town or district is concerned, no real change is visible. The world goes on its way and the dance and picture-shows are still crowded: but in revival the fear of God lays hold upon the community, moving men and women who, until then, had no concern for spiritual things to seek after God. [116]

The Distinction between Revival and Revivalism.

The distinction between revival and revivalism, therefore, has been blurred by the term "revival" being used to denote both revival as a direct visitation from God and high-powered evangelistic meetings, in which there have been many professions of conversion as a result of a lengthy, persuasive appeal to make an immediate and public confession of faith. The early "protracted meetings" tended to create a charged emotional atmosphere, in which religious excitement was generated and public decisions were easier to obtain. Also, the short-circuiting or simplifying of the need to repent, believe and confess Christ, by the physical act of going forward to the front of a church or to an inquiry room, or of "submitting to God" by standing up or kneeling down, led to numerous false and temporary decisions. In practice, however, the distinction between revival and revivalism is not always easy to make. Many books on revival confuse the issue, by describing as revival what is clearly revivalism or as revivalism what may have been revival. This is seen in the two major English works on revivalism, by John Kent from a liberal viewpoint in 1978, and Iain Murray from an evangelical, Reformed viewpoint in 1994,

---

[116] Peckham, Colin, N., "The Lewis Awakening, 1949-1953", in _Heritage of Revival_, p. 165

which deal with American and British evangelists who played a leading part in seeking to revive British churches in the mid-Victorian period. Both describe as revivalism, preaching in the 1860s and later, some of what was perhaps genuine revival, when the so-called "1859 Revival" was still ongoing in Britain.

The Major Nineteenth Century Revivalists in Britain.

After Lorenzo Dow, in the first two decades of the century there were, later, more widely influential revivalists, such as the Rev. James Caughey, Dr. Walter and Phoebe Palmer and William and Catherine Booth. The Rev. James Caughey toured Britain during 1841-1848 and claimed twenty-two thousand conversions. William Booth was influenced by his ministry and immediately began street preaching. During this time Caughey promoted revivalism among Methodist leaders and, according to Kent, he was a "hero" of the Wesleyan Reformers. His high-pressure methods, however, caused a lot of concern among the leaders of Wesleyan Methodism, as did the reliability of the published conversion figures. It was said that, in his eagerness to get results, Caughey would walk up and down the church aisles shouting, "Come out man and save your soul"! By 1844, an attempt was made by the Wesleyan Conference to restrain Caughey's efforts, but it failed. In 1846, one minister from a circuit where Caughey had held a mission warned the Methodist leader, Jabez Bunting that:

> A class of men exists among us who, if not sufficiently superintended, will soon bring the regularly instituted ordinances of God into utter contempt. These men are always boasting of their doings and making little or nothing of sound and wholesome teaching and, in spite of the fearful declensions caused in certain circuits, some of which have

been made red hot with the ism, they go on their own ways, no man forbidding. I glory in real revivals of experimental and practical Christianity but I abhor self-sufficiency and absurdity. O how I frequently long and sigh for the orderly and solemn services of London Methodism. [117]

Bunting tried to get the American Bishops to recall Caughey, without success; though they expressed regret that English Methodism might "possibly suffer some degree of inconvenience from his proceedings". From 1847, he was refused the use of Wesleyan Methodist premises for his missions and, finally, he was not allowed in their pulpits. After leaving Britain in 1848 he returned, in 1857, and again preached in numerous cities, mostly in Methodist churches and claimed scores, if not hundreds, of converts in each place. Spurgeon, in a sermon in 1858, referred to Caughey and the reported "revival, in a certain place in our country" (Sheffield).

As you are aware, I have at all times been peculiarly jealous and suspicious of revivals. Whenever I see a man who is called a revivalist I always set him down for a cypher. I would scorn the taking of such a title as that to myself. All that I call a farce (the reported "revival" in Sheffield). There may be something very good in it; but the outside looks to me to be so rotten, that I should scarcely trust myself to think that the good within comes to any great amount. [118]

All, however, did not share the criticisms of Caughey's ministry and methods. He was esteemed among the New Connection Methodists and they regarded his revivalism as the hallmark of their own cause. They reported his campaign in Sheffield

---

[117] Murray, Iain H., *Revival and Revivalism*, pp. 394, 395
[118] Ibid., pp. 406, 407

in 1859 as a "Pentecost" and a great revival and the revivalist paper, *Wesleyan Times,* stated that it proved the truth that revival could be brought about by special efforts. The paper asserted that the promotion of revivals was a fact and regretted that, because so few other preachers followed Caughey, the result was "the limitation of the revival to the one place where he happens to work". It added that, in commenting upon the labours and successes of Mr. Caughey, they have always said that there is no reason why, but for the unfaithfulness of others, a Christian church, wherever it is, should not experience similar a success to his.

Dr. Walter and Phoebe Palmer.

Dr. Palmer was a medical doctor and Methodist layman but, in the preaching tours of Britain, which he and his wife undertook, his wife usually gave the addresses. They tended to follow in the steps of Caughey and visit his contacts. After being stirred by the beginning of the North American revival in Ontario in 1857, they evangelized in Britain from 1859-1864. Their first mission, in 1859, was in Newcastle-on-Tyne and *The Times* reported that the town had experienced a religious Awakening equalling that in America and Northern Ireland and, it was said, one thousand four hundred converts were registered and many filled with the Holy Spirit. Early in 1860, they campaigned in Carlisle and their work was reported as "the revival of Carlisle". In several other places "an extraordinary work of the Holy Spirit" was reported. A month's mission in Cardiff, in which the churches co-operated, is said to have affected the whole city, bringing hundreds to the meetings and changing public morals, so that police testified that the city was a different place. The Palmers were criticized, however, for their altar calls and removing church seats to allow inquirers to go forward! The main Methodist body stood aloof from them, as they did from Finney and Caughey and, in 1862, the Wesleyan Conference forbade them to use their Methodist premises. Also, the Primitive Methodists, who had been involved themselves in revivalism earlier, issued a booklet, in 1862, in which the special efforts of revivalists, excited prayer meetings and penitent forms were called into question.

William and Catherine Booth

William Booth was a Methodist New Connection minister in Gateshead and experienced much blessing there at the time of the 1859 revival, his church being known as "the converting shop". Influenced by Phoebe Palmer, Catherine also began to preach and formed, with William, another husband and wife itinerant revivalist team. Also, as a result of the Palmer's influence, the Booths began to preach a version of perfectionism, that is, the possibility of instantaneous sanctification through an act of consecration and faith. Their method was to preach to the believer first, on the same principle as Evan Roberts' dictum later, "Bend the Church and save the world". They exercised an itinerant ministry throughout the country including, as mentioned in chapter six, missions in 1861 in various Cornish towns, which lasted in all for eighteen months, where remarkable results were recorded.

Perhaps the most difficult evangelist to assess, in terms of revivalism, is D.L. Moody who, undoubtedly, was the greatest evangelist to work in Britain in the last century, as Billy Graham was in the twentieth century. Iain Murray, who has written what is, perhaps, the most extensive and definitive work on revivalism regards him as a revivalist and has written:

Certainly Moody gained near unanimous support in Britain and in him revivalism was met at first with tolerance and then with an enthusiasm new to the country. In part this was due to his personality and in part to the low-key way in which he sought for immediate public decision. Aware that the altar-call had never been accepted in Britain, Moody substituted an invitation to go to the inquiry room. As this novelty was not accompanied by any instantly apparent doctrinal deviation, it was commonly regarded as simply a matter of method, and few recognized the long-term change which was being introduced into evangelism. It may well be that Moody himself was unconscious of how the practice of calling for instant physical action at the close of a service was related to theological belief. [119]

In associating Moody with revivalism, however, Iain Murray attributes an evangelism which calls for an immediate decision with revivalism, but Moody's missions at least were not characterized by a pressurized revivalism, and, at this distance in time, it may be impossible to determine to what extent, if any, there was genuine revival in his meetings. Certainly, Moody made no serious attempt to find out how many were converted or were influenced by his campaigns. Moreover, he distinguished between his work and spontaneous revival and never spoke of "having a revival" rather, towards the end of his life, he said wished in his lifetime to see a revival like that in 1858-1859. In J. Edwin Orr's view, Moody's campaigns constituted the second phase of the 1859 revival in Britain. He believed Moody's united prayer meetings; his co-operative evangelism; his zeal for home and foreign missions, which gave new life to the missionary movement in Britain; his promotion of lay ministry and his development of leadership

---

[119] Ibid., p. 399

and dependence upon the Scriptures-all these were already in evidence in the movement of 1858 in America.

Also, an influential Scottish professor and editor wrote of Moody's Edinburgh mission as "revival without revivalism". *The Christian* compared it to the awakening in New York in 1858, and others spoke of it as "the greatest revival since Wesley". At the time, hyper-Calvinists maintained that fellow Calvinists only supported Moody because of his success and believed that more good would have been done, and the harm of the Decisionist evangelism avoided, if the teaching had been sounder and the appeal system avoided. Many Christians today would also deplore any unscriptural means which were used to get results but few, perhaps, would wish to criticize the ministry of Moody, or of Billy Graham, although Graham had less support from evangelicals than Moody did, possibly because he put more emphasis on the appeal.

Revival in Revivalism and Revivalism in Revival.

What is significant about the missions of Finney, Caughey, the Palmers and the Booths, at least, is that although they used the revivalist methods of the protracted meeting, the "anxious seat" and the altar call or inquiry room, they worked at a time of real revival. It is difficult, therefore, to assess accurately the effectiveness of their ministry, since many who responded were, no doubt, independently under the conviction of the Holy Spirit, although the preacher's urgent appeal probably precipitated a response. At the same time, the intrusion of overzealous, persuasive methods led to numbers of spurious conversions. Iain Murray makes the valid point that:

> Once methods to induce and multiply a public response
> to the gospel are introduced, it becomes very much

harder to distinguish between the genuine and the merely temporary. If the apparatus for the decisions is established and the immediate public visibility of professed converts is encouraged, then the sheer weight of numbers 'responding', comes to be taken as indisputable proof (of the validity of the methods).

What is least important, because it is no real evidence of divine power, becomes the great subject of interest and attention. Instead of warning against the superficial, the new evangelism came to regard the institution of the public appeal as no small part of its strength. [120]

It seems clear, therefore, that in some movements, including the 1904 Welsh Revival, both revival and revivalist elements were present. There was, initially in Wales, genuine revival but then, on some occasions, revivalist phenomena appeared, such as unrestrained emotionalism, which caused concern to many ministers. Conversely, in a revivalist campaign, revival can break out, as apparently happened in some campaigns of Caughey, Finney, the Palmers and the Booths. A true revival, therefore, is not always an unmixed blessing and a revivalist campaign is not necessarily an unmitigated disaster. In the former there are often tares, sown among the wheat, and in the latter there is almost always wheat, despite the tares.

The nineteenth century revivalist phenomena, including the encouraging or emphasizing of physical prostrations as evidence of a work of the Spirit, has been repeated recently in some churches, during the popularity of the "Toronto Blessing" experience, by making provision for people to "fall down", etc. As the volume of prayer for revival seems to be continually growing worldwide, the challenge to the Church

---

[120] Ibid., p. 411

today, as it has been in the past two centuries, is to be aware of settling for mere physical phenomena or religious excitement or even an Awakening in the local church fellowship. We need nothing less than an outpouring of the Holy Spirit which will affect the community and the nation. In short, we need to pray for a fulfilment of Acts 2:17-21, "In the last days, God says, I will pour out My Spirit on all people...and everyone who calls on the name of the Lord will be saved".

BIBLIOGRAPHY

Adams, Kevin, & Jones, Emyr, *A Pictorial History of Revival,* (Farnham, Waverley Abbey House, 2004)

Adams, Kevin, *A Diary of Revival,* (Farnham, Waverley Abbey House, 2004)

Ambler, R.W., *Ranters, Revivalists and Reformers: Primitive Methodism and Rural Society in South Lincolnshire, 1817-1875,* (Hull, Hull University Press, 1989)

Ayling, Stanley, *John Wesley*, (London, Collins, 1979)

Bebbington, D.W., *Evangelicalism in Modern Britain: A History from the 1730s to the 1980s*, (London, Routledge, 1988)

Bennett, Richard, *Howell Harris and the Dawn of Revival,* (Bryntirion, Evangelical Press of Wales, 1987)

Bewes, Richard, *John Wesley's England*, (London, Hodder & Stoughton, 1981)

Butler, Joseph, *Works*, David E. White, ed. (Rochester, Rochester University Press, 2006)

Campbell, Duncan, *The Lewis Awakening, 1949-1953*, (Edinburgh, The Faith Mission, 1954)

Clowes, William, *Journals*, (Stoke, Tentmaker Publications, 2002)

Cook, Faith, *Selina, Countess of Huntingdon, Her Pivotal Role in the 18th Century Evangelical Awakening*, (Edinburgh, The Banner of Truth Trust, 2001)

Dallimore, Arnold A., *A Heart Set Free: the Life of Charles Wesley*,
(Darlington, Evangelical Press, 1991)

Drummond, Lewis, *Eight Keys to Biblical Revival*, (Minneapolis, Bethany House, 1994)

Drummond, Lewis, A., *The Awakening That Must Come*, (Nashville, Broadman Press, 1978)

Duewel, Wesley, *Ablaze for God*, (Grand Rapids, Zondervan, 1989)

Duewel, Lewis, *Revival Fire*, (Grand Rapids, Zondervan, 1995)

Edman, V. Raymond, *Finney Lives On*, (Minneapolis, Bethany Fellowship, 1971)

Edwards, Brian H., *Revival: A people saturated with God*, (Darlington, Evangelical Press, 1990)

Edwards, Jonathan, *The select works of Jonathan Edwards*, 3 vols. (London, The Banner of Truth Trust, 1958, 1959, 1961)

Edwards, Jonathan, *Jonathan Edwards on Revival*, (Edinburgh, The Banner of Truth Trust, 1994)

Ellis, Robert, *Living Echoes of the Welsh Revival 1904-5*, (London, Delyn Press, 1951)

Ervine, St John, *God's Soldier: General William Booth*, (London, William Heinemann, 1934)

Evans, Eifion, *When He is Come: An Account of the 1858-60 Revival in Wales,*
(Port Talbot, Evangelical Movement of Wales, 1967)

Eifion Evans, *Daniel Rowlands and the Great Evangelical Awakening in Wales*,
(Edinburgh, Banner of Truth Trust, 1985)

Evans, Eifion, *The Welsh Revival of 1904*, (Bryntirion, Evangelical Press of Wales, 1987)

Evans, Eifion, *Fire in the Thatch: The True Nature of Religious Revival*,
(Bryntirion, Evangelical Press of Wales, 1996)

Evans, Eifion, *Revivals – Their Rise, Progress and Achievements,
(London, Evangelical Press*, 1960)

Fawcett, Arthur, *The Cambuslang Revival*, (Edinburgh, The Banner of Truth Trust, 1996)

Finney, Charles G., *Lectures to Professing Christians*, (London, Milner and Co., 1837)

Finney, Charles G., Lectures on Revival, (Minneapolis, Bethany House, 1988)

Finney, Charles G., *The Memoirs of Charles G. Finney: The Complete Restored Text*, eds. Rosell, Garth M., & Dupois, Richard A.G., (Grand Rapids, Academie Books, 1989)

Finney, Charles G., *How to Experience Revival*, (Pittsburgh, Whitaker House, 1994)

Fitzgerald, W.B., *The Roots of Methodism*, (London, Epworth Press, 1903)

Green, Richard, *John Wesley The Evangelist*,(Dickinson, Revival Press, 2017)

Griffin, Stanley C., *A Forgotten Revival: East Anglia and North-East Scotland, 1921*,
(Bromley, Day One Publications,

Hardman, Keith, J., *Charles Grandison Finney, Revivalist and Reformer*, (Grand Rapids, Baker, 1990)

Horne, C. Silvester, *A Popular History of the Free Churches*, (London, James Clarke, 1903)

Johnson, Henry, *Stories of Great Revivals*, (London, Religious Tract Society, 1906)

Jones, R.B., *Rent Heavens: The Revival of 1904: Some of its Hidden Springs and
Prominent Results,* (London, Pioneer Mission, 1948)

Jones, B.P., *The King's Champions 1863-1933*, (Redhill, Love and Malcomson, 1968)

Jones, B.P., *An Instrument of Revival: The Complete Life of Evan Roberts, 1878-1951*,
(South Plainfield, NJ., Bridge Publishing, 1995)

Jones, Brynmor P., *Voices From the Welsh Revival 1904-1905*, (Bryntirion, Evangelical Press of Wales, 1995)

Kendall, H.B., *The History of the Primitive Methodist Church*, (London, Joseph Johnson, 1919)

Kent, John, *Holding The Fort: Studies in Victorian Revivalism,* (London, Epworth Press, 1978)

Kirby, Gilbert, W., *The Elect Lady*, (Rushden, Trustees of the Countess of Huntingdon Connexion, 2003)

Lloyd-Jones, D. Martyn, "*Revival: An Historical and Theological Survey*", *in How Shall They Hear* (London, Puritan and Reformed Studies Conference, 1960)

Lloyd-Jones, D. Martyn, *Revival: Can We Make It Happen?* (Marshall Pickering, Basingstoke, 1986)

Lloyd-Jones, D. M., "Jonathan Edwards and the Crucial Importance of Revival" *&* "Howell Harris and Revival" in *The Puritans: Their Origins and Successors*, Edinburgh, (The Banner of Truth Trust, 1991)

M'Kerrow, John, History of the Secession Church, William Oliphant, Edinburgh, 1839

Macfarlane, D., *The Revivals of the Eighteenth Century, particularly at Cambuslang*, (Glasgow, Free Presbyterian Publications, 1988)

Macpherson, John, *Henry Moorhouse: The English Evangelist*, (Kilmarnock, John Richie, 2010)

Macpherson, John, *Duncan Matheson: The Scottish Evangelist*, (Kilmarnock, John Richie, 2015)

Matthews, David, *I Saw the Welsh Revival*, (Chicago, Moody Press, 1951)

Moody, W.R., *The Life of Dwight L. Moody*, (London, Morgan & Scott, 1900)

Morgan, J.J., *David Morgan the Revivalist*, (Edinburgh, Ballantyre Press 1909)

Murray, Iain H., (ed.) *George Whitefield's Journals*, (London, The Banner of Truth Trust, 1960)

Murray, Iain H., *The Puritan Hope: Revival and the Interpretation of Prophecy*, (Edinburgh, The Banner of Truth Trust, 1975)

Murray, Iain H., *Jonathan Edwards: A New Biography*, (Edinburgh, The Banner of Truth Trust, 1987)

Murray, Iain H., *Revival and Revivalism: The Making and Marring Of American Evangelicalism, 1750-1858,* (Edinburgh, The Banner of Truth Trust, 1994)

Murray, Iain, H., *Pentecost Today*, (Edinburgh, The Banner of Truth Trust, 1998)

Nuttall, G.F., *Howell Harris, 1714-1773: The Last Enthusiast,* (Cardiff, University of Cardiff Press, 1965)

Orchard, S.C., *Cheshunt College*, Saffron Walden, Saffron Walden Press, 1992)

Orr, J. Edwin, *The Second Evangelical Awakening in Britain*, (London, Marshall Morgan & Scott, 1949)

Orr, J. Edwin, *The Light of the Nations: Progress and Achievement in the Nineteenth Century*, (Exeter, Paternoster Press, 1965)

Orr, J. Edwin, *The Flaming Tongue*, (Chicago, Moody Press, 1973)

Paisley, Iain, *The Fifty-Nine Revival*, (Belfast, Martyr's Memorial Free Presbyterian Church, 1958)

Parker, P.L., (ed.) *Wesley's Journal*, (Chicago, Moody Press, 1951)

Peckham, Colin N., *Heritage of Revival: A Century of Rural Evangelism,*
(Edinburgh, The Faith Mission, 1985)

Penn-Lewis, Mrs. J., *The Awakening in Wales, and some of the Hidden Springs,*
(London Paternoster Press, 1905)

Phillips, Thomas, *The Welsh Revival: Its Origin and Development*, (Edinburgh, The Banner of Truth Trust, 1995)

Pollock, John, *John Wesley, The Preacher* (Eastbourne, Kingsway, 1989)

Pollock, John, *George Whitefield and the Great Awakening*, (Tring, Lion, 1986)

Poole-Connor, E.J., *Evangelism in England*, (London, F.I.E.C., 1951)

Poole-Connor, E.J., *Evangelical Unity*, London, F.I.E.C., 1941)

Pudney, John, *John Wesley and his world*, (London, Thames and Hudson, 1978)

Ravenhill, Leonard, *Why Revival Tarries*, (Bromley, Send the Light Trust, 1972)

Richie, Jackie, *Floods upon the Dry Ground*, (Peterhead, Offset Printers, 1983)

Rosell, G.M., & Dupois, R.A.G., (eds.) *The Memoirs of Charles G. Finney, The Complete Restored Text*, (Grand Rapids, Zondervan, 1989)

Ryle, J.C., *Five Christian Leaders of the Eighteenth Century*, (London, The Banner of Truth Trust, 1960

Seymour, A.C.H., *The Life and Times of Selina, Countess of Huntingdon*, (London. W.E.Painter, 1844)

Shelhamer, E.E., *Finney on Revival*, (Minneapolis, Bethany House, 1974)

Simon, J.S., *The Revival of Religion in England in the Eighteenth Century*, (London, Forgotten Books, 2015)

Smeaton, George, *The Doctrine of the Holy Spirit*, (London, The Banner of Truth Trust, 1961)

Sprague, William B., *Lectures on Revivals of Religion,* (London, The Banner of Truth Trust, 1959)

Spurgeon, Charles H., *Revival Year Sermons*, (Edinburgh, The Banner of Truth Trust, 1996)

Stout, Harry S., *The Divine Dramatist: George Whitefield and the Rise of Modern Evangelism*,
(Grand Rapids, W.B. Eerdmans, 1991)

Thomas, I.D.E., *God's Harvest: The Nature of True Revival*, (Bridgend, Bryntirion Press, 1997)

Tyerman, Luke, *The Life of the Reverend. George Whitefield*, (Oswestry, Quinta Press, 2010)

Wallis, Arthur, *In the day of Thy Power: The Spiritual Principles of Revival*,
(London, Christian Literature Crusade, 1956)

Werner, J.S., *The Primitive Methodist Connexion, Its Background and Early History*,
(Wisconsin, University of Wisconsin Press, 1984)

Welch, Edwin, *Spiritual Pilgrim, A Reassessment of the life of the Countess of Huntingdon*, (Cardiff, Cardiff University Press, 1995)

Wesley, John, *Works*, (Ada, M I, Baker Books, 2007)

Whitefield, George, *Select Sermons of George Whitefield*, (London, The Banner of Truth Trust, 1959)

Whitefield, George, *George Whitefield's Journals* ((London, The Banner of Truth Trust, 1960)

Wilkinson, John T., *Hugh Bourne, 1772-1852*, (London, Epworth Press, 1952)

Wood, A. Skevington, *The Inextinguishable Blaze: Spiritual Renewal and Advance in the Eighteenth Century*, (Exeter, Paternoster Press, 1967)

Wood, A. Skevington, *The Burning Heart: John Wesley, Evangelist*, (Minneapolis, Bethany House, 1978)

Woolsey, Andrew, *Duncan Campbell: a biography; the sound of Battle* (London, Hodder & Stoughton, 1974)

Workman, H.B., *Methodism*, (Cambridge, University Press, 1912)

Acknowledgements

I am grateful for permission from The Evangelical Library to use the illustration, from its 1991 Annual Lecture, of the eighteenth century religious leaders that is inserted in chapter one. Thanks too to Day One publications for the use of the pictures in chapter eight from its book, "A Forgotten Revival", by Stanley C. Griffin. I am also indebted to the Faith Mission of Scotland for supplying the rare photos of Duncan Campbell for chapter nine. The Library staff of the University of Gloucestershire kindly photocopied several of the illustrations in the book. My thanks too to my son, Tim, who helped by formatting the Table of Contents and to Phil for encouraging me to publish. Finally to Leila of Acorn Publishing for her advice in the publishing process and to my wife for her patience during the long hours of research and writing!